STARTUP CITIES

WHY ONLY A FEW CITIES DOMINATE THE GLOBAL STARTUP SCENE AND WHAT THE REST SHOULD DO ABOUT IT

Peter S. Cohan

Apress®

Startup Cities: Why Only a Few Cities Dominate the Global Startup Scene and What the Rest Should Do About It

Peter S. Cohan
Marlborough, Massachusetts, USA

ISBN-13 (pbk): 978-1-4842-3392-4   ISBN-13 (electronic): 978-1-4842-3393-1
https://doi.org/10.1007/978-1-4842-3393-1

Library of Congress Control Number: 2018932402

Managing Director, Apress Media LLC: Welmoed Spahr
Acquisitions Editor: Shivangi Ramachandran
Development Editor: Laura Berendson
Coordinating Editor: Rita Fernando

Cover designed by eStudioCalamar

Cover image designed by Freepik (`www.freepik.com`)

Distributed to the book trade worldwide by Springer Science+Business Media New York, 233 Spring Street, 6th Floor, New York, NY 10013. Phone 1-800-SPRINGER, fax (201) 348-4505, e-mail `orders-ny@springer-sbm.com`, or visit `www.springeronline.com`. Apress Media, LLC is a California LLC and the sole member (owner) is Springer Science + Business Media Finance Inc (SSBM Finance Inc). SSBM Finance Inc is a **Delaware** corporation.

For information on translations, please e-mail `rights@apress.com`, or visit `www.apress.com/rights-permissions`.

Apress titles may be purchased in bulk for academic, corporate, or promotional use. eBook versions and licenses are also available for most titles. For more information, reference our Print and eBook Bulk Sales web page at `www.apress.com/bulk-sales`.

Any source code or other supplementary material referenced by the author in this book is available to readers on GitHub via the book's product page, located at `www.apress.com/9781484233924`. For more detailed information, please visit `www.apress.com/source-code`.

Printed on acid-free paper

To Robin, Sarah, and Adam.

Contents

About the Author

Peter S. Cohan is Lecturer of Strategy at Babson College. He teaches strategy and entrepreneurship to undergraduate and MBA students at Babson College. He is the founding principal of Peter S. Cohan & Associates, a management consulting and venture capital firm. He has completed over 150 growth strategy consulting projects for global technology companies and invested in seven startups—three of which were sold for over $2 billion. Peter has written 12 books and writes columns on entrepreneurship for Forbes, Inc, and The Worcester *Telegram & Gazette*. Prior to starting his firm, he worked as a case team leader for Harvard Business School professor Michael Porter's consulting firm and taught at MIT, Stanford, and the University of Hong Kong. Peter earned an MBA from Wharton, did graduate work in computer science at MIT, and holds a BS in Electrical Engineering from Swarthmore College.

Acknowledgments

This book has benefited greatly from the help of many people.

I could not have embarked on this project without the enthusiastic support of Nan Langowitz, who chairs the Management Division at Babson. My Babson colleagues Allan Cohen, Alexandra Nesbeda, Keith Rollag, Jonathan Sims, Siddharth Vedula, and Richard Wang all provided helpful suggestions. Thanks also go to my colleague Bruce Henderson for his insightful feedback on some of the book's exhibits and Gaurav Tuli at F-Prime Capital Partners for his comments on Chapter 2. Finally, thanks go to my Babson students with whom I visit many of the Startup Cities described in this book.

Without Apress this book would not exist. I am most grateful to Susan McDermott for her enthusiastic support of the idea for this book and for the outstanding editing and project management help from Laura Berendson, Rita Fernando Kim, and Shivangi Ramachandran.

Finally, I could not have completed this book without the help of my wife, Robin, who patiently read and commented on many of the chapters and my children, Sarah and Adam, who always make me proud.

Introduction

Who I Am and Why I Wrote This Book

I was the poster child for a confused adolescent. In college, I stumbled through a series of seemingly random career aspirations—concert pianist, poet, and architect—before realizing in my senior year that I wanted a career that combined my interests in computers and business strategy. So I set my sights on becoming a strategy consultant to help companies identify, evaluate, and profit from growth opportunities, which I have done in various guises ever since.

Back then, consulting firms hired newly minted MBAs rather than college graduates as they do these days.

While doing graduate studies in computer science at MIT, I met with the director of career counseling at its Sloan School of Management who introduced me to Index Systems, a consulting firm founded by three former Sloan School professors. I found out that consulting firms hired very talented people and provided opportunities for traveling and working on a variety of interesting projects. Index focused on helping managers use technology to boost business performance.

I decided that I was most interested in strategy work so after earning an MBA at The Wharton School, I went to work for Monitor Company, a strategy consulting firm co-founded by Harvard Business School strategy guru Michael Porter. My years there were a supremely intense learning experience. Thanks to what partners saw as a talent for turning Porter's ideas into processes for leading client teams, I was quickly promoted to managing consultant teams. Ultimately, the demanding travel burned me out and I spent the next few years working as an internal consultant in the banking and insurance industries.

In 1994, I took a chance and started my own consulting firm that provided strategy consulting for large high technology companies. This happened at a lucky time in economic history; the Internet was emerging as a major force for business growth. My consulting business boomed, I wrote several books, including *Net Profit*, which made me a regular on TV networks such as CNBC and an in-demand speaker at business conferences around the world. I also began investing in startups; since then, I have funded seven private companies. Three of them were sold for over $2 billion.

In 2001, I began teaching at Babson College, which *U.S. News and World Report* has ranked the top U.S. entrepreneurship school for the last two decades. After teaching part-time, I became a full-time lecturer in 2014 and was promoted to a Lecturer of Strategy in 2016. I teach MBA and undergraduate courses such as Strategy and the CEO, Strategic Decision Making, Strategic Problem Solving, and Foundations of Entrepreneurial Management. I also created and lead Electives Abroad to Hong Kong and Singapore, Israel, Spain and Portugal, and Paris.

This brings me to why I wrote this book—the idea that despite the wide popularity of the "World is Flat" mindset, when it comes to startups the opposite is true. Namely, where you locate a startup matters, and as you'll see below, location can make a big difference in whether a startup succeeds or fails.

This topic is of more than academic interest to me. I was born in Worcester, Mass. and come from a long line of entrepreneurs. For example, my great-grandfather started an ice and oil delivery business in the late 1800s. One of my grandfathers started a jewelry retailing business; my other grandfather started and built one of the largest independent accounting firms in central Massachusetts. And with his MIT roommate, Amar Bose, my uncle founded Bose Corporation. While my parents' generation operated many successful businesses in Worcester, my generation left town to seek our fortunes elsewhere. For example, one of my classmates moved to New Hampshire to start Cabletron Systems, a publicly-traded network equipment maker that was closed in 2013 while another started Acme Packet, a Bedford, Mass.-based, publicly-traded telecommunications equipment maker bought by Oracle that same year, leading to the question of why. More specifically, given that Worcester is the second largest city in New England and that it has 11 institutions of higher learning, why did so many of its most talented people leave town? I began looking into this question when I became a columnist for the local newspaper, Worcester's *Telegram & Gazette*, in 2011. In May 2013, I hosted an event at Worcester's DCU Center called the Worcester Startup Common Forum to look into this question and to urge changes that would reverse this leakage of talent.

At the same time, I was interviewing entrepreneurs and investors around the country for my eleventh book, *Hungry Startup Strategy*. In December 2011, I interviewed Kevin Hartz, co-founder of Eventbrite, an event ticket-seller. A graduate of Stanford who earned a Master's degree from Oxford, Hartz vaguely described something that he called "Silicon Valley's startup commons." Likening it to open source software, he described this startup commons as an ecosystem of mentors and young entrepreneurs that could learn from each other and ratchet up the entrepreneurial effectiveness of the region. I thought about this idea and began conducting more interviews focused specifically on developing the elements of what I call here the Startup Common. In so doing, I began to realize that the relative strength or weakness of a city's Startup Common had a major influence on whether valuable startup talent would be attracted to or repelled from a specific city.

The Startup Common idea was very helpful for my Babson Electives Abroad which addresses three questions:

- Why do some countries attract more private capital flows than others?

- Why is startup activity so concentrated in a small number of cities?

- What makes the difference between the small number of highly successful startups and the rest?

I have written books that address the first and third questions (*Capital Rising*, co-authored with Srini Rangan, and *Hungry Startup Strategy*, respectively). However, while I have published articles about the second, I wanted to investigate it further and *Startup Cities* is the result. This raises another question: who do I think should care about this question and what does this book offer them? Here are some thoughts:

- **Government policymakers**: Provides valuable lessons to city leaders on how to boost regional startup activity based on successful and failed efforts from cities around the world.

- **Entrepreneurs**: Supplies key insights into which criteria they should use to evaluate where to locate critical business functions.

- **Universities**: Equips university administrators and faculty with key insights from the most and least successful cities on how best to spur local entrepreneurship.

- **Capital providers**: Offers capital providers valuable lessons in how to select emerging regions in which to invest with the most attractive returns and how to build networks that supply access to the most promising ventures.

How I Researched the Startup Common

I began researching the Startup Common in 2011. It was an idea that emerged from an interview with the CEO of Eventbrite, one of about 160 startups I interviewed for *Hungry Startup Strategy*. Since then, I have developed the Startup Common concept, conducting many additional interviews to explore how entrepreneurs and investors have approached it. I published several papers on the concept and in 2012 began using the Startup Common concept with students in my Electives Abroad. During our annual visits, I have interviewed entrepreneurs, investors, university leaders, policymakers, and leaders of startup accelerators to deepen my understanding of the Startup Common in these locations.

To write this book, I compared pairs of cities in regions around the world. These pairs consisted of cities like Cambridge, which has enjoyed robust startup success, to Worcester, the second largest city in Massachusetts, which has been less successful. The other city pairs include Beijing and Hong Kong in China, Paris and Lyon in France, Tel Aviv and Haifa in Israel, Stockholm and Lund in Sweden, and Silicon Valley and Los Angeles in California. Within each city, I interviewed entrepreneurs, investors, university leaders, policymakers, and leaders of startup accelerators.

The Startup Common Roadmap

This book presents the findings of this research in two sections.

Part I. Exploring the Startup Common

Chapters 2 through 7 examine more deeply each of the six elements of the Startup Common: pillar companies (Chapter 2), universities (Chapter 3), human capital (Chapter 4), investment capital (Chapter 5), mentor networks (Chapter 6), and values (Chapter 7).

For each of these chapters, Section I covers the following topics:

- Definition of the Startup Common element
- Summary of the chapter's key takeaways for Startup Common participants
- Case studies of successful and less successful efforts to use the Startup Common element to spur startups
- Lessons learned from the cases about what to do and what to avoid
- Questions to spur action by Startup Common participants
- Conclusion

Part II. Implications for Cities

This second section of the book consists of its concluding chapter in which I summarize the key insights from the preceding chapters to help cities boost their economic growth.

In Chapter Eight, I do the following:

- Summarize key insights from Chapters 2 through 7
- Supply case studies of cities that have revived their economic growth by applying some of these insights

- Draw lessons from the successes and challenges presented in the case studies

- Present a methodology for leaders seeking to strengthen their Startup Common

If you want to do more to boost your city's economic vitality, turn the page to get started.

Exploring the Startup Common

What Is the Startup Common?

Location matters to startups because the people who provide them with the resources they need to grow—revenues, talent, capital, advice—are more than producers of code or PowerPoint decks. They live in houses or apartments and commute to offices. They attend meetings and bump into each other randomly at coffee shops and in hallways. And company founders seeking to build, develop, and sustain vital trust relationships with their startup's customers, suppliers, employees, mentors, and investors must meet with people in person repeatedly. Startups thrive or fizzle depending on the quality of these people and the strength of those relationships. And part of that quality depends on where a startup locates. Pick the right one and the startup gets the resources that it needs to grow. Pick the wrong place to run the company and it withers in the struggle to get those resources.

Think of these locations as Startup Commons. To understand this notion, go back to old England where farmers brought their animals to graze in a field at the center of their village. If farmers' animals ate too much, the Common would desiccate and the community would scatter, yielding the Tragedy of

© Peter S. Cohan 2018

P. S. Cohan, *Startup Cities*, https://doi.org/10.1007/978-1-4842-3393-1_1

the Common. But if each farmer's animals limited their consumption and the farmers added fertilizer and seed, the Common and the surrounding town would survive. Much in the world has changed since those days of yore, so the comparison between a village Common and a Startup Common is imperfect. That said, the energy going into both Commons must equal the energy they consume. In old England, the grass produced had to at least equal the amount the animals ate. And a Startup Common's cash, talent, and mentoring must at least equal the amount that entrepreneurs consume; otherwise startup CEOs will move to another Startup Common that supplies the resources their ventures require. Just as farmers did in old England, today's entrepreneurs and capital providers both compete and cooperate. And a Startup Common's values determine whether the balance between cooperation and competition tips the periodic cycle of startup success and failure towards ever-growing abundance or self-immolation.

Startup Commons of varying success span the globe. And the one whose arc bends the most towards ever-increasing abundance is Silicon Valley. In the second quarter of 2017, it attracted $7.75 billion in venture capital (combining San Francisco's $4.14 billion and Silicon Valley's $3.61 billion), which constituted 42% of the total capital invested during that period and was way higher than the $2.78 billion invested in the New York metro area, the $1.4 billion invested in New England, and the $1.1 billion poured into Los Angeles/Orange County.

The capital invested in these regions is attracted to the different kinds of world-class talent that flock there. And that talent attracts capital providers who can offer the cash and often the mentoring those startups need to grow. Therefore, entrepreneurs should locate in the Startup Common that best fits their venture's market and stage of development. Through deeper insights into how entrepreneurs make these choices, government policymakers can boost the odds that the most pioneering entrepreneurs will locate in their regions.

The idea of the Startup Common fits within my work on what drives capital to different countries. *Capital Rising* identified four factors that help explain country-specific differences in private capital flows. We dubbed these factors—corporate governance, financial markets, human capital, and intellectual property protection—the Entrepreneurial Ecosystem (Figure 1-1).

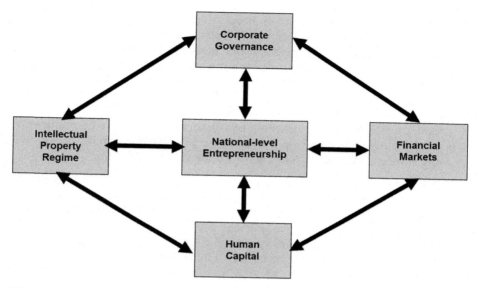

Figure 1-1. Entrepreneurial ecosystem diagram (Source: P.S. Cohan and U.S. Rangan, *Capital Rising: How Global Capital Flows Are Changing Business Systems All Around the World*, Palgrave Macmillan, 2010.)

The EE is useful for country-level policymakers and capital providers such as venture capitalists and hedge fund managers in the following ways:

- **Government policymakers:** Government leaders can change the EE to make a country more attractive to capital providers. Capital providers may boost their allocations to a country if its policymakers improve, say, corporate governance—by imposing stronger protection for minority shareholders; enhancing financial markets by strengthening financial reporting for public companies; bettering human capital by investing in the country's educational system; and tightening protection for intellectual property.

- **Capital providers:** Venture capitalists and private equity investors like investing in countries such as China or India with faster-than-average economic growth because fast growth can boost investment returns. However, we found that capital providers conduct deeper analysis, investigating, and adapting around a fast-growing country's EE. For example, a Boston-based venture capitalist found that Vietnam had weak intellectual property protection so it invested in a mobile payment service whose business model did not depend on proprietary technology, earning a 100-fold return on its investment.

But the EE's explanatory power ends at the country border. That's because the EE elements within a country are mostly the same in all its regions. For example, there is no significant difference between corporate governance in, say, Manhattan and San Francisco, nor are the rules for capital markets or intellectual property protection different in these two regions. The one EE element with significant differences across regions is human capital. For example, skilled engineers proliferate in the San Francisco area while Manhattan has a disproportionate share of investment bankers and traders. The EE framework is not sufficiently robust to help entrepreneurs decide the specific region of a country where it makes the most sense to locate their startup.

Simply put, the Startup Common can take up the EE's slack in helping entrepreneurs decide where to locate, capital providers where to invest, and government policymakers how to create an environment that will draw entrepreneurs. Taking Hartz's general concept a bit further, I defined the Startup Common (Figure 1-2) as six elements that get strengthened in each generation of startup successes and failures. Unfunded startups tap the Startup Common for capital, people, and advice—a small percentage of which are funded. A few of the funded startups succeed and their investors and founders reinvest their capital and know-how into the Startup Common. Even some of the many failed startups give back to the Startup Common as their people and technology are composted and become part of the Startup Common.

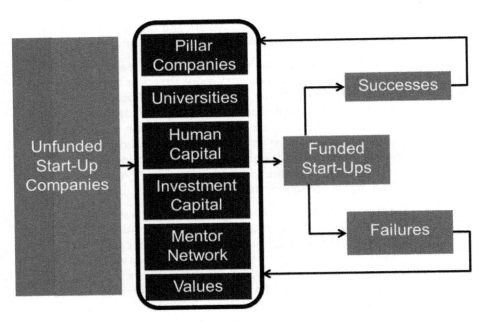

Figure 1-2. Startup Common

To understand why Silicon Valley leads, let's examine each Startup Common element in more detail, illustrated with examples from Silicon Valley:

- **Pillar companies:** In Silicon Valley, pillar companies like Apple, Google, Facebook, Oracle, and Cisco Systems help startups in three ways. They serve as early-adopter customers; provide capital from seed to exit; and supply talented executives, engineers, and sales people.

- **Universities:** Among the world's best sources of intellectual property and talent, Silicon Valley hosts Stanford, University of California, Berkeley, and Santa Clara University. Although Y Combinator is not a university, its intense learning environment adds valuable skills to its participants. Moreover, Ryan Sutton-Gee, whose startup PlanGrid graduated from Y Combinator, estimated that its roughly 600 graduates have a probability ranging from 2% to 3% of creating a $1 billion company, compared to the Silicon Valley average of 0.01%.

- **Human capital:** Coming from the pillar companies, universities, and talent from around the world, Silicon Valley has an ample, if expensive, pool of startup CEOs and other C-level executives, functional vice presidents, and engineers, sales people, and marketers. And Silicon Valley is able to provide this human capital with startup opportunities that do not require a change in their commuting patterns. As Chuck Eesley, Assistant Professor and Morgenthaler Faculty Fellow at Stanford, explained, "When someone's been working at Google or Facebook and they want to start a company, they don't want to leave and move their whole family, so they start where they are. Similarly, it's less risky for someone to start or join a startup in Silicon Valley because if it fails, they don't have to pick up the family and move to join another startup because they're all co-located; you don't need to move the family and buy a new house. For someone working at IBM in upstate New York, if they leave IBM to join a startup, it's much riskier because there [isn't] a cluster of other startups or large companies to go to if the startup fails."

- **Investment capital:** Startups need different kinds of capital at different stages: bootstrapping, founder financing, or friends and family money to get a business model; angel capital to win customers in a specific market segment; and venture capital to expand globally and broaden the product line. Silicon Valley has deep pools of all these kinds of capital. For example, in 2016 Silicon Valley VCs raised $41 billion from limited partners, a 10-year high.

- **Mentor network:** Experienced investors and executives mentor companies and talented professionals. At the corporate level, such mentoring includes help with strategic vision, acquisitions, raising capital, performance monitoring, organization design, culture, hiring and firing, product development, and getting customers and partners.

- **Values:** Finally, Silicon Valley has a unique set of values that guide the way people behave. As former Twitter executive Elad Gil explained, it puts a premium on giving back without expectation of short-term gain; taking a risk to disrupt big markets, which includes an acceptance of failure; and intellectual humility. These values help to expand the size of the opportunity available to entrepreneurs and investors in the region. Stanford Business School professor George Foster is impatient with this clichéd "embracing failure" formulation; he argues that rather than embracing failure, Silicon Valley "tolerates smart failure."

How Wayfair Tapped the Boston Startup Common

Entrepreneurs benefit from picking the right Startup Common. Wayfair, a $3.4 billion (2016 revenues) home hard goods e-tailer, clearly benefited from locating in Boston. Thanks to the capital and talent Wayfair accessed there, it was able to grow from a collection of 200 specific hard goods websites founded in 2002 to a $1.3 billion company that went public in October 2014. By August 2017 Wayfair's shares had risen 85%, yielding a stock market capitalization of $6.1 billion.

Former Cornell engineering classmates Niraj Shah (a Pittsfield, Mass. native who rejected working in New York and happily moved to Boston) and Steve Conine founded what is now Wayfair. In 1995, they started Spinners, an IT consulting business, which they sold in 1998 to interactive advertising firm iXL for $10 million. After two years with iXL, in 2001 they launched Simplify Mobile, which made mobile-phone software for corporate users but it never got off the ground. Almost a year's worth of hard work was gone without much to show for it. So as they considered their next move, Conine and Shah were determined to think big—really big. "We had aspirations," said Shah.

In 2002, they founded CSN Stores (after the initials of their last names) not long after the dot-com bubble had burst. According to *Fast Company*, "Shah knew a woman working out of her spare bedroom and making a quarter of a million dollars a year selling birdhouses online. He and his partner decided to sell products that would be hard to find in Best Buy or even Walmart. They wouldn't stock TVs or other electronics; instead they would offer every possible TV stand or rack to hold those TVs." Their first site was racksandstands.com, which sold only TV and speaker stands. A gym in Houston ordered eight television mounts and they added a second site that sold TV mounts and related accessories. Soon thereafter they added sites for outdoor, bedroom, and office furniture, ultimately controlling 200 sites in 15 categories such as exercise equipment, home improvement, pet and garden supplies, rugs, baby strollers, toys.

Amazingly enough, they accomplished all this without raising outside capital because their niche sites were generating cash. By 2011 CSN had reached $500 million in sales and was the largest home-seller on Amazon and eBay and the largest marketplace partner at Walmart. However, Shah noticed that they were not getting enough repeat customers because they did not have a strong brand. So they decided to reorganize the company around a strong brand which they called Wayfair, with help from Michael Estabrook, art director of the Newton, Mass.-based branding firm BrandEquity. To finance the creation of that brand and to offset the losses they expected as they moved those 200 individual sites under that one brand, the company raised $200 million from Boston venture capitalists Spark, Battery, Great Hill, and Harbour Vest. That money came in handy as they moved the individual sites to Wayfair in "waves, and, as they expected lost 50% of their traffic at the microsites that redirected to Wayfair, taking a 30% hit on revenue."

By 2012, Wayfair had a significant share of the $200 billion furniture market, of which a mere 5% was transacted online. One of the keys to Wayfair's success was its ability to offer excellent delivery service to consumers, which in turn depended on its ability to form partnerships with furniture manufacturers who would ship most customer orders directly to consumers. Although they added two warehouses in 2011, 90% of their products were shipped directly from their suppliers, and this was managed through computer systems that in 2012 coordinated the order flow and logistics of the more than 4,000 suppliers that shipped out an average of 93,800 items each week. As Alex Finkelstein, general partner of Spark Capital, a Boston venture capital firm, explained, "In my mind, that's the secret of the business—teaching thousands of small, mid, and large manufacturers how to do drop-ship so well. That's what really enables the engine behind the engine to work."

Shah located in Boston because he saw that its advantages outweighed its disadvantages. For example, he concluded that its talent was the best available for Wayfair. As he told *The Boston Globe*, "Boston's got an incredible amount of talent: it's got a lot of consumer-oriented brand talent, it's got a lot of traditional retail talent, a lot of technology talent. So it's got a lot of not just technology skills, but a lot of other skills that are highly relevant when you think of consumer Internet. What we found was that to some degree it's almost a better place [for hiring] because you talk to companies that you'd think would have a very easy time recruiting in [Silicon] Valley, and they'll share with you stories where they can't get engineers because basically Facebook and Google are in a bidding war against each other, and everyone else is just collateral damage." Shah also believes that "Boston has to be one of the top markets because it has all these universities and a diversity of industries: healthcare, academia, and retail. It's one of the best places to be in terms of hiring people across different skill sets." As he told me in March 2013, Wayfair hired more than 100 interns from Northeastern University's co-op program and Shah said he was very impressed with MIT graduates' skills in robotics, networking, and data management.

Despite these strengths, Shah believes that Boston could be better. For example, as he explained in a February 2013 interview, he thinks its Startup Common could use more "$10 billion plus" publicly-traded technology companies. He views such companies as "great places for people to gain experience and get wealthy through stock options." Often, Shah observes, this happens because Boston entrepreneurs "sell before they scale." Whereas in Silicon Valley, startup CEOs are willing to wait "to get a 100 times return on their investment; in Boston, entrepreneurs generally have not yet had a big score so they sell their companies when they have only made a 10x return."

While Wayfair's decision to base itself in Boston does not explain its success, Shah and his team have benefited from Boston's deep pool of talented people, particularly in key functional areas such as branding, marketing analytics, and logistical systems, as well as in access to investors who provided capital and excellent advice.

What Makes The Startup Common Different?

The Startup Common is a new way to think about questions that academics have been exploring for centuries. For example, the question of why some locations have more business activity than others has led academics to conclude that local agglomeration—the concentration of businesses and people in a specific location—can initially enhance and ultimately be the result of a region's comparative advantage. But it has only been in the last several decades that venture capital and the startups they finance have emerged as powerful economic forces. The Startup Common adds specificity to the dynamics of how a region becomes a hub for startup activity, the six specific elements that make up this local resource, and the way those elements develop and interact over time. To be sure, many of academics I interviewed cited the importance of universities, talent, and capital to a region's rise as a startup hub. However, they did not as often consider the important role of pillar companies, mentoring, and values to that region's emergence as a startup hub.

The Startup Common framework places a clear emphasis on the role of these other elements and thereby helps explain the rise and fall of a region as a startup hub based on the success or failure of a region's pillar companies to adapt to changing technologies, upstart competitors, and evolving customer needs. For example, in the 1950s, Detroit was the world leader in the automotive industry; however, in the 1970s, Japanese rivals began taking its market share and Detroit's pillar companies were slow to respond and never able to re-establish a lead over these rivals. Hence a Detroit renaissance, which might have been fueled by the revival of GM, Ford, and Chrysler or the emergence of pillar companies in new industries, never emerged.

The central role of values within a Startup Common is particularly significant. As you will see throughout this book, there are many cities that host universities, but only a handful of these university towns become a breeding ground for startups. For example, one reason that Cambridge and Palo Alto are such important startup locations is the value their leading universities, MIT and Stanford, respectively, placed on their professors doing work that was both at the cutting edge of thought and useful to industry. Worcester, Mass., a mere 45 miles from Cambridge, has eleven colleges and universities that do not place the same value on such academic interaction with industry. Entrepreneurial talent educated in Worcester flees to places like Cambridge and Silicon Valley to realize their dreams.

These observations emerged from my interviews with over a dozen leading business school professors from Stanford, MIT, and Harvard Business School. These experts commented on questions such as: What is a startup? Does it matter where startups locate? Why do a few regions have the most startups? How do these startup-rich regions achieve their status?

It is important to distinguish between a company founded to support its CEO and staff and companies funded by venture capital firms seeking rapid growth that culminates in an initial public offering or acquisition. Jan Rivkin, Harvard Business School Bruce V. Rauner Professor of Business Administration, pointed out that this statement is not precisely true because it depends on how you define startup. If a startup is a small, private company, such as a restaurant, that is intended to help a founder and its employees to make a living, such startups are widely distributed geographically. However, if a startup is thought of as a small private company whose goal is to get big fast, whose investors hope to get richer when the company is acquired or goes public, then startups are concentrated. The Kauffman Foundation refers to such fast-growing startups as gazelles, emphasizing that such startups are distinguished by their ability to grow quickly while continuing to develop new products, win customers, and deliver a high level of service. Kauffman argued that gazelles account for 50% of new jobs, they expand into new geographies, and they create growth in related industries.

Gazelles concentrate in specific locations because of the overwhelming advantages that those locations provide to entrepreneurs and investors. Rivkin suggested that gazelles have good reasons to locate in a relatively small number of specific cities such as Boston, Silicon Valley, and Los Angeles. As he said, "Venture capital is spiky. The top 50 metro areas receive 97% of the venture capital. 83% of the venture capital investment goes to places like San Francisco, Boston, and Southern California." Such concentration happens because it works. "It goes back to Alfred Marshall in the 1890s. Agglomeration happens for a reason: there are positive feedback loops between skilled labor and specialized inputs such as venture capital. Computer scientists want to be in the Bay Area; biotechnologists flock to Boston and Cambridge; media people go to New York. As Marshall wrote, 'Mysteries are as if they were in the air,'" explained Rivkin.

And while universities are often a starting point for a successful startup region, the magnetic power of its talent network is able to overcome the economic barriers imposed by high housing costs, congestion, and exhausting commutes. Stanford Business School Fred H. Merrill Professor of Economics Paul Oyer explained "it is almost impossible for cities that attempt to make themselves into the next Silicon Valley. [Startup cities] get started thanks to research and education. Towns with noted universities like Silicon Valley, Research Triangle Park, and Austin get people who graduate, live there, and get together. The network is valuable." Oyer points out that universities are a necessary but not sufficient condition. "If universities alone were all that was needed, Missoula, Mont., where University of Montana is located, would be a startup hub. You also need companies. For example, Stanford had Hewlett Packard and Schlumberger." Oyer sees many factors that could, but don't, destroy Silicon Valley as a startup hub. "It is hard for other cities to break in because of the power of the network that gets created, which grows as each new person comes here. And venture capitalists want to be where the talent is. The strength of the network overwhelms all the factors that should kill Silicon Valley, such as the high cost of living and high tax rates," he explained.

These regions are irresistible to entrepreneurs because they enable gazelles to raise capital and hire talent in large enough blocks to get big fast. As Harvard Business School Professor of Management Practice Shikhar Ghosh said, "A company like Facebook, which is trying to get big fast, can get the resources it needs in Boston when it's small, but if it wants to get really big, it needs to move to a place like Silicon Valley where it can more easily raise the capital it needs in big increments. A company that ultimately wants to employ 20,000 to 30,000 people will move to an area that has the capital to help it raise Series B, C, and D funding."

Another key resource that gazelles need to hire in big chunks is talented people. George Foster, Konosuke Matsushita Professor of Management at the Stanford Graduate School of Business, said "In Silicon Valley an entrepreneur hires 500 software engineers quickly. And China is becoming another such place. It produces 200,000 engineers a year and 2,000 of them are truly great." If talent is concentrated in a specific region, the risk of going to work for a startup there declines substantially.

An interesting development over the last five to 10 years has been the movement of that talent into cities, thus replotting the center of gravity for Silicon Valley to San Francisco and from Massachusetts's Route 128 to Boston and Cambridge. Harvard Business School Associate Professor William Kerr explained, "Culture favors some places over others. People want to be in places where everyone idolizes entrepreneurs. They want to be where you can try and fail and not be ostracized. In the Boston area, young talent wants to live in cities, which is making it hard for me to find a buyer for my three-acre property in [the upscale, rural suburb 25 miles from Boston] Lincoln."

Startup-rich regions such as Silicon Valley and Cambridge achieved their status as world leaders over many decades. In looking back over those decades, experts note that the initial spark for their emergence as leaders was the presence of outstanding leaders who started successful companies close to universities with startup-friendly values. These startups grew, went public, and became local pillars. New companies spun off from these pillars attracted new capital and fresh talent eager to partake in similar startup success. Before getting into how they evolved, it is worth noting that MIT and Stanford have created a tremendous amount of wealth. Eesley reported that by 2014 MIT alumni had created 30,200 companies with $1.9 trillion in revenue, which employed 4.6 million people. Stanford had done even more: by 2011 Stanford alumni had created 39,900 companies with $2.7 trillion in revenue and 5.4 million jobs.

As mentioned earlier, great leaders spurred the emergence of Silicon Valley and Cambridge. For example, as MIT Sloan School Lecturer Jorge Guzman pointed out, Silicon Valley would still be peach orchards were it not for William Shockley, the inventor of the transistor who moved west to found Fairchild Semiconductor. MIT Sloan School David Sarnoff Professor of Management of Technology Ed Roberts noted that Frederick Terman, an MIT professor who came to Stanford and helped two of his students, William Hewlett and David Packard, to found HP, helped HP succeed by connecting the company to Defense Department contracts. In Cambridge, there likely would be no venture capital industry were it not for Harvard Business School professor Georges Doriot and MIT alum Ken Olson, who founded Digital Equipment Corp. with funds from Doriot's American Research and Development. As MIT Professor of Technological Innovation, Entrepreneurship, and Strategic Management James Utterback explained, "From a 50-year career perspective, the key to the success of Cambridge and Silicon Valley is leadership within a context."

As Utterback implied, great leaders can't build companies all by themselves. For that they need talent and fresh ideas that come from local universities. As Roberts pointed out, MIT was started in the 1861 with the motto *Mens et Manus* (Latin for mind and hand), meaning that its mission was to make cutting edge ideas useful to industry. What's more, MIT encouraged professors to do research for industry to supplement their low professor's pay. Thus there was a natural flow of talent between MIT and industry, which in other universities is frowned on. Roberts believes that Terman took that same philosophy to Stanford and that has made much of the difference.

Capital, talent, and pillar companies follow initial startup success. Venture capitalists are pack animals; if they see that another firm has profited through an investment, they will seek out similar ones. So an initial success will attract more capital, and if that new capital is successful, a snowball effect will be created. If some of the startups go public and scale, then they become pillar companies that reinvest their capital and talent in the region. And that local success attracts more people in the local universities to go into startups. As Foster said, "The most important factors that cause scale up are opportunity and people. But there is a debate over whether the best talent will find the biggest opportunity" or vice versa.

As these experts explained, the emergence of a local startup hub takes decades. The Startup Common is different in that it provides a way to explain how over time specific regions may rise and fall based on the relative strength or weakness of the six startup common elements, many of which were mentioned by the experts I interviewed. What makes the Startup Common valuable is that it integrates all the components into one model that can help leaders to explain where a region is now, the vision for its success as a startup hub, and point the way to closing the gap.

Creating Pillar Companies

What Are Pillar Companies?

Pillar companies are local, publicly-traded firms that provide startups with talent and capital by using their products and sometimes by acquiring the startups once they've grown to their full potential as independent firms. Pillar companies are important to a region's startup ecosystem for four reasons:

- **They boost local entrepreneurship culture.** A pillar company's success provides local entrepreneurs with a compelling example of the advantages over big company employment of taking the risk to start a company or work with a startup. A region's first pillar companies can spur cultural change, magnetically pulling local talent towards entrepreneurship.

- **They create a new generation of entrepreneurs or angels.** A local startup's successful IPO creates a windfall for some of its employees, particularly members of the startup's top management team and other significant outside shareholders. The boost in their wealth and experience leading a successful company makes it possible for them to start companies themselves or invest in local startups as angel investors.

P. S. Cohan, *Startup Cities*, https://doi.org/10.1007/978-1-4842-3393-1_2

- **They bring outside capital into the region.** A pillar company's successful IPO often enriches the VC firms that invested when it was private. Rival VCs who missed out on this bonanza may investigate that region in order not to fall further behind their more fortunate peers. If the new VCs invest in startups near the pillar, and some of those startups go public or are acquired, the resulting snowball effect will strengthen the region's magnetic pull on outside investors. Moreover, VCs may see a pillar company's interest in a startup as a weak signal of an emerging market opportunity.

- **They create opportunity umbrellas for local startups.** A successful pillar company often ends up with surplus capital and talent. Moreover, due to its relatively large size and growth objectives, it may only be interested in investing in very large markets. If a pillar company's employees see a market opportunity that the pillar views as too small, the pillar may encourage its employees to start a company, with financing help from the pillar, and use the startup's product in its own business. More generally, a pillar may view support of local startups as a potentially profitable way to outsource some of its new product development.

Pillar companies are not always good for a city's startup scene. In fact, if a city's major employers are pillar companies, the city will be in trouble if those pillar companies decline or get acquired by a company outside the region that may cut back on local staff during an economic downturn. For example, the decline of Massachusetts pillars such as Digital Equipment Corporation and Wang in the 1980s threw many people out of work, as did the later implosion of many local networking companies such as Sycamore Networks after the dot-com crash. Hence the most vibrant startup cities have a constant stream of new startups with the potential to grow into pillars so that the maturing and decline of its older pillar companies will not send the city into a longer-term economic funk.

Eight of the 12 cities I researched for this book (Los Angeles, Hong Kong, Stockholm, Lund, Paris, Lyon, Worcester, and Haifa) have no pillar companies at all while four (Silicon Valley, Beijing, Boston, and Tel Aviv) have many pillar companies. By looking at the development of startup scenes in the six city pairs introduced in Chapter 1, a common pattern emerges for how a region can go from no gazelles to hosting many vibrant pillar companies that contribute to the region's continued growth.

The process starts with the arrival of an exceptionally talented entrepreneur to a region. That founder's reputation attracts talented cofounders and capital. Local universities supply talent and intellectual property. If the startup goes public or is acquired, the newly wealthy cofounders start new companies or provide seed capital for other entrepreneurs. If the next generation of entrepreneurs and VCs build successful companies, they add to the collection of compelling stories that change the local culture, which draws in more entrepreneurs and capital to keep the cycle moving forward.

This is an approximation of how Silicon Valley went from fruit orchards to the world's leading startup region. Leslie Berlin, Project Historian of the Silicon Valley Archives at Stanford, believes that people need to get beyond the region's myths. As she said, "Companies like Apple, HP, and Google are not just about the garages where they were founded. Institutions mattered tremendously in their development. HP and Google came out of Stanford. Apple's success was embedded in Silicon Valley's Homebrew Computer Club. The Defense Department provided R&D funding for semiconductors. And immigration is essential. Fifty percent of Unicorn cofounders were born outside the U.S." Culture and luck also play a role. As Berlin said, "Silicon Valley has a culture of openness and stock options. And it got very lucky that the ailing mother of William Shockley, who in 1956 founded Mountain View, Calif.-based Shockley Semiconductor, lived in Silicon Valley where he moved [to take care of her when she became ill]." In 1957, eight of Shockley's researchers left to start Fairchild Semiconductor, which played a major role in the growth of the local semiconductor industry. Indeed Fairchild, HP, and others spawned new companies such as Intel and Apple (co-founder Steve Wozniak was an HP engineer). And as we will explore later in this chapter, Google helps to spur more startups in Silicon Valley through a variety of corporate investment initiatives.

My research into pairs of startup cities suggests that there is a logical progression from no pillar companies to many that target large market opportunities, what I call the Pillar Company Staircase (Figure 2-1).

- **Level 0: No Pillars, No Gazelles.** Cities like Worcester, Mass. have no pillar companies and no gazelles. However, startups have some local support from universities and the local government. Since these startups generally lack entrepreneurs with the potential to scale the companies rapidly, they are unable to attract capital from outside the city. Thus there is little likelihood that any of these startups will become pillar companies. The city may have universities and local, publicly-traded technology companies; however, those companies do not engage with, support, or invest in local startups.

- **Level 1: No Pillars, Some Gazelles.** Cities like Lyons, France also lack pillar companies but they do have some gazelles. Thanks to support from local universities and government, which supplies seed capital for these gazelles, they are able to demonstrate the viability of their business model on a small scale. However, these cities lack the higher amounts of capital and mentor networks needed to help them scale. As a result, they tend to relocate to cities that can provide the larger increments of capital and talent they need to grow. If some of the companies founded by these local entrepreneurs go public or are acquired, some of the cofounders could return to the city of origin to invest some of their capital in local startups.

- **Level 2: No Pillars, Acquired Gazelles.** Cities like Stockholm, Sweden have no pillar companies; however, many of their gazelles have been acquired by large, publicly-traded companies like Microsoft. What's more, such cities have large, publicly-traded companies that dismiss talented workers during an economic downturn. Many of the enriched gazelle cofounders start or finance startups. Some of the talented former corporate engineers start companies and others go to work for these new startups. If some of these startups go public or acquired, eventually the city develops enough talented people to create a pillar company and sustain its growth as a public company.

- **Level 3: Some pillars in niche markets.** Cities like Boston, Mass. have some pillar companies in a variety of important areas of technology that support good-sized companies, but no huge ones that drive the global economy. Boston's pillar companies are in fields such as online marketing (Hubspot), hard goods e-tailing (Wayfair), broadband network operations (Akamai), robotics (iRobot), travel search (TripAdvisor), and orphan disease research (Vertex Pharmaceuticals). These pillar companies are a source of talent and capital for new startups, some of which are founded by their alumni. These cities also host universities that supply considerable talent and intellectual property for startups; they have ample venture capital; and their cultures encourage talented people to start companies to solve difficult technical problems.

- **Level 4: Many pillars in huge markets.** Silicon Valley is the only region with many pillar companies that participate in and create huge markets. Those markets (and sample pillar companies) include social networking (Facebook), computer network equipment (Cisco Systems), semiconductors (Intel), search (Google), smart phones and other personal computing hardware (Apple), data storage and analysis (Oracle), and electric vehicles (Tesla). Not only does Silicon Valley host successful pillars now, but it has created new ones in the wake of the maturation of many of its earlier pillar companies. While Silicon Valley's pillar companies compete for talent with startups and contribute to a higher cost of living and traffic congestion, these startup impediments have yet to diminish the region's magnetic pull for the globe's most talented entrepreneurs.

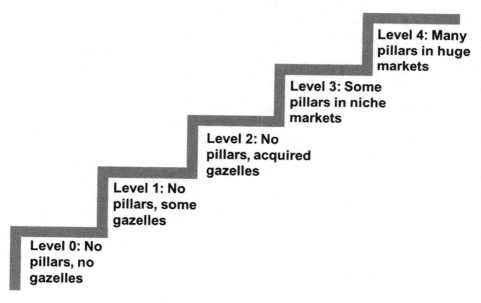

Figure 2-1. Pillar Company Staircase

Takeaways for Startup Common Stakeholders

The implications of the Pillar Company Staircase vary by Startup Common stakeholder.

- **Local policymakers:** Policymakers must identify their city's level in the Pillar Company Staircase and set their policies accordingly. For example, a city at Level 0 might want to consider investing in high-speed Internet and creating an incubator space in order to attract gazelles. Policymakers for a region at Level 4 may want to invest to make sure that roads and other infrastructure, including housing, are sufficient to support continued growth in the region.

- **Entrepreneurs:** Company founders must consider whether they will need the support of pillar companies, if they exist in their industry, early in their development. If so, they should consider locating in regions at Level 3 or Level 4. For example, a startup seeking to develop technology that will boost Google's productivity might benefit from locating near its headquarters. By contrast, a startup that will not need the talent and capital of pillar companies might be more flexible regarding where to locate initially.

- **Universities:** University leaders also ought to vary their actions based on a city's level in the Pillar Company Staircase. Indeed, many of the cities I studied lack pillar companies so they are establishing incubators for student entrepreneurs and adding courses and programs in entrepreneurship. By contrast, cities that host pillar companies, such as MIT and Stanford, have a long tradition of encouraging their faculty to start companies.

- **Capital providers:** Venture capitalists concentrate in regions with a large number of pillar companies and migrate to new regions after they've reached Level 2. By contrast, since private capital is unlikely to take a risk on a region that has had no prior success, some regions at Level 0 or Level 1 of the Pillar Company Staircase try to jumpstart the local ecosystem by financing startups at the seed stage through government grants.

Pillar Company Success and Failure Case Studies

Level 0: No Pillars, No Gazelles

Success Case Study: Zephyr Workshop Forges Ahead in Worcester with Limited Local Support

Introduction

While it hosts many lifestyle businesses, Worcester has no pillar companies and no gazelles. Interestingly, Worcester County does host a very successful, publicly-traded technology company, Oxford, Mass.-based fiber laser maker IPG Photonics, which is not a pillar because it does not provide resources for local startups. Founded in 1990 by a team of PhD physicists from Moscow, IPG went public in December 2006 and its stock soared 835% to about $242 a share, a stock market value of $13 billion, as of November 24, 2017. Its revenues grew 48% to $393 million in the third quarter of 2017 while its net income increased 68% to $116 million. Sadly, IPG's billionaire founder, Valentin Gapontsev (estimated net worth $3.1 billion), has not viewed his success as a reason to give back to the local startup community.

Though lacking in pillar companies and gazelles, Worcester's 11 institutions of higher learning educate students, most of whom choose to leave the city after they complete their education. Happily, Worcester's Becker College hosts a nationally ranked game design program, some of whose graduates have started game design companies in Worcester. Unfortunately, none of these startups have grown very rapidly, but one has at least been able to survive for a few years.

Case Scenario

Zephyr Workshop, a game developer, was founded by Oxford, Mass. native Breeze Grigas. He hoped to build it into a significant company in Worcester. In 2015, his company was selected to be part of StartUp Worcester, a program that selected a dozen local startups for a year's worth of free office space in a local incubator called Running Start. Grigas started his gaming career in Charlton, Mass. and was thrilled when he learned about Becker College's game design program. "I went to Bay Path Regional Vocational Technical High School in Charlton for programming and com-puter-aided drafting with the intent of pursuing game design," he said, "and when I saw Becker's ad for their game design program, I was instantly interested." After graduating with a major in interactive media design, with a concentration on art, Grigas decided he wanted to build games that he would want to play, so he started a company. "Originally, I created a game with another graduating senior, and we built a company around that product. I really enjoy creating things and working on my own projects, making things that I would want to play. It's why I pursued the game design industry to begin with." Grigas believed that as a college graduate, he would have a difficult time finding an entry-level position that offered what he wanted, so he decided not to take a job with someone else. As he explained, "The game industry is harsh and it's very hard to find entry-level work in a desirable position, on a project or team that's fulfilling. I personally have a bigger need for creative fulfillment right now, so I'm going for it, while keeping an eye out for that one really great opening to work on something really cool. A lot of game companies also look for experience on shipped products in a specific role, and one of the best ways to gain that experience is to self-motivate and create your own great games."

Grigas saw an enormous opportunity and believed his strategy would enable his company to gain a meaningful share. As Grigas said, "Our games target the 12- to 34-year-old male demographic, a large chunk of game players. We estimate the dollar value of our target market to be between $125 million and $175 million. Board and card games have had very large resurgence in recent years, being worth around $700 million in North America total, and the market value of the genre of games that we specialize in is about 18 to 25% of that." He believed Zephyr Workshop would grow because it would offer complex games at a much lower price. "We believe that we can offer a type of games that are traditionally very expensive and complex, and bring them to a broader audience for a lower price, with more content. We're shooting for the $30 to $50 range for our games, in a sector that normally has a buy-in of $80 to $150 for beginning players. Our overall model is to offer our initial products at that comparatively low buy-in and then continue to release additions and expansions at the $20 to $50 range also on a set schedule, building on the popularity of the product and keeping its lifetime long and players invested."

Zephyr Workshop's money came from "personal savings and revenue from previously sold iterations of our game." And while Grigas declined to comment on the company's revenues or customer count, he did express satisfaction with its progress. As he said, "We've had a good success across a number of conventions and festivals across the region and have completely sold through two print runs of our self-published game."

By August 2017, Zephyr Workshop, after a second year in StartUp Worcester, was still struggling towards its goals after raising funds from a Kickstarter. In 2016, the company had made some progress developing a game called A.E.G.I.S. and by 2017, it succeeded in raising $40,000 after its second attempt at a Kickstarter campaign. In 2016, Grigas felt that his company had made progress with partners and customers. As he said, "On top of celebrating a second year in StartUp Worcester, (we have) been moving forward on several projects in big ways. We've partnered with artist Emily Hancock and Cambridge-based Mob Made Games to produce the mobile tablet game Florafiora, which is due out in 2017. That game won the Indie Alpha and People's Choice categories at the MassDiGi Game Challenge in February 2016. We made a trip out to San Francisco for Game Developer's Conference for the first time to expand our network. Most importantly, in conjunction with our Marlborough, Mass.-based publisher, Greenbrier Games, we've finalized the assets for the wide release of our game A.E.G.I.S., which is still aiming for Kickstarter this year," said Grigas. He placed a great value in StartUp Worcester. "We applied to StartUp Worcester again because the Running Start space is indispensable for us. As a company with mainly remote workers that specializes in physical products, having a central space where we can congregate to develop and test our games is key. Through StartUp Worcester, we were also able to grow as a company and went from one game in development to having several, with a proper pipeline and a larger team to accommodate it." Zephyr Workshop hoped that by 2017 A.E.G.I.S. would "be on shelves and we'll be able to sell it direct to consumer at events," said Grigas.

Zephyr Workshop stumbled initially when it tried to raise funding through a Kickstarter but ultimately prevailed, raising at least $40,000. In October 2016, Zephyr tried to raise $40,000 for A.E.G.I.S. through a Kickstarter but did not meet its goal. In May 2017, Grigas tried again and had better results. As he said in a May 23 e-mail "our brand new Kickstarter campaign [was] completely revamped [since last October] and [was] extremely successful. We reached our goal in nine hours and have currently raised over $40,000!" [Most of the money] will go to "manufacturing the game and shipping it around the world and the rest will go towards marketing the game and selling the rest of the stock, as well as creating more content for the game in the future." [Ultimately, Zephyr aspires to get A.E.G.I.S. on retail shelves by] "selling and marketing at conventions such as GenCon and Penny Arcade Expo, where we traditionally have had the most interest and sales, and using the network we've built over the last few years to get in touch with distributors," he said.

Case Analysis

Zephyr Workshop is not a clear success story, yet as of August 2017 it had made the most progress of the 36 companies that participated in StartUp Worcester between 2015 and 2017. What does this case reveal about a location that lacks pillar companies or gazelles?

- **Pillar companies are evidence of a highly developed startup scene.** Worcester's startup scene has been trying to get off the ground for several years and has yet to produce any gazelles. If a region hosts enough gazelles, odds improve that perhaps one or two will grow to the point where they can be acquired. And perhaps some of those acquired companies will produce the entrepreneurial skills and capital needed to create the region's first pillar company. Worcester is in the early stages of the process of creating pillar companies, but there is little evidence so far that it will get beyond this step.

- **The absence of pillar companies makes it more difficult for startups to expand.** Pillar companies emerge from many startups in a location, most of which fail. The general challenges facing a startup in any location are even greater in a region without pillars. For example, without pillar companies, a founder lacks role models for success, has fewer sources of talent, struggles to get access to capital, and may find it more difficult to get mentorship. Zephyr Workshop seems to be coping with these challenges, but it is hard to tell whether it will survive.

- **Government and local universities may be the best resources available to startups in such locations.** Worcester is one of several regions I've seen—in Europe, local governments in Lisbon, Paris, Lyon, and Barcelona—that provide some seed capital and other forms of support for local startups. Worcester has the benefit of schools like Becker College which attract students with skills in game design and encourages them to start companies. Ultimately, such government pump priming can help create startups in a region; however, such regions will only become self-sustaining if private sector actors, particularly VCs, step in to finance fast-growing startups.

Unsuccessful Case Study: Hopkinton's EMC Squashes a Startup by Suing a Former Executive

Introduction

In April 2013, I asked a group of Cambridge-based venture capitalists whether Hopkinton, Mass.-based data storage suppler EMC was a pillar company. They made it very clear that EMC was the opposite. How so? Instead of supplying startups with talent and capital, it sought to use the legal system to destroy them. Specifically, EMC was Massachusetts's leading advocate for so-called non-compete agreements, which block former employees from leaving the company and working for a competitor for a period of time, even after the employee had been dismissed through a layoff.

A leader in Boston's venture capital industry believes that EMC put the region at a competitive disadvantage. Paul Maeder, co-founder and Chair of Highland Capital Partners, with offices near MIT and in Palo Alto, Calif., is sanguine about Boston's startup scene. But he recognizes many of Silicon Valley's advantages, one of which is its relatively large number of pillar companies—locally-headquartered, publicly-traded technology companies that supply local startups with talent, capital, and a willingness to use the startup's product. More importantly, large Boston-area technology companies differ from those in Silicon Valley by enforcing non-compete agreements intended to block former employees from taking jobs at rivals or founding startups. As Maeder explained, "While I am not sure that pillar companies confer a big advantage to startups since a lot of the ideas we see come out of universities, there are tons of pillar companies like Google in Silicon Valley which gives it an advantage over Cambridge. Worse than Boston's lack of pillar companies is the persistence of non-compete agreements, which were heavily advocated by Joe Tucci, former CEO of EMC (which is now a Dell subsidiary)."

Case Scenario

A case in point is SANgate Systems, a data storage company that was co-located in the Boston area and in Israel. In 2000, an EMC executive bolted to take over as SANgate's CEO. EMC sued the executive, charging him with violating the terms of his non-compete and EMC prevailed, so SANgate replaced him as CEO with a Canadian executive who lasted about a year before the company's CFO took over and shut down its Israeli operation. Ultimately, SANgate failed—a victory for EMC and a sadly powerful demonstration of the power of an anti-pillar company to stifle a region's startup community. It remains to be seen whether Dell will continue to suppress entrepreneurship by following in Tucci's footsteps.

In 2000, Doron Kempel, a former leading Israeli military figure with a law degree from Tel Aviv University and an MBA from Harvard Business School, was an EMC executive. Since 1997, Kempel had been VP and general manager of EMC's media solutions group, responsible for creating streaming video servers. He joined EMC from Imedia, a streaming video router company he helped create and sell to Terayon Corp to for $100 million. Prior to that he was a venture capitalist at Israel Corp.

His EMC tenure ended in 2001 when he was among the thousands of employees laid off as EMC's sales and profits plummeted, but that September he was appointed CEO of Southborough, Mass.-based SANgate Systems, a start-up data storage company established in 1999 with an Israeli center to develop software for a product that allowed data sharing between open systems and mainframes. EMC sued Kempel for violating the terms of his non-compete agreement, which barred him for a year for working for a competitor. But Kempel argued that his EMC work focused on so-called rich media, video server development, and the delivery of streaming video, of which storage was just a component. He argued that SANgate was working on a technology that did not overlap with what he did at EMC. EMC prevailed, forcing Kempel to give up the SANgate job on the grounds that he had violated his non-compete agreement. Its approach to Kempel reflected EMC's two-pronged strategy: publicly deny that startups were a threat while privately spending heavily to restrict their operations by suing key executives.

SANgate's troubles continued after Kempel was replaced as its CEO, ending with its demise. Under its first CEO, Alan Davis, SANgate focused on technology to move data from mainframes to storage systems. Kempel was hired to replace Davis and was forced to leave. Patrick Courtin took over and began to develop products to shift data from networked servers to storage devices. Courtin left and was replaced by George McHorney, formerly SANgate's CFO. In July 2003, SANgate shut its Israel-based operations, dismissing 24 of its 26 Israeli workers after having raised $25 million in three financing rounds. In December 2003, the company was closed.

Case Analysis

EMC's role as an anti-pillar—actively squashing startups that tried to hire its people—shows the power that a large, publicly-traded company can have over a region's startup scene. Indeed, EMC's conduct cast a shadow not only on Worcester County, where it was headquartered, but on Boston's efforts to spur startups as well. Here are two implications of this case scenario:

- **Policymakers must resist the pull of an anti-pillar's campaign cash.** In 2016, despite vocal advocacy from the New England Venture Capital Association, Massachusetts failed to pass non-compete reform. Associated Industries of Massachusetts, an industry lobbying group whose most vocal non-compete advocate was EMC, effectively kept Massachusetts from passing non-compete reform, leaving unresolved the tension between separate bills passed in the Massachusetts House and Senate. Sadly for the state's declining share of venture capital and startups, local policymakers were unable to resist the pull of EMC's lobbying efforts. In light of EMC's acquisition by Dell, it is possible that non-compete reform may have more hope for passage in the future.

- **Entrepreneurs who might depend on an anti-pillar's talent should locate elsewhere**. Until such reform is a reality, entrepreneurs who depend on hiring talent from public companies who enforce non-competes may want to move to other states, such as California, where non-compete contracts are generally prohibited. Should such reform in Massachusetts be delayed or deferred, the state may continue to lose its ability to retain locally-educated talent who decamp for more accommodating regions that lack non-competes.

Principles

A region with no pillars and no gazelles faces such enormous hurdles to becoming a vital startup hub that its leaders may decide that there is little point in trying. Consider the costs and benefits of trying to boost local entrepreneurship in such a region. Government policymakers would need to assemble a team of local university leaders, business executives, philanthropists, and investors to identify the challenges facing the region in competing for top entrepreneurial talent and spurring the talent to start fast-growing companies. Overcoming such challenges might require significant capital investment to transform a city into a place where such talent would want to live and work—with no guarantee that such investments would yield the level of startup activity required to justify the investment. Despite these costs, leaders could be spurred to take these risks if they believed that not doing so would cause the region to lose an opportunity to broaden its local economic base before its existing industries declined even further.

The case studies reveal key issues that a region's stakeholders ought to consider when trying to decide whether to boost its startup ecosystem and some principles to guide those decisions:

- **Government policymakers:** Politicians focus on reelection so civil servants must keep their ears attuned to politicians' changing priorities. Politicians consider whether action to boost a region's entrepreneurial ecosystem will increase their reelection prospects. If so, they must decide what they should try to do and how they should try to do it. Such decisions should be guided by analysis of four questions: Can the actions generate momentum quickly to help build support for further action? Have such actions worked for similar regions and what can be learned from those cases? Do the actions build on the region's competitive advantages? Can the region finance the actions?

- **Investors:** Such regions often lack local venture capital firms although they may host angel investors and philanthropists. VC near but outside the region may not want to finance its startups, perhaps hoping others will pioneer investment in its startups and then they will follow those pioneers quickly if they are successful. Unless a venture capitalist has an emotional attachment to the region, he or she may not want to be that pioneer.

- **Business leaders:** Local business leaders in such regions might be professional managers rather than entrepreneurs or their firms might be lifestyle businesses, slowly growing or static companies that support their founders and staff. Such leaders should consider whether supporting the local entrepreneurial ecosystem would benefit or threaten their company. As you'll see, some local business leaders view startups as a threat to be blocked through the legal system. Others see no benefit to supporting the local startup community and thus ignore entreaties to participate, for example, by sponsoring a local startup accelerator or offering internships to local university students.

- **Student entrepreneurs:** Local university students in such regions are often inclined to leave after they graduate. After all, there is little reason for them not to move to regions with far more robust entrepreneurial ecosystems. Why should they be pioneers and start companies near the local universities? Most students conclude that they lack the commitment to the region and the talent to overcome the odds against success in a place where there are no local role models. On the other hand, locally-educated students who decide to start companies nearby may benefit from lower real estate and salary expenses and less competition for access to talent.

Level 1: No Pillars, Some Gazelles

Success Case Study: Check Point Software's IPO Spawns Spinoffs That Go Public

Introduction

In the early 1990s, Israel lacked pillar companies. But a fast-growing Internet security company founded in 1993 by a college-skipping veteran of the Israeli army's information security unit, the 8200, and two fellow programmers went public in 1996. That company, Check Point Software, makes firewall software that protects networks from being accessed by unauthorized insiders and outsiders. In 2016, Check Point's sales had reached $1.7 billion, net income was $725 million, and on August 23, 2017, its stock market capitalization stood at $18 billion. What's more, Check Point's founders, most notably Shlomo Kramer, had spawned numerous other companies that were either acquired or taken public. In this way, a country that lacked pillar companies ended up creating many new gazelles that in turn became pillar companies.

Case Scenario

Jerusalem native Gil Shwed skipped college, but that did not stop him from being one of Israel's most successful entrepreneurs. When he was 10, Shwed (net worth $2.9 billion on August 22, 2017) began taking weekly computer classes in Jerusalem. At 12, he got a summer job coding for a language-translation software company. In high school, at age 14, he started an almost full-time job as a system administrator at Hebrew University in Jerusalem. From 16 to 18, he ran its computer systems, after which he spent four years in Unit 8200 where he built military computer networks that blocked confidential information from all but the most privileged and trusted users. After the army, Shwed took a software development job at Israeli startup company Optrotech where he met Marius Nacht. Shwed, Nacht, and an army friend, Shlomo Kramer, saw the potential of technology to filter and control traffic to separate computers on business networks from the wider Internet, the basis of Check Point's first product, FireWall-1, which was developed in April 1993. Shwed, Kramer, and Nacht drank Coke and ate pizzas in Kramer's grandmother's apartment for a year while they developed FireWall-1, which they debuted in 1994 at the NetWorld Interop show in Las Vegas. That year, Ramat Gan, Israel-based Check Point signed an OEM agreement with Sun Microsystems, followed in 1995 by a similar deal with HP. Check Point went public in 1996.

While not at the scale of Silicon Valley's PayPal mafia whose alumni went on to found companies like Tesla and Yelp, Check Point's original founders started and took public or sold an impressive collection of information security companies. In 2011, Kramer raised $90 million for the IPO of Redwood Shores, Calif.-based web application firewall provider Imperva, which lost $70 million on its $264 million in 2016 sales. And in 2013, one of Check Point's original employees, who also served in the 8200, Nir Zuk, took his enterprise network firewall maker, Palo Alto Networks, public. Zuk kept starting companies after leaving Check Point. In 2002, Zuk sold OneSecure, a company he had founded, to NetScreen Technologies for $45 million and became its chief technology officer. Zuk became Juniper Networks' vice president of data security after it bought NetScreen in 2004 for $4 billion in stock. In 2005, he left Juniper and founded Palo Alto. It had 2016 sales of $1.4 billion and a net loss of $225 million, in which Kramer also invested prior to its IPO. In 2013, I estimated Kramer's net worth at about $1 billion after he sold Trusteer to IBM for about $1 billion. By August 2017, Kramer was CEO of Tel Aviv-based Cato Networks, a wide area network communications service, with executives from some of the other companies he founded.

Case Analysis

The Check Point case is a compelling example of how a gazelle can become a pillar, enriching its founders and giving them the experience they need to get new ventures off the ground and into the hands of public investors, thus creating a virtuous cycle of new pillars that create new opportunities for local entrepreneurs to start fast-growing startups. Here are some takeaways for government policymakers, investors, and entrepreneurs:

- **The right training grounds produce more and better aspiring entrepreneurs.** Israel's disadvantage of being a small country surrounded by enemies makes mandatory military service critical for survival. Those who serve in its elite units, such as the 8200, develop technical and leadership skills that translate well for starting companies. In this way, Israel develops aspiring entrepreneurs who have many role models for entrepreneurial success. Government policymakers in regions without pillar companies should consider whether it may be possible to create analogous opportunities to develop entrepreneurial talent.

- **Investors should network with entrepreneurial training grounds.** Capital providers who develop relationships with those who deliver training to aspiring entrepreneurs can pinpoint leaders with the greatest potential. In so doing, those capital providers can access the best investment opportunities. If these capital providers are fortunate enough to invest in a gazelle that becomes a pillar, they may gain access to a broader set of future opportunities as those newly wealthy cofounders seek to start their own companies.

- **Aspiring entrepreneurs should join gazelles with great leaders.** Those who wish to start companies in the future ought to recognize what strengths they bring to a startup and what they need to learn in order to develop into effective entrepreneurs. Then they should seek startups where they can bolster their weaknesses. That experience will put them in a better position to create pillar companies.

Less Successful Case Study: RedMart Grows Fast, Loses Money, Gets Acquired For Half Its Capital By Deep-Pocketed Alibaba

Introduction

Singapore has made substantial progress since it became independent of Malaysia in 1965. While the city-state has excellent educational institutions, an increasing number of startup accelerators, and some venture capital, it has not yet turned any gazelles into pillar companies. Like many countries in Asia, the high real estate prices in Singapore make it very difficult for university graduates to afford a place to live unless they can find employment in a high-salary job such as investment banking or consulting. As a result, local entrepreneurs are often not native Singaporeans. Without local pillar companies, Singapore's entrepreneurial ecosystem lacks local talent with the experience of growing a gazelle into a pillar company; as a result, founders are not always well-enough prepared for the challenges of scaling a startup.

Case Scenario

A great example of this is RedMart, an online grocery delivery service in Singapore. Founded in 2011, it ran out of money, was unable to raise more, and in November 2016 was acquired for less than the total amount of capital it had raised. But this story had a happier second act. By January 2018, RedMart was enjoying the benefit of a Chinese owner who was willing to invest to support its rapid gain in market share and its goals for Southeast Asian expansion. RedMart's cofounders met in their MBA program at the INSEAD campus in Singapore and while they both had impressive backgrounds in finance, neither had previous experience in the online grocery industry or even working in Singapore. For example, RedMart's CEO, Roger Egan III (whose father had been an executive at insurance broker Marsh) had previously been an Associate at hedge fund Omega Capital before starting an insurance brokerage company that went on to raise $320 million in venture capital. Vikram Rupani, RedMart's COO and CFO, had previously worked as an investment banking analyst at JPMorgan, a research analyst at a hedge fund, and had completed the groundwork for a polyester and alkyd resin manufacturing plant in Bahrain. The pair concluded that their lack of industry experience was not an impediment. Egan got the idea for online groceries because his job as a banker denied him the time to shop properly for groceries. And Rupani believed that his lack of experience would enable him to look at the industry with fresh eyes, envisioning a better experience for customers and building the operations required to realize that vision.

They soon realized that the typical online grocery idea would not be profitable. As Rupani told TechInAsia, "The margins were very low on this business. To be successful as a retailer; you need very large volume and extremely efficient logistics. We thought about how we could change the business model to make the idea of competing with large established retailers as a startup sound a little less crazy."

They concluded that RedMart could be profitable if manufacturers used its service to bypass supermarkets and sell directly to consumers. In so doing they would offer manufacturers advantages, such as better marketing information to help them target ads to consumers that would boost their likelihood of buying by analyzing consumer demographics and purchasing information; eliminating fees to list their products; and allowing them to set their own prices. They hoped that this business model would be more sustainable than an online grocery service because it would add more sources of revenue from its data analytics and marketing services and operate with lower costs due to lower overhead, which would enable them to charge consumers lower prices for personal care items and other non-perishables than did local supermarkets.

RedMart, founded in November 2011, was able to raise a total of $55.1 million in six rounds from 18 investors to target what Egan then said was the $4.2 billion Singapore grocery market which fueled rapid (revenue up 267% from 2014 to 2015) but unprofitable growth. After two months, they received seed funding from INSEAD professors Patrick Turner, Serguei Netessine, and Neil Bearden in the form of a convertible note and funds from Skype co-founder Toivo Annus's venture firm ASL. By its fourth round of financing in July 2013, a Series A round "in the millions," RedMart had raised $4.6 million. By July 2013, RedMart said it had $5 million in sales, 10,000 registered users paying $59 per order, 25 employees at headquarters, and 50 in the warehouse. RedMart also hired Tim Klem, a product manager from the failed online supermarket WebVan; Trudy Fawcett, previously a buyer at Sainsburys supermarkets; and Todd Kurie, former marketing director at eBay. In January 2014, RedMart, which then said it was growing at 20% to 30% per month and had increased its employee count to 175, raised $5.4 million in "bridge financing" from investors including Facebook co-founder Eduardo Severin and Asian online real estate mogul Steve Mellhuish, bringing its total financing to $10 million. In August 2015, RedMart raised $26.7 million "in preparation for a Series C for expansion into Southeast Asia" and hired former Amazon executive Colin Bryar who replaced Rupani as COO, naming Rupani president, as the company expanded at what Egan said was 12% to 15% per month in the "$16 billion Singapore grocery market." With all this growth, RedMart was falling short of its hopes for profitability; revenues were $1.5 million in 2013, $9.6 million in 2014 (while posting a $21 million net loss), and $27 million in 2015 with a nearly $71 million net loss. RedMart said it expected to be "self-sustainable by mid-2017."

RedMart could not convince investors to put more money in and the company was acquired for an undisclosed amount, estimated at $30 million to $40 million. In January 2016, rumors abounded that RedMart was seeking to raise $100 million in Series C funding. When that financing failed to close, RedMart sought investments from NTUC, a leading Singapore grocery chain and Singapore's sovereign wealth fund. However, those efforts failed and instead RedMart was sold on November 2, 2016 to Lazada (a German electronics, fashion, and baby items e-tailer that had obtained *a $1 billion investment from Alibaba CEO Jack Ma) for between "$30 million and $40 million." Happily for RedMart's employees, Alibaba saw the company as a way to build up a strong position in the Southeast Asian grocery delivery market.*

Case Analysis

RedMart's fate may be seen in the future as a promising though unprofitable experiment in turning a gazelle into a pillar. However, given the structure of its financing, which included bridge loans and preferred stock, it is highly likely that its investors suffered a significant loss. Here are some of the takeaways of this case for investors and entrepreneurs:

- **Investors should examine closely the fit between founders' strengths and the requirements for the company's success.** The prominence of RedMart's early investors helped it raise capital, whom later investors may have assumed had done excellent due diligence. However, while it was clear that Egan and Rupani had relevant experience in raising capital and developing business plans, they lacked prior experience in building and growing a logistics-intensive hard goods delivery business. Investors likely knew about the fate of Webvan and the difficulties that Amazon encountered with its efforts to deliver groceries ordered online. In retrospect, such examples ought to have made investors more skeptical that a pair of former financiers would be able to solve the considerable operational problems they would face. Egan and Rupani were fortunate that Alibaba — with its deep pockets and huge ambitions — was willing to provide the funds that its initial investors lacked.

- **Founders should locate in a region where they can hire people who complement their strengths.** In retrospect, Egan and Rupani were over-confident. To their credit, they did try to hire people with skills that could bolster their team's skills in marketing and operations. However, by locating their company in Singapore, which lacked pillar companies in relevant industries, they were unable to get the talent or practical advice that might have helped them create a path to profitability. Rupani's initial conclusion that the online grocery business would not be profitable was proven correct by their experience, and it does not appear that they were ever able to realize their "eBay of consumer packaged goods" vision.

Principles

Regions with no pillars and some gazelles have a good chance that some of those gazelles will become pillars or at least be acquired, thus enriching the gazelle's founders, some of whom will decide to start companies of their own. If this happens, the region's leaders will find that they have more wind at their backs as sails of capitalism swell with the hope of high return on investment.

The case studies reveal key issues that a region's stakeholders ought to consider when trying to decide whether to boost its startup ecosystem and some principles to guide those decisions:

- **Government policymakers:** Politicians eager for actions that will boost their reelection prospects will want to be seen as helping a successful gazelle so it will have a profitable exit and thus enrich founders who start companies in the region. Politicians may wish to consider offering tax incentives or government grants to entice entrepreneurs to base a startup in the region rather than leaving for better established startup hubs. As you will see later in the book, such government financing can work well in some cases, as it did when it gave government contracts to Silicon Valley companies and less well in giving grants to startups who agree to locate in Chile for a time.

- **Investors:** If a local gazelle is growing rapidly and appears to be on the path for a successful exit, some venture capitalists outside the region will hold back and wait to see whether the gazelle is acquired or goes public before scouting out the region.

- **Business leaders:** Local business leaders may recognize that the growth of nearby gazelles could lead to more competition for their most talented employees as new ventures are formed by the newly-enriched cofounders. While many business leaders will not change their posture, some might respond by raising the compensation for their best people or invest in local startups should their talented people choose to join them.

- **Student entrepreneurs:** Local university students in such regions may change their minds about leaving town after graduation. Instead, those local students might seek out internships and full-time employment with the fast-growing gazelle. Or they may be more inspired to start their companies near their university.

Level 2: No Pillars, Acquired Gazelles

Success Case Study: Cofounder Reinvests Proceeds of Selling Skype Twice in Stockholm Startups

Introduction

Stockholm lacks pillar companies; however, some of its founders have sold their gazelles to U.S. acquirers. Fortunately for Stockholm, many of those founders have chosen to reinvest their winnings into the local startup scene. As a result, Stockholm has attracted outside capital, begun to establish a helpful mentor network for entrepreneurs, and raised the level of startup skills in Sweden's capital. In 2016, 375 Swedish startups attracted $1.6 billion in growth capital; that's more than twice the $787.6 million of venture and growth capital invested into Swedish companies in 2014. In 2016, 38 Swedish tech companies raised $160 million in capital through IPOs. Indeed, in 2015 at 6.3, Sweden had the second largest concentration of $1 billion companies per capita, behind Silicon Valley's 8.1. Therefore, despite the absence of local pillar companies, Stockholm has reason to hope that some of the gazelles that are growing there now could someday become local pillar companies.

Case Scenario

Niklas Zennstrom is a good example of a Stockholm entrepreneur who sold his company and reinvested the proceeds in local companies. In October 2005, eBay paid $2.5 billion for Skype, the Internet phone service he cofounded in 2003. But Skype was loaded up with debt and losing money, so in 2009 eBay sold 70% of Skype to private investors including Silver Lake Partners, Index Ventures, and Andreessen Horowitz for $2.75 billion. In 2011, Microsoft bought Skype for $8.5 billion in cash and $686 million in assumed debt. Zennstrom, who previously cofounded Kazaa, a peer-to-peer music and movie-sharing service, made money on both transactions and decided to give back to Stockholm. As Olle Zetterberg, CEO of Stockholm Business Region, said, "Zennstrom, who founded Skype, made an exit twice and he reinvested in Stockholm startups which drew capital from the UK and U.S. investors. He did not buy a Beverly Hills mansion [as did the founder of game-maker Mojang], which is important for developing the startup community."

Zennstrom founded London-based Atomico, a venture capital firm, in 2006 and by late 2013 it had raised a $476 million fund. Atomico has invested in Swedish companies including Klarna, a payments processor; Truecaller, an advanced caller ID *service; and closed-loop shower maker Orbital Systems. These Atomico investments did well. Klarna was a $460 million (estimated 2016 revenue) Stockholm-based payment service founded in 2005 with 25 million consumers in 15 countries, 45,000 retailer partners, and 1,200 employees. Klarna raised $521 million in 10 rounds from 19 investors as of August 2017. Stockholm-based Truecaller, a mobile app that enables users to see who is calling and to block unwanted calls, raised about $93 million in six rounds from nine investors, valuing the company at $1 billion. When Atomico invested in Truecaller in December 2014, Zennstrom said, "It is great to see a team from Sweden that's rethinking how we communicate and scaling their technology globally. We look forward to working with the team to help them reach the next 100 million users." Zennstrom also contributed to a $16 million investment in Orbital; its product is a shower that recycles up to 90% of the water. Mehrdad Mahdjoub, CEO at Orbital Systems, said, "In the last two years, we've realized that the technology works just as well on Earth as it does in space." In February 2017, Atomico announced that it raised $765 million to invest in EU startups.*

Case Analysis

Zennstrom's decision to invest some of his Skype profits into Stockholm-based startups benefits its startup scene. In so doing, local entrepreneurs whose companies are acquired help a region in three ways:

- **Role models that change culture:** Zennstrom is seen as an inspiration to aspiring Swedish entrepreneurs. His success is far more powerful to Stockholm students than marveling at the accomplishments of, say, Silicon Valley entrepreneurs. Moreover, his decision to reinvest his capital in Stockholm also sets a good example that can ultimately strengthen the local startup scene by encouraging other entrepreneurs to give back.

- **Capital providers who attract outside investment:** Zennstrom's success with Skype enriched Silicon Valley venture capitalists. This created a compelling reason for other Silicon Valley VCs to seek opportunities to invest in Stockholm, many of which have also invested in Klarna and Truecaller. This snowballing effect has the potential to create more successes like Skype, which will attract even more capital to the Stockholm startup scene.

- **Developers of local startup talent:** Entrepreneurial skills are best developed by putting people into startups and seeing how far they can grow with them. While Zennstrom's experiences may never lead him to take a company public and sustain its growth to the size of a company like Facebook or Amazon, his investments in promising Stockholm startups could help some of their people to develop the skills needed to create a local pillar company.

Unsuccessful Case Study: Joost's Failure Shows the Limits of Zennstrom's Peer-To-Peer Startup Magic

Introduction

It is unreasonable to expect one individual who has sold his startup at a big profit to single-handedly support a city's startup ecosystem. One of the risks of depending on a successful entrepreneur in this way is that he may be good at only one thing—and that skill may not be guarantee success for every business he funds. This comes to mind in considering the fate of Joost, a peer-to-peer video platform backed by Zennstrom and his Skype cofounder, Janus Friis.

Case Scenario

Joost, invented by Zennstrom and Friis, was originally called "The Venice Project" and was intended to be a peer-to-peer (P2P) TV network. Joost recruited Cisco Systems executive Mike Volpi as CEO and partnered with CBS and Viacom to provide online distribution; both companies later invested. Joost's ability to sell this vision and raise $45 million was directly tied to its founders. Joost had problems with its P2P architecture, its bulky software player, and its content library. After launching in September 2007, it never took off. Instead, Hulu, a joint venture between News Corp., NBC, and Disney, became the most popular site for TV episodes on the web. Joost's remnants were sold in late 2009.

The buyer, Adconion Media Group, did not disclose the terms of the November 2009 acquisition; however, it was thought to be a fire sale that would not deliver returns to Joost's investors. In June 2009, Joost announced it would change its strategy to provide video platforms for branded services providers. Indeed, Adconion announced a long-term licensing partnership as the exclusive display and video ad-serving solution for the Goldbach Media Group in Europe. Joost's backers had included Index Ventures and Volpi. TechCrunch's Michael Arrington said, "Here's what I learned from Joost's failure: celebrity founders, celebrity CEOs, and tons and tons of cash can be a recipe for disaster. Applying yesterday's solutions to today's problems isn't an interesting business. And finally, knowing when to throw in the towel and just return what's left of capital to investors is an important skill as well. That way everyone can move on and focus on real value-add opportunities. There's no room for Joost in the consumer online video space, and there's almost certainly no room for them in white label video, either. Time to call it a learning experience and move on."

Case Analysis

Joost's failure reveals the limits of a successful entrepreneur's efforts to spur his city's startup scene. Zennstrom's mastery of P2P technology was clearly not sufficient to enable Joost to build a successful service for viewing video content online. As Hulu's success reveals, building such a business depends on attracting many users quickly. And in order to do that, it's critical for a service provider to have access to popular content that can't be gotten as easily anywhere else. Zennstrom did not recognize the importance of this capability and did not hire a team that could bolster Joost's weakness here. Had Joost succeeded, it might have become a pillar company that brought more capital and a new skill set to the Stockholm startup scene. But in retrospect, it's clear that Joost should have located closer to the talent that could either create popular video content or negotiate effectively to make it available on the Joost platform.

Principles

Regions with no pillars and acquired gazelles can host founders, some of whom will decide to start companies of their own. If this happens, the region's leaders will find that they have more wind at their backs as sails of capitalism swell with the hope of high return on investment.

The case studies reveal key issues that a region's stakeholders ought to consider when trying to decide whether to boost its startup ecosystem and some principles to guide those decisions:

- **Government policymakers:** Politicians eager for actions that will boost their reelection prospects want to help successful gazelles and encourage their newly enriched founders to start companies in the region. They may wish to consider offering tax incentives or government grants to entice these entrepreneurs to create startups in the region rather than leaving for better established startup hubs.

- **Investors:** After a local gazelle gets acquired, VCs will learn about the high returns earned by peers who financed these winners. Outside VCs may visit the region to explore whether they should help finance the startups that the acquired gazelle is likely to spawn.

- **Business leaders:** Local business leaders may recognize that the success of nearby gazelles could lead to more competition for their most talented employees as new ventures are formed by the newly-enriched cofounders. These business leaders might respond by raising the compensation for their best people or may invest in the startups that their talented people choose to join.

- **Student entrepreneurs:** Local university students in such regions may change their minds about leaving town after graduation. Instead, those local students might seek out internships and full-time employment with the successful gazelle and its spinoff companies. Or they may be more inspired to start their companies near their university.

Level 3: Some Pillars in Niche Markets

Success Case Study: Telecom Billionaire Xavier Niel Propels Paris's Startup Scene

Introduction

A city with publicly-traded technology companies in niche markets has the potential to keep growing. But whether that company becomes a pillar depends largely on the CEO's attitude towards the local startup ecosystem. If the CEO decides to focus solely on the company's success, the city will certainly benefit from the taxes it pays and the people it employs. However, if the CEO has greater ambitions—to change the city's startup culture by investing in local startups, educating talented technology workers, and building a local incubator—the city's startup ecosystem has a greater chance of adding more pillar companies. What's more, such a publicly-traded tech company becomes a role model for pillar companies, thus inspiring more local startup activity.

Case Scenario

This comes to mind when considering French billionaire Xavier Niel, who came from the wrong side of the tracks of Parisian society, built his Iliad into a public company by offering a bundle of telecom services at a discount to that of rivals, and as of August 2017 had a net worth of $9.5 billion. He became an entrepreneur at 16 without family money or a university education, building a sex chat service for France's Minitel. Niel also started France's first Internet provider WorldNet in 1993 at the age of 25 and selling it for $50 million in 2000. He invested in sex shops and in 2004, just a few months after Iliad's successful IPO, was held in prison when officials discovered that one of them was a front for prostitution. He was found not guilty of having known what was going on, but was fined €250,000 for embezzling €200,000 from the shop. Niel's wealth is tied significantly to his 55% stake in Iliad, the publicly traded parent company of Free Mobile, which sells unlimited calls, texts, and Internet for half the price of similar services sold by France's other three telecom networks. Niel continues to expand especially in Italy. He sold a 15% stake in Telecom Italia and agreed to buy assets from CK Hutchison Holdings Ltd. and VimpelCom Ltd. to create a fourth mobile-phone network in Italy. Niel also owns Monaco Telecom and Orange Switzerland, for which he paid $2.9 billion in 2014. He also owns a controlling interest in French newspaper Le Monde.

Niel personally, rather than Iliad, is giving back to the Paris startup ecosystem. Niel invested €70 million to finance 42, a free coding academy (named for a line in The Hitchhiker's Guide to the Galaxy; it's the answer to the greatest question about life and the universe) for young people in Paris and other locations, which he created in 2013. He started 42 to give back. As he told VentureBeat, "The first [reason I created 42] is a sentiment that is really specific to French people and not to Americans: It's the notion of giving back. Once I had made a lot of money in France and in the U.S.—and I hope it will be the case in many other countries as well—I always asked myself, 'How can I give back some of the money I have made in those places?'" In addition, he spent €250 million to turn an abandoned train station in Paris called Station F into the world's largest startup incubator, which will host 1,000 startups. It opened in July 2017. Niel's venture capital firm, Kima Ventures, invests in two start-ups a week, many in Paris.

Will his efforts make a difference in Paris's relative position in the startup world? Venture capitalists invested €874 million across 590 French startups in 2016, ahead of Britain's 520 deals. Niel believes that Paris is now fully equipped to attract more innovative companies than London and dominate Europe's startup scene. As he opened Station F, he told Reuters, "It's something that is achievable in the coming months. We're of course helped by Brexit." Meanwhile, Niel's friend, President Emmanuel Macron, wants to transform France into a startup nation through business-friendly reforms and the launch of a €10 billion fund to invest in French startups.

Case Analysis

Strictly speaking, Iliad is not a pillar company because it does not supply capital and talent for startups in Paris. However, Niel does that and more. In that sense, Niel is a pillar of the Paris startup community. At the same time, his success and his willingness to give back reveals an important reality for cities seeking to create pillar companies. They must somehow attract extremely talented outsiders who are driven to succeed and use that success to defy traditional norms. Indeed, my visits to Paris have revealed that Niel is the opposite in many ways of Macron, who followed the tried and true path of graduating at the top of his class from Sciences Po and going into banking and government. It is too soon to know whether Niel's investments in the Paris startup scene will yield a new crop of pillar companies, but he is clearly acting as a role model for other aspiring entrepreneurs and using his capital and talent to make Paris a leader in Europe's startup community.

Less Successful Case Study: Boston's Pillars Produce Mostly Tepid Outcomes

Introduction

What Niel has accomplished in Paris has contributed considerably to its chances for ultimately emerging as a location with many pillars targeting large markets. It is perhaps equally likely that Parisian business culture is so slow to change that Niel ends up being an outlier whose success is difficult for others to replicate. Indeed, there are other locations with a fairly small number of pillar companies that spawn spinoffs after their IPOs, when their talented and newly-enriched executives start their own companies. While, as you'll see later in this chapter, Silicon Valley was able to spawn large pillar companies capturing large market opportunities, such a snowball effect is far from guaranteed. Indeed, if a region's venture capitalists prefer to invest in companies that target relatively small problems facing businesses, the spinoffs might struggle to repeat the success of their pillar "parents."

Case Scenario

This comes to mind in considering an analysis of the spinoffs from a handful of Boston pillar companies, a list compiled by a Boston-based venture capital firm. The following is an analysis of the capital invested in these 127 spinoffs from six current or formerly publicly-traded Boston technology companies (Genzyme and Kayak went public and were acquired): Akamai (39 spinoffs), Genzyme (28), Hubspot (28), TripAdvisor (11), Wayfair (10), and Kayak (11). The one biotechnology company in the lot yielded far more impressive investor returns than the other five information technology pillars. Genzyme is the hero of this collection of pillars: of its 28 spinoff companies, seven raised outside capital totalling about $110 million, according to Crunchbase, with total exit values of $19.5 billion. Two of these were acquired for a whopping $14.9 billion in total, three others went public with one, Madison, Wisc.- based molecular diagnostics supplier Exact Sciences, achieving a $4.6 billion market capitalization and the other two, Medford, Mass-based biopharma PixarBio and Maryland-based drug developer Spherix, holding much smaller stock market values totalling $33 million as of August 25, 2017. While it is too bad for Boston that Exact Sciences moved from Marlborough, Mass. to Wisconsin, the corporate "children" of Genzyme, which Sanofi acquired for $20 billion in 2011, were the most successful of the ones analyzed.

Sadly, the Boston information technology pillars yielded a far less impressive outcome. These five pillars' 88 spinoff companies consumed a total of $814 million in capital to yield a total exit value of a mere $722 million. Most of that exit value came from one spinoff of Akamai Technologies, a San Francisco, Calif.-based marketing analytics firm called Krux Digital that was acquired by Salesforce in

November 2016 for $700 million after raising $50 million in capital. While this was a very good outcome for Krux's investors, the success no doubt was a far bigger benefit to San Francisco than it was to Cambridge, home of Akamai. What is also less than optimal about these 88 spinoff companies is that only seven of the other ones had exits, meaning that they were acquired. And of those, five were acquired for such a small amount that the prices were not disclosed. The other two were acquired for decent multiples of the amount invested; Portland, Oregon-based Database-as-a-Service provider Orchestrate raised $4.2 million in capital and was acquired for $10 million and Cambridge-based small business marketing service provider ThriveHive raised $4.5 million in capital and was bought for $11.8 million.

Case Analysis

As an investor in startup companies, this case reinforces the idea that the magnitude and frequency of Boston information technology investment successes are more muted than those in Silicon Valley. Boston's pillar companies generally take a long time to reach sufficient scale to be able to go public and once they do, these pillars spawn many spinoff companies, the vast majority of which go nowhere. By contrast, the relatively compelling results of Genzyme's spinoff companies suggest an important general principle: it is best to invest in the startups of regions that have the world's best talent targeting the largest market opportunities. Biopharmaceutical companies are more likely to be able to generate profitable exits if they make more progress in new drug research than their publicly-traded peers. This tends to generate sufficient investor interest to yield a solid IPO. By contrast, Boston's information technology pillars tend to focus on smaller markets with more significant competitors. As a result, the capital required to build them is significant and the chances of earning high returns are lower.

Principles

Regions with pillars in niche markets tend to have all the resources they need to grow on their own and to help along their spinoffs as they see fit. However, the role of government policymakers in such regions shifts fairly dramatically from helping to encourage startup activity in the region to removing threats to its further development while maintaining the support of local voters who may not be benefiting directly from the startup activity.

The case studies reveal key issues that a region's stakeholders ought to consider when trying to preserve the benefits of robust local entrepreneurship against its costs:

- **Government policymakers:** Policymakers in such lively startup hubs may realize that growth is beneficial for the region because it is raising tax revenues and local housing prices, but at some point such growth strains local infrastructure. Such policymakers may be considering whether to invest in more roads, utilities, sewer systems, and housing in order to prevent high housing prices and congestion from forcing citizens to leave the area. If financing for such expansion can be obtained and those blocking change can be mollified, politicians should expand the local infrastructure.

- **Investors:** Investors in such regions are likely to find themselves facing more competition for participation the best startup investment opportunities as VCs from around the world flock to the region. As a result, such investors may be forced to specialize in specific industries where they have the greatest expertise or move into new geographies that can benefit from that unique skill.

- **Business leaders:** Local business leaders may see greater opportunity in supporting local entrepreneurship than in fighting it. Indeed, they may respond by setting up their own incubators to attract locally educated talent and by financing spinoffs in order to benefit from their new products and ultimate financial success.

- **Student entrepreneurs:** Students who have expertise in the fields in which the local pillar companies specialize may choose to work at those local pillars to develop their skills before going out on their own. Or the success of those local pillar companies may be sufficiently inspiring that they decide to found their own companies in the region.

Level 4: Many Pillars in Huge Markets

Success Case Study: Alphabet Invests Billions in Startups Through GV, Capital G, and Gradient Ventures

Introduction

Silicon Valley has a relatively long tradition of gazelles becoming pillar companies. Employees of those pillar companies start aspiring gazelles and some of them become new pillar companies. For example, after the so-called Traitorous Eight left Shockley to start Fairchild, where Mike Markkula, who later became Apple's third employee, worked between 1967 and 1969, then counted at least eight spinoffs launched by Fairchild alumni, including Intel (which Markkula joined) and National Semiconductor. Fast forward to 2017 and it's clear that this tendency of pillar companies to beget spinoffs, some of which become new pillar companies, persists. These days, some of the pillar companies in Silicon Valley not only supply talent to spinoffs and other start-ups but they also supply capital and other valuable assistance such as introductions to potential customers, help with hiring and product development, and so on. As a result, some of today's pillars are able to capture some of the value of this trend for their own shareholders.

Case Scenario

Alphabet, the parent of Google, has numerous ways of investing in Silicon Valley start-ups. These include GV, formerly known as Google Ventures, which as of August 2017 had $2.4 billion in assets under management and intended to invest $500 million annually in startups; CapitalG; Gradient; and strategic investments from the parent company and specific business units. GV was founded in 2009 and its investments (in companies in North America and Europe) include Egnyte (online storage), Docusign (digital signatures), Slack (collaboration software for businesses), Stripe (online payments), Uber (ride-hailing), Walker + Co. (beauty products); plus drone and robotics start-ups like Abundant Robotics, Airware, and Carbon. Seven GV companies were later acquired by Google, most notably home automation startup Nest, which Google bought for $3.2 billion in 2014. By August 2017, GV had announced about 30 new investments. Capital G (formerly Google Capital, founded in 2013) invests in the tens of millions of dollars range to obtain stakes in later-stage companies around the world, including India and China. Its portfolio includes short-term rentals platform Airbnb, daily fantasy sports app Fanduel, and Glassdoor, a site that provides salary data and employee reviews of their companies. Capital G also invested in Snap and Care.com, both of which are now public.

Alphabet also provides capital for mission-specific startups and funds non-profit and other philanthropic organizations. Gradient Ventures, an AI-specialized venture fund, was founded in July 2017 and its portfolio included Algorithmia, Aurima, Cape, Cogniac, and Dyndrite. Parent company Alphabet, which has the goal of running its data centers on 100% renewable energy, has invested "billions into clean power-generating projects and renewable energy startups." In March 2017, its health-focused division Verily invested in Freenome, a start-up developing a blood test to detect cancer. In 2015, Alphabet's urban development-focused Sidewalk Labs invested in Intersection, a supplier of public internet kiosks in New York. X, a "skunkworks" lab at Alphabet, took an equity stake in a spin-out company called Dandelion that helps homes use geothermal energy for heating and cooling. In addition, Alphabet makes non-equity investments in non-profits and start-ups through Launchpad, an incubator space for early-stage start-ups, and its philanthropic arm, Google.org.

While it is difficult to know how much value Alphabet creates through these investments, a look at the private market value of some of the startups in which it has invested suggests that the returns are likely enormous. For example, the private market value of 10 of the GV portfolio companies totalled about $120 billion as of August 2017. These include Uber ($68 billion), Airbnb ($29.3 billion), Stripe ($9.2 billion), Slack ($3.8 billion), DocuSign ($3 billion), and eight others worth over $1 billion.

Alphabet is likely to continue such investments. For example, GV in Europe intends to provide capital for life sciences, development tools, and fintech. As of March 2017, for example, GV had invested about a third of its funds in life sciences such as publicly-traded Foundation Medicine which focuses on oncology. GV also saw opportunities to invest in development tools, such as Stripe and Currencycloud, which Google's platform can help to grow. And talent in London's financial district presents the possibility that GV could invest in fintech startups there and later sell those stakes to "double-digit numbers of businesses that can buy a fintech company for over $1 billion."

Case Analysis

Alphabet's extensive venture portfolio reveals important reasons why pillar companies can be powerful contributors to a region's growth. Indeed, the venture portfolio of a pillar company like Alphabet that operates globally has an impact not solely on its headquarters region but in all the locations where it invests. A pillar company's venture investments provide a range of benefits:

- **Boost the value of the parent's company's investment capital:** While it is unclear what the rate of return that GV and CapitalG have earned on their investments, the roughly $120 billion value of some of the private companies in which GV has invested suggests that this return could be considerable.

- **Enhance the startup ecosystems in locations where it operates:** Startups in locations that receive capital from Alphabet benefit from the funding and potentially from the growth potential that Google's platform may be able to offer them.

- **Provide career-broadening opportunities for talented employees:** Alphabet hires some of the world's most talented people. While many of them work there for the professional branding and experience, Alphabet may want to groom some of them for more senior positions. Alphabet could invest in startups founded by employees, help those companies grow, and then acquire the companies, folding the successful leaders of these startups back into the company.

- **Further socially-beneficial goals:** Alphabet has invested in companies that help detect cancer and others that are intended to power Google's operations with renewable energy. To the extent that such investments achieve their lofty aims, society benefits along with Alphabet.

Unsuccessful Case Study: Alphabet Abandons SideCar For Uber, Which Alphabet Later Sues Over Waymo

Introduction

Pillar companies that get too powerful can stumble with their startup investments. That's because their surplus of capital and power can lead them to make investments that may end up conflicting with each other. And when that conflict becomes significant enough, the pillar companies may be forced to make choices that end up damaging all of the companies involved in the conflict. This outcome could be attributable to bad decision-making or it might reflect decisions that are thought to benefit the pillar company over the long run, even though the decisions damage some of the portfolio companies involved in the conflict.

Case Scenario

This comes to mind in considering the fate of SideCar, a ridesharing company in which GV invested in 2012, only to sink $258 million the next year into its much bigger rival, Uber. SideCar shut down in 2015 with GM buying its scraps. In 2017, Alphabet sued Uber citing theft of trade secrets from Waymo, its autonomous vehicle subsidiary. SideCar was founded in 2012 and deemed itself "the leading crowd-sourced transportation network," claiming that as of October 2012 it had "facilitated nearly 50,000 rides in San Francisco." With plans to enter new markets, SideCar raised $10 million that month from Lightspeed Venture Partners and GV. Joe Kraus, partner at GV said, "The transportation industry is going through a major transformation. With ridesharing gaining popularity, SideCar is in a strong position to quickly become a leader in the space. We are thrilled to partner with Sunil as he scales the company to change the way we think about commuting."

SideCar probably questioned the benefits of GV's investment when less than a year later it invested $258 million in Uber, whose success likely contributed to SideCar's demise. GV's investment was the biggest part of a $361.2 million funding round which valued Uber at around $3.4 billion pre-money and $3.76 billion post. Though it was a later-stage deal, which should have been part of Google Capital, given the latter's later-stage focus, GV provided the capital, which represented 86% of its $300 million annual fund. Google CEO Larry Page outlined how Google's resources could "bolster Uber co-founder Travis Kalanick's grand plan to offer everything via iPhone." This news must have been received as bad news by SideCar, which ceased operations at the end of 2015 after raising a total of $39 million. Although SideCar invented many of the ride-sharing industry's features, such as "casual drivers using their own cars, driver destinations, shared rides, upfront pricing, and back-to-back rides," it was unable to grab and keep the lead. CEO Sunil Paul explained the failure as follows: "We were unable to compete against Uber, a company that raised more capital than any other in history [$6.61 billion as of the end of 2015] and is infamous for its anti-competitive behavior. The legacy of SideCar is that we out-innovated Uber but still failed to win the market. We failed, for the most part, because Uber is willing to win at any cost and they have practically limitless capital to do it." Paul decided not to point out that one of his early investors, GV, supplied a significant portion of Uber's capital that Paul blamed in part for SideCar's demise. Ultimately, Paul's team sold SideCar's technology and assets to General Motors for an undisclosed price.

From Alphabet's perspective, SideCar's 2015 demise might not have been seen as terrible news. After all, its investment in Uber rose some 14-fold from $258 million (2013) to $3.5 billion (2016) in the following three years. But that was before Alphabet sued Uber, alleging theft of trade secrets when an engineer from Alphabet's self-driving car unit Waymo transferred thousands of confidential files, including designs for a self-driving truck that he used to start and quickly sell his company, Otto, to Uber. Uber concluded that Alphabet's claims were baseless. After GV's 2013 investment in Uber, the two companies tussled. For example, Uber wanted a discount on Google Maps software, which it did not get, and Google did agree to give Uber a way to let users hail an Uber ride from Google Maps, although its implementation was slow and initially disappointing. Then Uber decided to hire 40 experts from Carnegie Mellon to set up a self-driving lab in competition with Waymo, and Google set up a carpooling service through Waze, which threatened Uber. In January 2016, Anthony Levandowski, a key engineering manager at Waymo quit Alphabet to form the self-driving truck start-up Otto, which Uber acquired later that year for $680 million. Alphabet alleged that Levandowski downloaded "14,000 proprietary *design documents and used them to create Otto's—and later Uber's—version of a key autonomous vehicle technology called Lidar, which uses light pulses reflected off objects to gauge their position," according to Reuters. Uber and Levandowski denied the allegations. By the end of July 2017, no settlement was in sight and a trial had been scheduled for October 2017. As of August 2017 some investors had marked down the value of their Uber holdings by up to 15%.*

Case Analysis

Alphabet's venture capital investments in the ridesharing industry reveal the complex effects that a pillar's money and capabilities can have on a region's startup ecosystem. While GV helped Uber through its capital and adapting Google Maps to boost Uber revenues, the two companies also battled in the autonomous vehicle industry. Moreover, by making such a significant investment in Uber, GV contributed to the demise of its first ridesharing investment, SideCar. Meanwhile, with its future uncertain, Alphabet's lawsuit against Uber does nothing to increase the value of GV's investment in the ridesharing industry leader. In retrospect, Larry Page is probably wondering whether GV should have invested in Uber and no doubt Sunil Paul is wishing GV had decided to invest more in SideCar instead of buying $258 million worth of Uber.

Principles

Regions with many pillars in huge markets tend to have dominant control of a region's economic levers. Indeed, they may be so influential that they can find politicians who support policies favorable to them and provide financial and other support they need to get elected. The danger in such regions is that local infrastructure becomes so stretched and the cost of living becomes so high that only the very wealthiest people can afford to live near their workplaces and provide decent educations for their children.

The case studies suggest the following principles that stakeholders should consider in such regions:

- **Government policymakers:** Politicians in such regions may be powerless to lower housing prices or increase the region's road and other infrastructure capacity enough to keep middle and lower income residents from leaving the region or from suffering a deterioration in their quality of living (e.g., percent of income going to housing and two- or three-hour commutes to work) if they stay.

- **Investors:** Investors in such regions may find that the competition for the best deals is so intense that they look to regions where they can find good investment opportunities with far less competition.

- **Business leaders:** The ranks of business leaders in the region will be dominated by local pillar company CEOs who are likely to have the power to encourage government policies that help their companies. The risk to the region is that what benefits these companies in the short term may hurt the region in the long term.

- **Student entrepreneurs:** Student entrepreneurs are highly likely to seek employment with the best local pillar companies or start their own firms. However, once launched, the startups may struggle to compete for talent with the pillar companies and better-funded local startups backed by local VCs.

Table 2-1 below summarizes the principles for each step in the Pillar Company Staircase.

Table 2-1. Principles by Step in Pillar Company Staircase

Pillar Company Stair	Principles
Level 0	Policymakers should create an environment where talent will want to work, live, and play.
Level 1	Gazelles should scale by seeking capital, talent and customers from outside the region.
Level 2	Investors and founders of acquired gazelles should reinvest to turn gazelles into pillars.
Level 3	Pillars in niche markets should invest in gazelles and apply capabilities to new opportunities.
Level 4	Pillars in huge markets should fund gazelles and help expand housing and infrastructure to keep pace with growth.

Are You Doing Enough To Nurture Local Pillar Companies?

Each region's stakeholders must make decisions about how to shape its local startup ecosystem based on its unique strengths and weaknesses. To evaluate whether your region is doing enough, consider these six questions:

- Where does your region fit in the Pillar Company Staircase?

- Has your region formed a team of local leaders to boost the startup ecosystem?

- Has this team evaluated policies to boost the region's startup scene?

- Do the selected policies build on the region's greatest competitive strengths?

- If your region hosts gazelles, is the region helping them become pillar companies?

- If your region has pillar companies, do they invest capital and talent into the local startup scene?

Conclusion

Different regions have varying levels of current or potential pillar companies. In this chapter, you explored five such levels in the Pillar Company Staircase and found that the roles of stakeholders in the region's startup ecosystem vary dramatically as the role of local pillar companies becomes more important. The case studies highlight some of the benefits and risks at each of the levels. Ultimately, each region must identify its position in the Pillar Company Staircase and use the principles explored here to take action based on its own strengths and weaknesses. In Chapter 3, you'll examine the role of universities in shaping a region's entrepreneurial ecosystem.

Launching Startups from Universities

How Do Universities Shape the Startup Common?

Universities have a profound effect on the trajectory of a city's startup scene. Universities do the following:

- **Attract professors and researchers:** University professors and researchers develop ideas and technologies with the potential to solve significant societal and economic problems. If professors work with these startups, either as part-time advisors or executives, they may help build successful companies, and students will see them and the companies they build as entrepreneurship role models.

- **Create and license intellectual property:** Licensing university intellectual property (IP) to startups or larger companies generates cash for the university, individual departments, and/or specific professors. If some of the

© Peter S. Cohan 2018
P. S. Cohan, *Startup Cities*, https://doi.org/10.1007/978-1-4842-3393-1_3

startups that license the IP become successful, more professors and researchers will want to license their IP, which could in turn result in more successful startups.

- **Admit and educate future entrepreneur students:** University admissions committees decide which students to admit and their departments and faculty committees create and deliver programs to develop students' abilities. Such students complete their education and may work for startups, either out of school or after several years at a more well-established company; they may ultimately become entrepreneurs.

- **Operate incubators and internship programs:** Universities can operate incubators and internship programs admissions that connect students to the local startup community. The incubators encourage students to start companies while giving them access to local mentor networks and capital providers. The internship programs help students explore their interests and develop their skills by working with businesses, some of which are local startups. Such programs can increase the number and variety of a region's startups.

- **Promote values that shape attitudes towards entrepreneurship:** Universities ultimately have a profound effect on a region's attitude towards entrepreneurship. If local universities encourage professors aspiring to win tenure to publish in narrowly circulated academic journals and shun those who get involved in commerce, this is likely to put the region at a competitive disadvantage when it comes to entrepreneurship. By contrast, if a university admires and rewards professors who create ideas that result in successful businesses and bring the resulting insights into the classroom, the demonstration effect could make entrepreneurship a more attractive career option, thus helping the region become and remain a leading startup hub.

Takeaways for Startup Common Stakeholders

The Startup Common's stakeholders ought to consider and make choices regarding the role of universities in the local startup scene.

- **Universities:** University leaders must decide whether to change their institutions to make them more effective contributors to the local startup scene.

- **Invest more in IP licensing.** If a university's professors and researchers have created commercially valuable IP, the university may want to assess whether it should allocate more resources to technology licensing.

- **Add departments in fields that produce valuable IP.** Universities may also want to consider whether they could add or enhance academic programs in fields such as artificial intelligence and biotechnology, which might produce valuable IP in the future.

- **Help students start ventures.** The universities should assess how well they are providing opportunities for students to do internships with companies founded by alumni and to offer programs in entrepreneurship and operate incubators for student-led ventures.

- **Encourage professors to start companies.** Universities might also consider whether they should encourage professors to start companies both as a way to create entrepreneurial role models for students and researchers and to enliven class discussions with insights from their startup work.

- **Government policymakers:** Local government officials seeking to boost their city's level of startup activity could explore ways to collaborate with nearby universities. In particular, government policymakers could consider doing the following:

  - **Provide financial incentives for accelerators and incubators.** Local government leaders might consider whether they should offer tax or other financial incentives to encourage universities to create spaces for local entrepreneurs.

  - **Expand startup-friendly infrastructure.** Local government leaders might assess whether locally educated students are eager to stay in the city. If so, they should plan to expand roads, housing, shopping, office space, and other infrastructure to assure that the region can handle the growth. If not, they should assess whether to develop the city to encourage students to stay.

- **Student entrepreneurs:** Students who aspire to start businesses must decide whether to do so near their universities or elsewhere. Every aspiring student entrepreneur who leaves the university's region to start a company is a missed opportunity to boost the region's startup scene. Student entrepreneurs should do the following:

  - **Participate in incubators.** If a university offers an incubator program, student entrepreneurs should participate in it. If not, they should encourage the university to create such a program,

  - **Network with alumni entrepreneurs.** Student entrepreneurs should take the initiative to identify and contact alumni entrepreneurs. They should also take advantage of the university's programs for creating internships with their companies. If such programs do not exist, students should encourage the university to create them.

  - **Consider the advantages of starting up near the university.** If most students leave the city after they graduate, student entrepreneurs should consider whether they might be better off starting the company nearby so they can enjoy easier access to local mentors and talent.

- **Capital providers:** Startup capital providers, from friends and family to venture capital firms, may find opportunities to collaborate with universities. Capital providers should do the following:

  - **Work with university technology licensing offices.** If a university has technology licensing office, capital providers should seek to build relationships with that office in order to gain access to potentially valuable IP.

  - **Serve as mentors at local accelerators.** Capital providers should also establish relationships with university-led accelerators so they can identify and help talented student entrepreneurs in whom they might invest.

University Success and Less Successful Case Studies

In Chapter 2, I introduced the Pillar Company Staircase. By examining how universities attempt to spur local entrepreneurship at each of its five levels, a link emerges between a university's policies towards entrepreneurship and the vitality of its local startup scene.

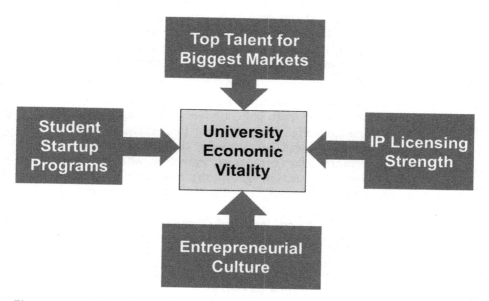

Figure 3-1. The four drivers of university startup vitality

Specifically, the strength or weakness of four university policies—the four drivers of university startup vitality (Figure 3-1)—seems to determine the vitality (or lack thereof) of its pillar companies:

- **Ability to attract world-class professors, researchers, and students in fields with greatest market opportunity.** Universities that attract the world's best talent that can be applied to the largest market opportunities tend to spawn more pillar companies. Conversely, universities whose talent is strongest in fields that are not valuable to large opportunities or are not world-class tend to have fewer pillar companies.

- **Strength of IP licensing.** Universities whose programs produce IP with the most market value tend to produce pillar companies if their technology licensing programs are staffed by experts who can connect that IP to the right entrepreneurs or companies and overcome the challenges of turning the IP into revenue-generating products. Universities without strong IP licensing are not as effective at creating pillar companies.

- **Culture that encourages professors and researchers to start companies.** Universities that encourage professors to create world-class IP and to apply it to solving real-world problems by starting companies tend to produce pillar companies, whereas universities that do not value that and instead encourage professors to publish in academic journals tend not to produce pillar companies.

- **Programs that promote student entrepreneurship.** Universities that help students gain experience in startups and offer programs that help students turn entrepreneurial ideas into growing companies tend to produce more pillar companies. However, while many universities offer such programs, the ones with the top talent focused in the right fields of study tend to produce pillar companies while those with less skilled talent focused on fields with less market impact tend to produce more acquired gazelles.

Level 0: No Pillars, No Gazelles

Success Case Study: U Mass Medical School Licenses Intellectual Property to Startups Outside of Worcester

Introduction

Worcester lacks pillar companies but it has at least one university, U Mass Medical School (UMMS), that licenses its IP to startups. Sadly for Worcester, none of the companies that have licensed this IP operate in town. Indeed, several of the startups using technology developed by UMMS professors are located in Cambridge. They choose to locate their companies over 40 miles away from Worcester because Cambridge has a relatively high concentration of scientific talent required to turn their ideas into a viable business. It is interesting to consider whether Worcester's startup scene would improve if the professors were required to locate their companies there as a condition of licensing their IP.

Case Scenario

UMMS's most significant contributions to entrepreneurship are the talented professors and researchers it has attracted to Worcester and the valuable IP that talent has developed. As Brendan O'Leary, UMMS Executive Vice Chancellor for Innovation and Business Development, said "UMMS has actively marketed its IP to companies for decades and this is a key component of our partnering activities with the private sector. The licensing fees we collect from companies [which totalled $570 million between 1994 and 2017 from 197 companies] help support our core mission of improving human health. In order to further advance all of our partnering activities, we created the new Office of Innovation and Business Development in 2014 which coordinates all of these activities and is charged with dramatically increasing the number, type, and potential value of our partnering efforts."

UMMS professors have also cofounded companies including three companies based in Cambridge. Guangping Gao, Professor in the Department of Microbiology and Physiological Systems, Director of the Gene Therapy Center and Vector Core, and Scientific Director of the UMMS-China Translational Research Initiatives, and Phil Zamore, Howard Hughes Medical Institute Investigator, Gretchen Stone Cook Chair of Biomedical Sciences, Professor of Biochemistry and Molecular Pharmacology, and Chair of the RNA Therapeutics Institute, are cofounders of Cambridge-based Voyager Therapeutics, a gene therapy company developing treatments for fatal and debilitating diseases of the central nervous system. This company went public in November 2015 and had a stock market capitalization of about $268 million on September 1, 2017. Michael Green, chair of UMMS's Department of Molecular, Cell, and Cancer Biology cofounded Fulcrum Therapeutics, a Kendall Square-based company focused on discovering and developing small molecules that modulate the on/off control mechanisms that regulate genes. Christian Mueller, Associate Professor at UMMS's Department of Pediatrics, cofounded Cambridge-based Apic Bio, a pre-clinical stage gene therapy company leveraging its proprietary platform to advance therapies to treat rare diseases with complex mechanisms.

UMMS also operates a program intended to help its researchers commercialize their IP. The MassTERi [Translation, Entrepreneurship, and Realization] program was founded by three UMMS faculty members: Anastasia Khvorova, Melissa Moore, and Celia Schiffer. MassTERi's goals are to "foster a culture of entrepreneurship at UMMS and facilitate dynamic partnerships with industry; bridge the gap between UMMS discoveries and their development into drugs, products, technologies, and companies; educate and nurture the next generation of translational scientists and entrepreneurs; and benefit the public good through development and commercialization of new therapies and creation of high-value life science jobs."

Case Analysis

UMMS has some impressive IP and is taking steps to help researchers commercialize their work. The most significant challenge for the Worcester community is that companies cofounded by UMMS professors are located in Cambridge. Since more of the talent required to build their companies is located in Cambridge, which is only 40 miles from Worcester, it makes sense to the cofounders to locate there. Should these companies grow and go public or find acquirers, there is a chance that the resulting gains could be invested in Worcester. But unless a critical mass of talent locates in Worcester, the local startup scene will not benefit from that success.

Less Successful Case Study: Some Clark University Alumni Build Successful Companies Outside Worcester

Introduction

Creating a local startup scene is not the principal aim of any university. What's more, a traditional liberal arts school tends to have a long tradition of considering business a less-than-noble calling for its alumni. It is not reasonable to expect a liberal arts school to produce much IP that it can license, with the possible exception of some professors from its Physics, Biology, or Chemistry departments. It is unreasonable to expect such a university to contribute much to a region's startup scene. However, with the growing popularity of entrepreneurship among students, it would be imprudent not to cater to those students' interests.

Case Scenario

Worcester's Clark University offers many courses in entrepreneurship, runs a program to connect students with businesses, and counts many successful entrepreneurs among its alumni. According to Director of Media Relations Jane Salerno, Clark's courses include Entrepreneurship: Art of the New, Entrepreneurial Design Thinking, Funding Ventures, Innovation and Societal Transformations Toward Sustainability, and Creating a Culture of Innovation. "There's more," said Ms. Salerno, "Approximately 300 students each year take entrepreneurship courses to learn, build, and strengthen their entrepreneurial mindset and thinking. Two student-run ventures, the Community Thrift Store and The Local Root, have successfully been operating with ongoing student leadership transitions for the past six years on campus. Sixteen teams entered the 2016 Ureka Big Idea Challenge and worked with alumni, faculty, and community mentors to shape a business model around their project. Three ideas split a $5,000 award." Clark's ClarkCONNECT "already has shown practical success in helping students discover direction and career opportunities. This initiative gives alumni and other Clark partners a forum in which to provide students with job market advice, industry expertise, and valuable post-Clark connections," said Ms. Salerno.

Clark also educated some very successful entrepreneurs, which appears to me to be a result of chance rather than Clark's intention. For example, Avenue Capital Group, a $10 billion Manhattan-based hedge fund, was founded by Marc Lasry '81, whose net worth Forbes estimated at $1.6 billion in September 2017. He's also co-owner of the NBA's Milwaukee Bucks. Ron Shaich '76, founder, chairman of the board, and CEO of St. Louis, Missouri-based Panera Bread Company, which his Au Bon Pain acquired, earned an estimated $400 million in July 2017 when he sold Panera for $7.5 billion to private equity firm JAB Holding.

One Clark alumnus founded a successful company in Worcester County. Arthur J. Remillard, Jr. '56 founded Webster, Mass-based The Commerce Group, which was sold to Spain's Mapfre in October 2007 for $2.2 billion soon after Remillard retired. And Jeffrey Lurie '73, owner of the NFL's Philadelphia Eagles, was a Boston University professor before taking a job at his grandfather's General Cinema. In 1994, he took out a loan to buy the Eagles for $185 million, which accounts for most of what Forbes estimates was his $1.85 billion net worth as of September 2017.

Moreover, a Clark MBA graduate cofounded a company that turns shipping containers into hydroponic farms. Thanks to customer profits, Boston-based Freight Farms lets customers "grow leafy greens, vine crops, and mushrooms hydroponically in insulated, climate-controlled containers." Freight Farms' founders, Brad McNamara (who earned a masters' degree in environmental science and an MBA from Clark) and Jonathan Friedman, were fed up with how inefficient it was to grow produce in a rooftop greenhouse. Friedman decided it would be better to use a shipping container. In 2009, they were working on the design of an urban rooftop greenhouse. According to Friedman, "I was frustrated with the technology for rooftop farming. Despite using double-walled polyvinyl chloride, it was inefficient since so much energy went for heating, cooling, and venting. You can't maintain constant internal temperature. The operating costs were too high. The numbers did not add up and it could not be done at scale." Friedman came up with the solution. As McNamara explained, "The problem was to come up with a large space but more efficient and with a smaller footprint. Jon came up with the idea—use a shipping container—it was a smack in the face. He decided that it would need to fit into a 40 foot by 8 foot space and would be efficient and profitable. And by using light-emitting diodes (LEDs), annual lighting power costs are only $2,600."

It took time to turn that idea into a working prototype. "In early 2010, we started working on the design—looking at components and technology. We needed money so we did a Kickstarter campaign, raising $30,000. The people who contributed money got the joy of helping us achieve our mission of taking local food global. They also got t-shirts, reusable grocery bags, and their names on the outside of our first prototype so the world would know that they were among the first to see the future of the food system," explained McNamara. After raising the money and building the prototype, they entered a local business accelerator, MassChallenge. And their business targets a specific market. "We decided to target a very specific part of the food system to start off. There are 4,400 institutional distributors of fresh fruit and produce to restaurants, hospitals, and universities. We are selling to small and medium *sized distributors with revenues between $3 million and $75 million, representing an $860 million opportunity." In December 2014, Freight Farms received an additional $3.7 million in venture funding from Spark Capital.*

And Freight Farms is helping these distributors that ship to customers throughout the year to reduce their costs. That's because they buy their fresh fruit and produce from local farms during the harvest seasons. But during the rest of the year, they have to source from further away. By using Freight Farms, the customer's costs have dropped. As McNamara explained, "One of our Boston customers imports basil from Mexico that is flown to California and trucked to Boston. He bought one of our containers for $60,000 and uses it to grow a third of his basil, 300 pounds per week, that he sells for $120,000. He used to pay between $3.75 and $4.00 a pound for that basil and with our product it costs him much less." Freight Farms has financed its growth through customer payments. "When customers place an order, they give us a down payment that we use to pay our contract manufacturer. We have one in Mansfield and another north of Boston," explained McNamara.

Case Analysis

As a liberal arts school, Clark is not dedicated to producing world-class IP, yet it has a surprisingly good record of startups founded by alumni. None of the alumni who have started companies in a variety of fields, mostly unrelated to their fields of study at Clark, have built those companies in Worcester. One reason for this could be that most students educated in Worcester want to leave town after they graduate because they view relatively nearby locations such as Boston and New York as much more attractive places to live and work.

Principles

At each of the five levels of the Pillar Company Staircase, university stakeholders should follow specific principles to boost their local startup scenes. At Level 0, the cases highlight the following such principles:

- **University leaders:** They should determine whether to maintain the current level of investment in activities to spur entrepreneurship or to invest more. If they choose to achieve more ambitious goals, they should team with key academic departments to agree on the goals, change values, and incentives, and implement initiatives such as investing more in technology licensing, boosting incentives for local faculty entrepreneurship, and introducing new programs to link students with alumni.

- **Government policymakers:** If university leaders decide that they want to encourage more of their locally-educated

students to stay in the city after graduation, they will need
to partner with government policymakers. The university
and government leaders should assess the opportunities to build real estate developments and boost cultural
activities that will encourage graduating students to live,
work, and play in the city after they graduate.

Level 1: No Pillars, Some Gazelles

Successful Case Study: HEC Helps Students and Alumni to Create Gazelles

Introduction

Paris does not have a true pillar company, although as you saw in Chapter 1,
the CEO of one of its publicly traded companies, Xavier Niel, is a billionaire
who is pouring his own resources into boosting Paris's startup scene. Paris
does have several gazelles and its leading business university, HEC Paris, is
a major contributor to their success. It remains to be seen whether any of
those gazelles will become pillars, but if they do it seems likely that HEC will
be seen to have contributed to their success.

Case Scenario

*HEC alumni have started large, traditional companies, turning their founders into bil-
lionaires, gazelles that were acquired for hundreds of millions of dollars, and gazelles
that have the potential to reach that scale. For example, Philippe Foriel-Destezet
(Forbes estimated his net worth at $2.9 billion in September 2017) founded his
staffing company, Ecco, in 1964; by the 1980s it was France's largest supplier of
temporary personnel. He merged the firm with Klaus Jacobs's Swiss firm Adia to create Adecco in 1996. The company now employs more than 33,000 people full time
across 5,100 branches in over 60 countries. In 1966 Pierre Bellon (Forbes estimated
his net worth at $5.7 billion in September 2017) founded Sodexo, which started as
a catering and cruise service with one company restaurant in Marseilles. By 2017,
Sodexo was one of the world's 20 largest employers, with 420,000 employees. Pierre
Kosciusko-Morizet cofounded e-commerce company PriceMinister in 2001 after seeing that France lacked a website connecting buyers and sellers. PriceMinister grew
to 200 employees and was acquired in 2010 for $350 million by Japan's Rakuten.
Kosciusko-Morizet's investments include BlaBlaCar, a leading French long-distance
car sharing app, on whose board he sits. Tatiana Jama and Lara Rouyres cofounded
LivingSocial, a Washington, DC-based daily deal site that raised $928 million and
after considerable layoffs was acquired in October 2016 for an undisclosed amount
by Groupon. Céline Lazorthes was CEO of payment app Leetchi that was acquired
by Credit Mutual Arkea for 50 million Euros in 2015. HEC alumni also include*

Boris Saragaglia, founder of online shoe retailer Spartoo, which raised $72 million in funding; Oleg Tscheltzoff, the founder of royalty-free image bank Fotolia, which was acquired by Adobe Systems in December 2014 for $800 million in cash; and Ning Li, cofounder of London furniture e-tailer Made.com, which raised $73 million by September 2017.

HEC Paris is pursuing several paths for producing more startups and otherwise contributing to Paris's economic growth. As Etienne Krieger, Scientific Director of the HEC Entrepreneurship Center, explained, "We do occasionally license our IP, generating not huge revenue streams. For example, ESA in Beirut launched a Master in Entrepreneurship in partnership with HEC Paris and the Chamber of Commerce, Industry, and Agriculture of Beirut and Mount Lebanon. Such a partnership entails an IP part, since we transfer our academic knowledge in entrepreneurship and innovation for degree programs as well as executive education programs. 137 full time HEC professors have started companies and continue running such companies while teaching at HEC Paris. These professors are mainly part of our affiliate faculty (30 full-time professors and several part-time professors) and they are CEOs, CFOs, and/or board members of several startups or small- or medium-sized enterprises. HEC also participates in incubators. For example, it operates one of France's largest startup incubators (70 startups) at Station F and cofounded IncubAlliance, France's biggest tech incubator, located on the Paris-Saclay cluster. HEC also offers numerous courses on entrepreneurship and innovation and has created MOOCs on entrepreneurship and innovation including an Online Masters of Innovation and Entrepreneurship. HEC connects students with alumni through its incubator, as well as during conferences, pitching events, and courses about startup creation and financing where students analyze real startups and meet the founders and potential investors. In addition, HEC is the cofounder of the Paris Saclay Seed Fund, whose Managing Partner is an HEC alumnus. HEC works with this fund to generate deal flow and help students understand the logistics of venture capital."

Case Analysis

HEC has educated many successful entrepreneurs. What's more, it offers many programs to help teach entrepreneurship through concepts and action, such as internships at startups and help with early-stage startup financing. Some of them have become huge companies, others have grown to the point where they were acquired for hundreds of millions of dollars, and a few are still fairly small but seem to have growth potential. Some of these successful founders are contributing capital and expertise to new startups, thus potentially creating a virtuous cycle. Nevertheless, HEC does not generate IP that has the potential to create significant revenue streams, which could limit its ability to contribute significantly to the Paris startup scene.

Less Successful Case Study: Two Hong Kong Gazelles Become Unicorns without Help from University of Hong Kong

Introduction

While Hong Kong has a long history of business success, including many family-run conglomerates, it has not yet established any high tech pillar companies. However, in recent years Hong Kong has hosted gazelles that were founded by Hong Kong natives who were educated in the U.S. and returned to start their companies. Two such gazelles have become so successful that their private market value exceeds $1 billion, making them part of the unicorn club. However, Hong Kong's universities have not contributed much to their success.

Case Scenario

Two Hong Kong gazelles are the Uber-for-delivery-vans-service GogoVan and WeLab, which operates a personal lending platform. The CEOs of both firms are originally from Hong Kong, earned their degrees outside Hong Kong, and returned there to start their companies. And both CEOs have overseen the growth of their companies to the point where they are valued in the private market at over $1 billion. However, the story of GoGoVan is loaded with drama whereas WeLab's ascent appears to have been smoother sailing. GoGoVan was started by Steven Lam, the son of a construction worker, who dropped out of high school, moved to the U.S. where he worked delivering Chinese food, excelled at a California community college, and was next admitted to the University of California, Berkeley, which he paid for by fixing iPhones and reselling them on eBay among other businesses he created. After graduation he returned to Hong Kong and operated a business that posted advertisements on top of Styrofoam Chinese food containers. One day he was waiting for a delivery truck to arrive so he could get an order to a client on time. But the driver was late and he could not get any information on when he would arrive. Lam went out in the street and saw a driver sitting in a delivery van doing nothing. Lam asked the driver if he could deliver his shipment and the driver told him that it was up to the radio dispatcher. In frustration, Lam came up with the idea of an app that would bypass the dispatcher, connecting drivers with people wanting things delivered. The result was GoGoVan, which was started in 2014 by five Hong Kong founders and raised over $26 million from investors, although many potential investors declined to lend him money because they were saving up to buy an apartment. In August 2017, GoGoVan merged with 58 Suyun, attaining a valuation of over $1 billion. 58 Suyun is owned by online classifieds giant 58.com and operates in over 100 cities in China with 1.2 million registered drivers, while GoGoVan had spread to eight cities in China, Taiwan, Singapore, Korea, and India. Alibaba invested in both companies: GoGoVan via its entrepreneurship fund, and 58.com's 58 Home subsidiary, which operates 58 Suyun, in a $300 million round in 2015. GoGoVan wants to raise $200 million for expansion into two or three new markets in 2018, and in the following year Lam wants to move Australia and Europe, and take the company public.

WeLab's story is less dramatic but another great example of a gazelle becoming a unicorn. Cofounder and CEO Simon Loong started WeLab in 2013 after over 15 years in the banking sector. Prior to WeLab, he held senior positions at both Citibank and Standard Chartered Bank. Most recently he was Standard Chartered's Regional Head of Northeast Asia, where he managed the personal loan and credit card businesses, "transforming it into one of the largest and most profitable businesses of its kind in Greater China. He also served on Standard Chartered's Consumer Bank Management committee in Hong Kong. Loong is a CPA who earned a Bachelor's in Commerce, with a focus on accounting and finance, from University of Sydney and holds a master's degree from Stanford Business School." Loong's experience made him familiar with the high costs and barriers to accessing credit faced by Hong Kong consumers. So he developed "a solution that circumvented traditional financial institutions." In 2013, he founded WeLab, a mobile lending platform that uses risk-testing technology to conduct credit assessments in seconds and enables customers to borrow money with a few taps of their smartphones. Now valued at more than $1 billion, it was Hong Kong's first tech unicorn and its WeLend leading online lending platform has sourced more than "$154 million in loan applications and 16,000 members." By January 2016, WeLab had loaned money to 2.5 million customers, the majority in mainland China. That month WeLab raised a $160 million Series B from Khazanah Nasional Berhad, Malaysia's strategic investment fund, with participation from ING Bank and Guangdong Technology Financial Group, which is run by the Chinese government, leading to total funding of $182 million. WeLab planned to use the funds to improve its technology, which uses non-traditional sources of data to assess a lender's risk profile, and form partnerships with companies and banks. WeLab also intended to partner with e-commerce platform Ule.com and the Postal Savings Bank of China to launch online financial products. In November 2017, WeLab raised even more capital — bringing its total to $425 million.

The Hong Kong University (HKU) is one of several universities participating in the local startup ecosystem; however, its professors and alumni have had more notable success in creating traditional Hong Kong businesses. HKU has licensed its technology to companies and trained talent, some of which goes to local startups. However, while some companies spun out of HKU have been successful, they have not achieved unicorn status as have GoGoVan and WeLab. According to a September 6, 2017 interview with Rhea Leung, HKU's Manager of the (Media) Communications and Public Affairs Office, "HKU established a wholly-owned technology transfer arm, Versitech Limited, to take care of the technology transfer and licensing matters of IPs to the industry. The company started its business operation in 1998 and the cumulative total revenue received from IP licensing exceeds $12.7 million as of June 2017. HKU has licensed its technologies to 22 companies so far where HKU professors were involved in the commercialization of their R&D projects. 19 of them were still in active operation as of June 2017. HKY offers formal courses in entrepreneurship; an entrepreneurship networking program called i-Dendron which organizes and coordinates entrepreneurship forums, mixers, events, courses, internships and competitions for HKU students, staff, and alumni; and in August 2017, a partnership between HKU and Cyberport was announced to establish jointly a HKUxCyberport Digital

Tech Entrepreneurship Platform with the objective of building a unique digital tech ecosystem for Hong Kong. HKU alumni established several well-known more traditional companies, including Hong Kong Economic Times, *the city's leading financial daily newspaper;VTech, a manufacturer of electronic learning products;Vitasoy, a beverage and desert maker; and Shun Tak Holdings, a conglomerate with interests in transportation, property, hospitality, and investment. HKU alumni also founded many startups including the following:*

- *Snapask, an education technology company that raised $5 million in seed funding in June 2017;*

- *9Gag, a user-generated video site that raised $2.8 million in seed financing in 2012;*

- *Innopage, a mobile app developer founded in 2010; and*

- *Athenex, a Buffalo, New York-based maker of pill versions of intravenous cancer drugs that was founded in 2003, raised more than $250 million in private financing, and went public on NASDAQ in June 2017, reaching a stock market value of $1 billion on September 8, 2017.*

Case Analysis

Hong Kong is a business-friendly city in which real estate is considered among the most prized investments. The emphasis on real estate puts pressure on college graduates to seek out high paying jobs in banking and money management so they can afford to buy or rent property, which is exceptionally expensive. In Hong Kong, high technology startups are seen as far riskier places to invest. Nevertheless, some Hong Kong natives who were educated in the U.S. return home with a different mental attitude and, as Lam and Loong have demonstrated, the ability to turn a gazelle into a unicorn. Unfortunately, HKU's efforts to use its IP and talent to create high tech gazelles have yet to yield significant success for Hong Kong's startup scene.

Principles

The Level I cases highlight the following principles that university leaders and government policymakers should pursue to boost the local startup scene:

- **University leaders:** The case studies reveal that HEC Paris and HKU have created some alumni startups that have been able to grow quickly but not big enough to go public. However, both universities have opportunities to teach aspiring students how to scale startups and run them as public companies. Such training would come from a combination of courses, internships, and mentoring from executives who have scaled their companies successfully.

- **Government policymakers:** The case studies reveal that local capital providers and financial markets are not deep enough to support the scaling of local startups to the point that they can go public. To remedy that deficiency, government policymakers should boost their expertise in how to build the legal, regulatory, and technology infrastructure needed to host such capital markets.

Level 2: No Pillars, Acquired Gazelles

Success/Opportunity for Improvement Case Study: KTH Supplies IP and Talent to Some of Sweden's Gazelles

Introduction

Stockholm hosts a remarkable number of gazelles given its relatively modest population. One contributor to Stockholm's startup success is the KTH Royal Institute of Technology, which was founded in 1827 and has "grown to become one of Europe's leading technical and engineering universities, as well as a key center of intellectual talent and innovation. [KTH is] Sweden's largest technical research and learning institution and home to students, researchers, and faculty from around the world dedicated to advancing knowledge." Moreover, KTH has been helping professors to commercialize their IP and students to learn about entrepreneurship and start companies.

Case Scenario

Since 2007, KTH Innovation has been the driving force behind commercializing KTH's new ideas. Specifically, in the last decade KTH Innovation has helped "over 1,900 new ideas from 1,080 students and 850 researchers, including 275 professors by offering free, objective, and confidential support in all areas relevant to taking an idea from research result to innovation." KTH Innovation employs 15 people who help researchers and students with business development, patents and law, funding, and project management. KTH Innovation also runs the "KTH Innovation pre-incubator and niche projects to draw attention to and aid innovation development and internationalization."

KTH alumni have started some remarkable companies. As Lisa Ericsson, CEO of KTH Innovation (who previously worked for McKinsey to spin off a business plan competition and has headed KTH Innovation for a decade) said in a September 4, 2017 interview, "KTH alumni's are very active in the Stockholm startup ecosystem and many of the most prominent startups have been started by them, for example Spotify, Prezi, and Tobii Technologies. Spotify [valued at $8.5 billion in June 2011] is a music, podcast, and video streaming service that was officially launched on October 7, 2008. It was founded by KTH alumnus Daniel Ek and most of the developers working there have been and are KTH alumni. It provides digital rights management-protected content from record labels and media companies. Prezi was founded in 2009 by KTH alumnus Peter Arvai in collaboration with Péter Halácsy and Adam Somlai-Fischer. The company's flagship platform is a visual storytelling software alternative to traditional slide-based presentation formats. Prezi presentations feature a map-like, schematic overview that lets users pan among topics at will, zoom in on desired details, and pull back to reveal context. Tobii was founded in 2001 by KTH alumni John Elvesjö and Mårten Skogsö with Henrik Eskilsson. Based on total market share, leading technology, and a comprehensive eye tracking patent portfolio, Tobii is the world leader in eye tracking. It provides conditions for new insights into human behavior and technology more adapted to humans, using eye tracking as their core."

KTH Innovation works with a different set of policies than those found at other universities discussed in this chapter. As Ericsson said in an August 31, 2017 interview, "In Sweden we have the professor's privilege, which means that all IP stays with the researchers and they are not obliged to inform KTH if they seek to commercialize it. I also run The Holding Company LLC, which is controlled by KTH, was started in 1994, and began acting in its current role in 2010. The Holding Company can invest in startups and serves as a parking place for IP. If a researcher has excellent IP and no interest in commercializing it, we offer to invest and share the profits with the researcher. Unfortunately, we are underfunded; we have only $50,000 per investment and we could do so much more. So we collaborate with angels and venture capital funds."

Since 2014, KTH has helped 70 companies founded by KTH faculty, including Volumental, Manomotion, and Adaptive Simulations. As Ericcson explained, "Volumental helps consumers find shoes that fit well. Researchers at the Computer Vision and Active Perception Lab Department at KTH's School of Computer Science and Communication developed the algorithms for Volumental, which uses the latest computer vision and 3D technology to make finding the perfect fitting shoe a breeze. To do this, they built the world's fastest and easiest 3D foot scanner, enabling brands and retailers to scan and analyze their customers, recommend great products, and provide the best, personalized service in the footwear industry. They are now laying the groundwork for the next huge step: enabling brands to bring custom shoes to customers all over the world using technology such as 3D printing. KTH Innovation supported the researchers behind Volumental from early 2012 to May 2013 through funding and investment, recruitment of co-founder/CEO, market verification, and IP strategy, after which they went on to the accelerator STING. ManoMotion provides a framework for real- time 3D gestural analysis. Using its unique technology users can grasp and manipulate objects in 3D spaces with the same feeling as they would have in the real world. All that's required is a simple RGB camera found in everyday smartphones. KTH Innovation helped the researchers behind Manomotion to address patenting issues, to obtain funding, and to recruit an external CEO."

"Adaptive Simulations offers a cloud-based service (SaaS), providing customers with fully automated flow simulations. Its automated cloud solution increases accuracy, flexibility, and cost efficiency when simulating flow. The accessibility and ease of use of the solution enables designers, engineers, researchers, innovators, and architects without any prior knowledge of Computational Fluid Dynamics or simulations to predict flow and improve their design. KTH Innovation has supported Adaptive Simulations since early 2012. The support has included funding, recruitment of an external CEO, and exposure to our network of private investors, KTH EarlyBird Network."

Since 2014, KTH Innovation has also helped a total of 22 student startups, including Greenely, Tinitel, and Shortcut Labs. As Ericsson explained, "Using a mobile application, Greenely visualizes and analyses a household's energy consumption to save money and preserve the environment. Researchers at the Department of Psychology at Stanford University have collaborated with Greenely for two years to study and develop new behavioral and communications technology with individual households to reduce their energy consumption. Together they are now launching Greenely Go in the US. Greenely was one of the first startups to join the KTH student incubator in 2013, receiving enhanced support in an accelerated process. It also received support in funding, business modelling, and business development. Tinitell is a wearable mobile phone for kids. It is simple, fun, and durable, perfect for outdoor adventures. Parents manage it from the Tinitell admin app and using the GPS tracker they can easily locate their kids. It is currently for sale both in Europe and the US. KTH Innovation supported the student behind Tinitell with market verification, funding, and patenting issues. Shortcut Labs developed the Flic button, a wireless Bluetooth button that can be used to control things around you. The button can be set up to perform a single action, such as turning on lights, or a series of actions with just one click. KTH Innovation helped the students behind Shortcut Lab with prototyping, funding, and patent search."

Case Analysis

KTH has produced a considerable number of alumni and professor-led companies. Many of them are gazelles and some of them have been acquired, as we explored in Chapter 2. KTH companies tend to focus on relatively narrow technical problems, most of which do not target sufficiently large markets to justify taking a company public or keeping it growing once it has completed its IPO. While KTH would benefit from providing more resources to its technology licensing efforts, it is clear that Stockholm has yet to develop the executive talent required to lead a company that can compete effectively after it goes public. Nevertheless, KTH has achieved much considering its relatively limited resources and the small size of its local markets.

Principles

The Level 2 case, KTH, highlights the following principles that university leaders and government policymakers should pursue to boost the local startup scene:

- **University leaders:** The KTH case is one of success, as demonstrated by the number of KTH gazelles that have been acquired and the unicorn status of some that are still independent, and opportunity for improvement due to the limited market opportunity facing many of its startups and the limited amount of capital available locally. University leaders may be able to improve on the weaknesses by offering programs that expose students, through internships, consulting assignments, and education abroad programs to U.S. or Israeli companies that have scaled successfully.

- **Government policymakers:** Sweden's financial markets are not deep enough to support the scaling of local startups to the point that they can go public. As a result, local entrepreneurs do not have good role models for how to run a public company from Stockholm. To remedy that deficiency, government policymakers should boost their expertise in how to build the legal, regulatory, and technology infrastructure needed to host such capital markets.

Level 3: Some Pillars in Niche Markets

Success Case: MIT Creates 30,200 Companies with $2.9 Trillion in Revenues

Introduction

MIT has had an enormous economic impact on the world. Its twin emphasis on creating innovative ideas and using them to solve real problems is at the core of its ability to boost economic activity. However, for reasons that may also have to do with its culture, companies produced by MIT, such as Akamai and iRobot, in recent decades are considerably smaller than ones based on Stanford's technology, such as Cisco Systems and Google. What's more, while Silicon Valley has been able to create new pillar companies for many technology generations, MIT spinoffs reached their peak of influence in the mid-1980s and have since waned in their global impact.

Case Scenario

This is not to diminish the awesome economic power of MIT (I was a graduate student in computer science there). According to a December 2015 report, "Innovation and Entrepreneurship at MIT," as of 2014 MIT alumni had "launched 30,200 active companies, employing roughly 4.6 million people, and generating roughly $1.9 trillion in annual revenues." A significant contributor to MIT's economic power is the talent it attracts and the IP that talent generates. According to my August 31, 2017 interview with Lesley Millar-Nicholson, Director of MIT's Technology Licensing Office, "Between 1991 and 2015, licensing MIT's patents has generated $1 billion in revenue. Since a licensing fee is roughly 2% of revenues, that represents $50 billion in sales generated by the IP. And that excludes the $24 billion spent on [MIT's defense research arm] Lincoln Labs."

While there is no MIT-wide list of its top 10 companies, some MIT departments do list their spinoffs. For instance, MIT's Media Lab has spurred the creation of "well over 150 companies" including a few that were acquired, such as Twitter's 2013 acquisition of Bluefin Labs, a social analytics company, for about $90 million. Lincoln Labs lists 107 companies on a list of its spinoffs, including Digital Equipment Corp which at its peak employed 114,000 and had revenues of about $14 billion before stumbling when its CEO struggled to see why anyone would need a PC and losing its independence in 1998 to Compaq. Then there's MIT's Computer Science and Artificial Intelligence Lab (CSAIL), which has spawned over 100 companies, including Akamai, Dropbox, iRobot, OKCupid, Rethink Robotics, and RSA. Sadly for MIT, the economic impact of these companies is relatively limited. For example, content delivery network service provider Akamai had 2016 sales of $2.3 billion; personal robot maker iRobot's sales were $661 million last year; Dropbox, OKCupid, Rethink Robotics, and RSA (which EMC acquired for $2.1 billion in 2006) are privately held so their sales are unknown. This compares unfavorably to just the two Stanford spinoffs mentioned above: Google (2016 sales of $90 billion) and Cisco ($48 billion).

Nevertheless, MIT has finely honed its skill at commercializing its IP. As Millar-Nicholson said, "Between 1991 and 2015, we made 11,000 total patent applications of which 4,000 issued patents have value to licensees and 437 companies licensed MIT-owned IP. After taking 15% to partially offset the TLO's costs ($30,000 to $40,000 per patent issued), a third of the remaining licensing revenue goes to MIT, a third goes to the inventor, and a third to the inventor's MIT department. And our office helps the inventor find a licensee that will best commercialize the invention." From there, other MIT programs help out. For example, In October, 2016, MIT launched The Engine to support startup companies "working on scientific and technological innovation with the potential for transformative societal impact." MIT supplements the inventor's skills by helping to find business people who can build a company around the IP, identify sources of capital, pick the right market on which to focus the invention, and test the value of the invention to potential customers. Ultimately, MIT's TLO helps "find a place we think is right for the technology," said Millar-Nicholson.

Case Analysis

MIT is a global pioneer in spurring local entrepreneurship. And while it continues to generate new ideas that result in new businesses, its economic impact is diminishing in relation to other regions. As you saw in Chapter 1, Silicon Valley garnered 42% of the venture capital invested in the second quarter of 2017 while New England (7.6%) fell way behind New York (15.1%). As a veteran Boston venture capitalist told me, after the telecom equipment boom in the 1990s, which led to the creation of companies like optical switch maker Sycamore Networks, which had a peak stock market value of $45 billion and liquidated itself in 2013, and was cofounded by Desh Despande, who helped start MIT's Deshpande Center for Technological Innovation, and Dan Smith, who started and sold Cascade Communications for $3.6 billion in 1997, Boston never figured out its next act. "Since then," he said, "Boston has lacked a flywheel, in which a company is either acquired or goes public and fuels the next generation of entrepreneurs that achieve the same or greater levels of success." This may be due in part to the culture of MIT; based on my experience, it has a strong preference for solving difficult and relatively narrow engineering problems and it is less interested than Silicon Valley seems to be in building startups based on a grandiose, world-changing vision. MIT's culture also affects the attitude of Boston-area venture capitalists who are often hesitant to invest in a startup until it can build a product and get confirmation from customers that they'll buy it.

Less Successful Case: Haifa's Technion Helps Launch 90 Companies 52 Miles Away

Introduction

Israel's startup scene, which boasts of the world's largest number of NASDAQ-listed companies per capita, is headquartered around Tel Aviv. As we explored in Chapter 1, the Tel Aviv area is the host of pillar companies such as Check Point Software, which spawned many other publicly-traded companies, creating the flywheel effect mentioned above. Haifa, 52 miles north of Tel Aviv, hosts the Technion, which is known as the MIT of Israel. However, most people who graduate from the Technion do not want to live or start companies there after they graduate. Although the Technion has licensed technology to companies that have gone public, most are not located in Haifa and are not pillars. Instead, they operate around the world.

Case Scenario

One former Technion professor does not seem troubled that Haifa does not host many Technion startups. As Shlomo Maital, an emeritus professor of economics at the Technion, explained in an August 6, 2017 email, "Israel is a very small country. Tel Aviv is less than an hour from Haifa by train. It is not clear that there are insights to be gained by looking at individual cities or neighborhoods instead of viewing Israel as a whole ecosystem." He does think Haifa has some strengths. As he said, these include "the presence of Intel Israel Development Corp. (IDC), established in 1974, which employs several thousand people. IDC employs star Technion students even before they graduate. IDC is located in merkaz ta-asiyat mada (MATAM). In addition, Haifa Science Park has a very strong cluster of high tech companies, including startups and global giants Elbit and Microsoft. Intel spins off startups when its engineers become bored and leave to launch their own firms. In addition, there is the new Haifa Life Sciences Park; its first building is completed and others are on the way. The Haifa Economic Corporation has partnered with MIVNE Real Estate Group to establish the Haifa Life Sciences Park, intended for companies with a clear affinity towards medicine and science, initiating and developing technological solutions and platforms for scientific breakthroughs. Leading companies from medical device developers and digital healthcare development companies to technological incubators are calling the Haifa Life Sciences Park home, thereby placing Haifa at the forefront of research and development of a wide spectrum of fields. This is a field of dreams project: if you build it, they will come. GE Healthcare is the first major occupant; we'll see if startups come here. The main life sciences incubator/accelerator is in Rehovot, near the Weizmann Institute. The Park's management invests a great deal in creating unique opportunities for the industry, while promoting integration of the biotech and medical equipment industries in Haifa, to enable strategic cooperation between academic institutions, medical centers, research institutes, and commercial entities in Israel and abroad."

With the exception of Elbit Systems, a $6 billion (September 8, 2017 stock market capitalization) aerospace and defense company, Haifa does not have pillar companies. But it does host satellite offices for Silicon Valley pillar companies such as Intel, Google, Apple, Yahoo, Philips, GE Healthcare, Cisco Systems, and Flextronics, according to Maital, who believes that the Technion is not eager enough to license its IP. As he said, "Hossam Haick, a Technion chemical engineer, developed an electronic 'nose' that became the basis of several startup ventures. I have a personal beef. Universities in general, Technion in particular, in my view, cling too tightly to IP developed within the university. This deters investors like citronella deters mosquitos. MIT let Bose use his Ph.D. results to launch a speaker company. Later, Bose willed the whole company to MIT! Technion does not following this model. I regret it. Technion is a public university, funded in part by government (at least, the operating budget). IP developed within Technion belongs to the people and should be more freely released. (Not everyone agrees)."

Among those who might challenge Maital is the CEO of the Technion's technology transfer office. According to an August 30, 2017 interview with Benjamin Soffer, CEO of Technion Technology Transfer, "We have 90 companies in our portfolio near Tel Aviv and Herzliya. Except for pharmaceuticals-related IP that we license directly to established companies, we license Technion IP to startups that do the technology transfer. Technion keeps half of the licensing revenue and the other half goes to the inventor. Our annual licensing income of $35 million covers a third of Technion's *research budget. Technion scientists can consult one day a week to the startups; we don't want to turn brilliant scientists into mediocre business people." Technion technology has found its way into 10 companies that went public including*

- ReWalk Robotics, an Israel and Marlborough, Mass.-based maker of exoskeletons for paraplegics with $6 million in 2016 sales, a $33 million loss, and a stock market value of $34 million as of September 8, 2017;

- Vancouver, B.C.-based medical diagnostics company Breathtec Biomedical with no sales, a $7 million 2016 net loss, and a stock market value of $4.4 million as of September 8, 2017;

- Waltham, Mass.-based vascular surgery robot maker Corindus Vascular Robotics with $3 million in sales, a $33 million 2016 net loss, and a stock market value of $305 million as of September 8, 2017;

- Caesarea, Israel-based orthopedics and neurosurgery medical device maker Mazor Robotics with $36 million in sales, a $19 million 2016 net loss, and a stock market value of $1.1 billion as of September 8, 2017;

- Yokneam, Israel-based pre-clinical medical device maker Microbot Medical with no sales, a $10 million 2016 net loss, and a stock market value of $35.5 million as of September 8, 2017;

- St. Helier, Jersey-based medical systems developer Novocure with $83 million in sales, a $132 million 2016 net loss, and a stock market value of $1.8 billion as of September 8, 2017;

- Haifa, Israel-based biotherapeutics supplier Pluristem Therapeutics with $3 million in sales, a $23 million 2016 net loss, and a stock market value of $113.7 million as of September 8, 2017; and

- Miami, Fla.-based diagnostics and pharmaceutical company Opko Health with $1.2 billion in sales, a $25 million 2016 net loss, and a stock market value of $3.5 billion as of September 8, 2017.

Maital is not optimistic about Haifa's startup scene. As he said, "The Haifa startup scene will decline in the next five years. Why? Tel Aviv is a magnet for startups and for young people is ranked fifth in the global list of best startup cities, and it's getting better. Haifa has a reputation of being a boring city, no night life, mediocre schools, and the sidewalks get pulled in at 8 pm. Even Jerusalem is ascending (now there's a paradox). The high-tech park in Jerusalem, with Mobileye, is right in the midst of an ultra-Orthodox neighborhood; the contrast is stark. But Jerusalem's mayor, Nir Barkat, was a successful entrepreneur and then helped fund Check Point. Haifa's mayor, Yona Yahav, is very far from that world. Haifa is asleep. A new high-tech area nearby, about 20 minutes away, is called Yokneam Illit, and it already has over 100 high tech companies in an area known as Startup Village. It's close to a major highway (Route 6) and has good schools and ample space."

Case Analysis

The Technion produces more world-class talent and IP than Haifa can absorb. Indeed, the headquarters of many of the largest Technion-linked companies are outside Israel. It does not appear likely that Haifa intends to change its attitude towards encouraging Technion students and professors to start companies near the school. What remains to be seen is whether the leaders of successful Technion-led companies ultimately return to Haifa to reinvest their gains in startups. While this could happen, it appears more likely that the Technion will remain a place where people study in relative isolation and leave to start companies.

Principles

The Level 3 cases, MIT and the Technion, highlight the following principles that university leaders and government policymakers should pursue to boost the local startup scene:

- **University leaders:** MIT has created successful companies around the world and many of them are located near the campus. Moreover, thanks to innovations from its Whitehead Institute, pharmaceutical and biotechnology companies have opened offices in Kendall Square as well. There is not much more that MIT could be doing to encourage local startups. In thinking about the relatively small scale of MIT pillar companies, it is clear that their CEOs are good at focusing on specific technical problems that have limited market potential. Were MIT to change its admissions policies and education programs to encourage what Stanford calls T-shaped students with breadth in a range of areas and depth in one, MIT's pillar companies might become more valuable. To be sure, such a change would take time: first, the T-shaped students would need to turn consumer-focused ideas into large startups, eventually causing a flywheel effect in the region.

- **Government policymakers:** Government policymakers in Cambridge and Haifa face very different challenges. Cambridge is growing rapidly and needs to build housing, public transit, roads, and other infrastructure to support growth that does not displace too many of its long-time residents and is convenient to work and play for newcomers.

Haifa needs to decide whether it wants to host Technion startups and, if so, must transform the region into a place that appeals to young people so they do not flee after graduation.

Level 4: Many Pillars in Huge Markets

Success Case Study: Stanford's $2.7 Trillion Startup Machine

Introduction

Stanford leads the world when it comes to producing both pillar companies and valuable startups and it has sustained that leadership for decades. It is highly unlikely that other universities will ever be able to match its accomplishments. Due to a combination of its talent, culture, and luck, Stanford has been able to sustain its leadership by creating new waves of technology that have overtaken the preceding ones.

Case Scenario

Like MIT, Stanford has created companies with revenues in the trillions of dollars with millions of employees. What makes Stanford the world's leader in creating pillar companies is the sheer scale of so many of those companies. According to Stanford spokesperson Ernest Miranda, a 2012 study estimated that companies formed by Stanford entrepreneurs generate worldwide revenues of $2.7 trillion annually and have created 5.4 million jobs since the 1930s, during which time Stanford alumni and faculty have created nearly 40,000 companies. Adding up the value of 15 well-known public companies founded by Stanford alumni yields a whopping $1.39 trillion in value: Charles Schwab & Company ($53 billion market capitalization as of September 12, 2017), Cisco Systems ($161 billion), Dolby Laboratories ($5 billion), eBay ($41 billion), E*Trade ($11 billion), Electronic Arts ($37 billion), Google ($651 billion), Hewlett-Packard Enterprise ($21 billion), HP ($33 billion), Intuitive Surgical ($39 billion), Netflix ($80 billion), Nike ($88 billion), NVIDIA ($101 billion), Tesla Motors ($61 billion), and Zillow ($8 billion). If you include the price at which another nine have been acquired—Instagram ($1 billion), LinkedIn ($26.2 billion), MIPS Technologies ($406 million), Odwalla ($181 million), Orbitz ($1.6 billion), Silicon Graphics ($275 million), StubHub ($310 million), Sun Microsystems ($7.4 billion), and Yahoo ($4.5 billion)—that adds nearly another $42 billion to that total. Then there are the well-known privately held companies—Gap, Trader Joe's, and Whole Earth Catalog—of unknown value. What's more, from its founding in 1970 to 2016, Stanford's Office of Technology Licensing has overseen the creation of more than 11,000 inventions and issued more than 3,600 licenses that have generated more than $1.7 billion in royalties, according to Miranda.

Beyond accepting many of the world's brightest minds, Stanford seems to attract people who combine technical strength with strong interpersonal skills. Stanford runs programs that connect students with alumni, many entrepreneurship programs, and a variety of startup accelerators. For example, there is the Stanford Technology Ventures Program in the School of Engineering, Start X, an educational, non-profit business incubator associated with Stanford which "helps entrepreneurs launch fledgling companies in a range of industries" while requiring neither fees nor equity in companies. Stanford also offers StartX Med for medical entrepreneurship.

Stanford got to be such a huge economic engine due to three factors: great men, the right culture, and California's values. Great men spurred Silicon Valley's initial success. For example, as MIT Sloan School Lecturer Jorge Guzman pointed out, Silicon Valley would still be peach orchards were it not for William Shockley, the inventor of the transistor who moved west to found Fairchild Semiconductor. MIT Sloan School David Sarnoff Professor of Management of Technology Ed Roberts noted that Frederick Terman, an MIT professor, came to Stanford in 1925 and later helped two of his students, William Hewlett and David Packard, to found HP. Terman helped HP succeed by connecting the company to Defense Department contracts. Another factor is Stanford's culture, which Roberts believes is based in part on MIT's. As Roberts pointed out, MIT was started in the 1861 with the motto Mens et Manus (Latin for mind and hand), meaning that its mission was to make cutting edge ideas useful to industry. What's more, MIT encouraged professors to do research for industry to supplement their low professor's pay. Thus there was a natural flow of talent between MIT and industry which in other universities is frowned on. Roberts believes that Terman took that same philosophy to Stanford and that has made much of the difference.

A third factor is California's pioneering spirit. According to William F. Miller, a physicist who was the last Stanford faculty member recruited by Terman and later became provost, the relationship between Stanford and Silicon Valley is related to Stanford's founding. "This was kind of the Wild West. The gold rush was still on. Custer's Last Stand was only nine years before. California had not been a state very long—roughly 30 years. People who came here had to be pioneers. Pioneers had two qualities: one, they had to be adventurers, but they were also community builders. So the people who came here to build the university also intended to build the community, and that meant interacting with businesses and helping create businesses." Former Stanford President John Hennessy said that California's relative lack of traditions to be protected mean that "people are willing to try things. At Stanford more than elsewhere, the university and business forge a borderless community in which making money is considered virtuous and where participants profess a sometimes inflated belief that their work is changing the world for the better."

Case Analysis

Stanford's success at creating startups is exceptional; while other universities can learn from its success, they should not try to replicate it. Its undergraduate program has the lowest acceptance rate of any school in the world, which means it attracts the best talent. Stanford also provides programs that connect student entrepreneurs with mentors and offer accelerators that help startups progress. What's more, Stanford enables its professors and administrators to work with startups created by its students and to invest in those companies. While some of those startups will fail, this involvement in so many startups generally insures that Stanford does not miss out on any big successes that might survive the winnowing process.

Failure Case Study: Stanford Enables Enfant Terrible to Crash and Burn Clinkle

Introduction

Stanford's success in creating startups has a dark side. There is an incestuous relationship between student entrepreneurs seen as stars and professors and administrators who fear missing out on the next big thing. One example of this is Theranos, a blood testing company founded in 2013 by a Stanford dropout with help from her chemistry professor, Channing Robertson. Its value peaked at $9 billion in 2014, accompanied by fawning press, the year before a Wall Street Journal investigation of its practices—most notably making false claims about its blood tester—sent its value tumbling in the wake of lawsuits that left it in a precarious financial position. A few years before that collapse, another startup with even closer ties to Stanford had a rapid rise and fall.

Case Scenario

Clinkle was founded in 2011 by a superstar Stanford undergraduate. In 2013, Clinkle raised over $30 million in seed round with significant support from Stanford professors, administrators, and its entrepreneurship programs. In 2013, Lucas Duplan was the 22-year-old founder and CEO of Clinkle, a mobile payments app that aspired to replace cash and credit cards using high-frequency sound technology. Duplan got the idea for Clinkle on a visit to London after he had forgotten his credit card, leading him to walk around with pound coins "clinking" in his pockets. Soon after graduating from Stanford in June 2013, Duplan raised $25 million in seed funding from a coterie of Stanford affiliates. These investors included PayPal founder and fellow Stanford graduate, Peter Thiel; Mendel Rosenblum, a Stanford professor of computer science; Bob Joss, former dean of Stanford Business School; Mehran Sahami, its associate chair of computer science; and John Hennessy, a serial tech investor, Google and Cisco board member, and Crinkle's academic advisor; and Laura Arrillaga-Andreessen who teaches philanthropy at Stanford. Stanford professor Chuck Eesley's course helped direct Clinkle's development, staff its founding team, and find its initial customers. Eesley offered a year-long course, for which 16 teams of five students apiece were each assigned a pair of experienced mentors from Silicon Valley. Duplan recruited over 12 of his classmates to join Clinkle while Eesley helped convince some Stanford dining halls and cafés to trial the app. Clinkle also benefited from StartX, a Stanford accelerator program that offers office space, legal advice, and mentorship to Stanford start-ups. Of Clinkle, Duplan claimed, "This isn't the next social app. Clinkle is a movement to push the human race forward by changing how we transact."

By 2015, Crinkle was up in smoke thanks to a lack of board oversight and Duplan's capricious management style. But that was after Crinkle was able to raise even more money, bringing the total seed round to $30.5 million by October 2013 thanks to Duplan's skill at raising money. A former employee said Duplan "was charismatic when he wanted to be" and could "raise money in absurd abundance. It was his one skill." Though Clinkle lacked a public product, Forbes made Duplan the face of the 2014 30 Under 30 list for the finance category, while Clinkle was featured in profiles in The Wall Street Journal *and other publications. In 2014, Clinkle began to fall apart due to layoffs and departures of executives recruited from Netflix and Yahoo; plus a loss of momentum to competitors like Venmo, a peer-to-peer payments app, and later Apple Pay. At the beginning of 2015, Clinkle's headcount had tumbled from 70 to 30 and by May the rest had departed. One factor in the collapse was the lack of board oversight. Since Clinkle had raised small amounts from many investors, all had assumed that one of them was keeping an eye on their investment, but none of the investors took a board seat. That lack of oversight meant that investors did not realize that the video that dazzled investors (people who saw the demo described it as "mind-blowing") was not the app that Duplan said the company was poised to launch. Indeed the gap between Clinkle's sizzle and its reality was enough to get Chi-Chao Chang, a former Yahoo ad executive Duplan hired as VP Engineering in December 2013, to quit after his first day. Chang accepted an offer to join Clinkle just after Thanksgiving but was not confident because the company did not disclose information about its product during the interview process. On Chang's first day of work there, he found out that Clinkle was planning a round of layoffs, the second in two months; it intended to hire more executives; its product and marketing strategy was in poor shape; and Chang disagreed with the management team about Clinkle's direction. Chang told Duplan his reservations at the end of the day and that he would not return to Clinkle the next day. By 2015 Clinkle was no more. Duplan wrote, "Next-gen banking product. Low margin, high cost business, so discontinued."*

Case Analysis

Crinkle's collapse exemplifies the dark side to Stanford's startups. A young Stanford entrepreneur's ability to craft an exciting story that persuades well-known investors and executives to fear being left behind if they pass on writing a check seems to be a highly prized skill. Sometimes the entrepreneur has the talent to turn that exciting story into a real business, but occasionally Stanford students, professors, and administrators turn a wunderkind into a young tyrant who lacks the skills needed to build a company and the intellectual humility required to recognize key weaknesses and get help to bolster them. Given the way Stanford embraced Duplan as he was launching his company, it appears as though the people who invested either did not know his skills were limited when it came to building a company or they simply were too afraid to be left behind to pay attention to them. As you'll see in Chapter 4, local investors are more willing to bet on such enfants terribles than are more conservative regions, such as Boston, which prefer to invest in entrepreneurs who've proven they can build successful companies.

Principles

The Level 4 case, Stanford, highlights the following principles that university leaders and government policymakers should pursue to boost the local startup scene:

- **University leaders:** Stanford is the world's leader in producing successful companies. It appears that its leaders are unlikely to make changes to its policies. Nevertheless, the failures of Theranos and Clinkle suggest that the risks of professors and administrators getting deeply involved with student startups can cause considerable pain to investors and employees when student entrepreneurs get in over their head and fail catastrophically. Stanford's leaders ought to find ways to limit such damage without impeding students' efforts to start companies.

- **Government policymakers:** Silicon Valley policymakers appear to have lost control of the area's growth. Housing prices are so high that many long-time residents can no longer afford to live there and many workers spend as much as four hours commuting from an affordable location to their offices. Moreover, traffic and other infrastructure are overly-stressed. Government policymakers ought to find ways to solve these problems by building more affordable housing in locations closer to Silicon Valley businesses and they should build more public transportation to reduce clogging on local roads.

Table 3-1 below summarizes the principles for each step in the Pillar Company Staircase.

Table 3-1. Principles by Step in Pillar Company Staircase

Pillar Company Stair	Principles
Level 0	Encourage professor and student-led startups to operate locally.
Level 1	Use university network to find capital and talent to boost growth of locally-operated gazelles.
Level 2	Help university-funded spinoffs to raise capital from global investors and acquired gazelles and encourage their global market expansion.
Level 3	Maintain strong position by adding professors and students in new and important fields of technology.
Level 4	Tighten investment discipline to avoid backing 'enfants terribles'.

Are You Doing Enough To Launch Startups From Local Universities?

Universities must choose how much they want to try to spur entrepreneurship in their regions and other stakeholders such as government policymakers, student entrepreneurs, and capital providers must decide how they can collaborate with universities to enhance the local startup scene. To evaluate whether a region is doing enough, its stakeholders should ask themselves the following questions:

University administrators:

- Should we include a professor's entrepreneurial accomplishments in evaluating cases for tenure?

- Should we set more ambitious goals for IP licensing revenues and allocate more money to achieve them?

- Should we change the mix of faculty, researchers, and students to increase our economic impact on the local community?

- Should we engage more with local businesses and alumni startups to provide career opportunities for students?

- Should we start and operate incubators to spur startups in different disciplines such as life sciences and information technology?

- Should we fund such initiatives by cutting back on departments that do not help students achieve career goals?

Government policymakers:

- Can we help the university to win government funding for research that might ultimately yield valuable new technologies?

- Should we work with developers and others to convert empty office space into startup incubators?

- Could we alter regulations or lower financing costs to encourage more local startup activity?

- Could we spur a housing and office space development that would encourage locally educated students to live and work in the city instead of leaving town after graduation?

Student entrepreneurs:

- Do I have the skills needed to build and grow the venture?

- If not, does the university's region have the talent needed to build an effective team?

- Will the university supply resources such as incubator space, capital, and access to mentoring I will need to grow the business?

- Does the university's region offer lower cost real estate and salaries for comparable talent than Boston, New York, or Silicon Valley?

- Does the university's region supply housing, restaurants, and entertainment opportunities that would make it a compelling place to work?

- Would I be better equipped to run a startup after working for a larger company?

- If so, are the best opportunities to work at such companies near the university?

Experienced entrepreneurs:

- Does the university offer programs that can help my startup tap into its IP and talent?

- Can I mentor student and aspiring faculty entrepreneurs?

- Will the university supply resources such as incubator space, capital, and access to mentoring I will need to grow the business?

- Does the university's region supply housing, restaurants, and entertainment opportunities that would make it a compelling place to work?

Capital providers

- Should I mentor a university's startup accelerator?

- Should I help finance the licensing of a university's IP?

- Should I collaborate with professors who are developing potentially valuable technologies?

- Should I sponsor a university-run accelerator to learn about interesting startups and entrepreneurs?

Conclusion

There is wide variation in how much universities contribute to a region's startup success. Three big factors make the most difference between universities that contribute to local entrepreneurial activity and those that do not: the relative quality of the students and faculty they attract, the extent to which the university encourages that talent to start new companies, and the university's geographic proximity to a lively startup hub. Stanford and MIT attract world-class students and professors, and they encourage that talent to start companies. HEC Paris and KTH attract good talent that is not world class in key areas of technology; as a result, their alumni and professors do not tend to start companies that scale into pillar companies and create a virtuous cycle of startups within their regions. In Chapter 4, we examine how a region's supply of human capital helps determine whether startups will locate there or abandon where they started off and move to a region where they can hire the talent they need.

Deepening the Human Capital Pool

What Is Human Capital?

Human capital refers to the people a startup hires to achieve its goals. Founders deciding where to locate should consider the following human capital factors that make a region more or less compelling:

- **Different startups need different skills as they grow.** A startup's skill requirements will vary depending on its industry and growth goals. For example, a gaming startup that hopes to employ a founder and his friends from school may need only programmers and a sales person. However, a global payment services provider seeking to reach at least $100 million in revenue needs to hire people with different skills, such as engineering, sales, marketing, operations, and customer service, plus experienced executives to lead them.

© Peter S. Cohan 2018
P. S. Cohan, *Startup Cities*, https://doi.org/10.1007/978-1-4842-3393-1_4

- **Some regions lack all the skills needed for growth so founders seek them elsewhere.** For example, for decades Israeli entrepreneurs excelled at developing products but lacked world-class sales and marketing skills. As a result, many Israeli companies host R&D in Israel and operate sales, marketing, and key administrative functions out of U.S. offices in Silicon Valley or Boston.

- **In order to climb to the top of the Pillar Company Staircase, regions need more skilled CEOs.** Entrepreneurs fall into three categories:

  - *Amblers* seek to grow their companies at a leisurely pace, just fast enough to keep their friends and family employed. Such CEOs are common at Level 0 regions.

  - *Sprinters* aspire to take their companies public or sell the company to an acquirer quickly. Sprinters are often in a hurry to make a profit quickly from a startup exit and are less interested in running a large publicly-traded company. Such CEOs are common at Level 1 and Level 2 regions.

  - *Marathoners* build a company from an idea into a large, publicly-traded company with stock market valuations over $10 billion. Marathoners are very rarely first-time entrepreneurs such as Amazon's Jeff Bezos or Microsoft's Bill Gates. Often serial sprinters develop into marathoners because they realize that in order to achieve their ambitions, they must change their management style. Marathoners are most common in Level 4 regions, and Level 3 regions can best reach Level 4 by attracting or developing marathoners.

- **Regions with in-demand skills bid up salaries to prohibitively high levels.** Silicon Valley and Beijing, for example, pay artificial intelligence experts starting salaries in the $200,000 to $500,000 range, with some companies offering compensation packages reaching tens of millions of dollars. Such high compensation packages make in-demand skills unaffordable for all but the best financed companies.

- **Founders seek skills and cultural fit.** Startups seek people with the skills they need who fit with the startup's culture. Generally, CEOs look for individuals who will fit well with the personalities of the first 20 to 30 people. Often these cultures put a premium on individuals who are creative, bring new skills to the company, get along well with other people, and have relatively modest egos. CEOs like to hire people who are part of the professional network of the founding team and key early employees.

Takeaways for Startup Common Stakeholders

Most Startup Common stakeholders cannot do much to change a region's human capital in the short- to medium-term. For example, universities cannot rapidly change their departments, their faculty, or the nature of their student body. If it is not seen as an attractive place to stay after graduation, government policymakers can't make locally-educated students want to start companies and live in the city. And pillar companies take a long time to gestate.

Only entrepreneurs can deepen a city's human capital pool in the short- to medium-term by choosing where to start their companies. Before founding a company, entrepreneurs ought to ask themselves the following questions:

- Where do I and my family want to live and work?

- What skills will my startup need in order to achieve its growth goals?

- Does the place I want to live and work host the skills my startup needs?

- If not, what skills are missing and where can I hire them?

- If we open multiple offices that house all the skills we need, can we coordinate their efforts without putting too much strain on our people?

Human Capital Success and Failure Case Studies

Where a talented entrepreneur locates a startup has the potential to draw new talent to the region. As Figure 4-1 illustrates, if a pioneering entrepreneur builds the startup to the point that it is acquired or can go public, the success will attract more venture capital firms. Those VCs will look to invest in the most talented members of the founding team of the companies that enjoyed successful exits. If these new companies, in turn, become successful, they will draw more talent and capital to the city, thus converting more of a city's potential entrepreneurs into actual ones. And if local government policymakers can build a consensus, the region will invest in new housing and infrastructure to support the growth of these firms and keep the city from becoming so expensive and congested that new startups choose to locate elsewhere.

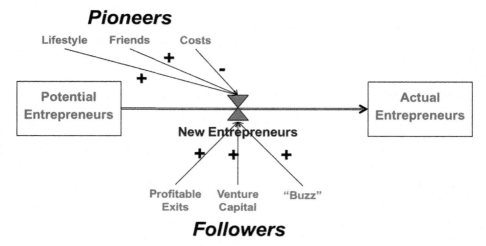

Figure 4-1. How entrepreneurs deepen a region's human capital pool

The pairs of successful and less successful case studies that follow show how that dynamic can play out at each of the five levels of the Pillar Company Staircase.

Level 0: No Pillars, No Gazelles

Success Case Study: Zephyr Workshop Finds Local Talent to Fuel Its Games

Introduction

Some cities host universities that train students with useful skills such as developing video games or operating pharmacies. While these skills enable people to support themselves and a modest number of employees, they might not necessarily provide the entrepreneurial tinder required to produce local gazelles. While the local schools may be able to supply the talent for a lifestyle business that does not increase employment at a rapid clip, the people who work at these companies are likely to be quite satisfied.

Case Scenario

A case in point is Zephyr Workshop, a game developer founded and staffed by graduates of Worcester's Becker College first discussed in Chapter 2. Zephyr Workshop assembled its team based on its balance of skills and personal fit. "We have four core team members and several collaborators and consultants. Originally it was only myself and a fellow graduating senior. We were paired together on our capstone project. After a few months, the team expanded to four more full-time members, Jesse Clark, Sarah Como, Ryan Richford and Bron Mitchell, most from Becker, to balance out our skill sets. We try to find good personality fits and particular skills, so the share of work is more evenly distributed," said Grigas.

Grigas hoped that Zephyr Workshop would reach its fifth anniversary as a profitable maker of popular games. Indeed by 2020, he aspired to make Zephyr Workshop "self-sustaining with an amazing portfolio of products and partnerships." To do that, he said he would ideally like to stay in Worcester because it "offers an affordable alternative to Greater Boston while still being in an accessible location for the team to come to."

Case Analysis

Zephyr Workshop appears to be sustaining itself through non-equity financing so that its employees, mostly Becker alumni, can work in Worcester on building its products and expanding their distribution. While it is possible that Zephyr Workshop will find a large audience for its games that could attract outside capital or the interest of a larger acquirer, it could also find itself running out of money and its staff could seek employment with a larger company. Regardless of the outcome, it appears likely that Grigas and his fellow employees have gained valuable startup experience which could ultimately pay off for them either at Zephyr Workshop or in future endeavors.

Less Successful Case Study: When It Comes to Freight Farms, Boston's Gain is Worcester's Loss

Introduction

A city with many universities has the potential to supply talent to startups founded by its alumni. However, if other cities supply deeper pools of human capital and other resources that a startup needs to grow, the students are likely to move away once they graduate. In this way, the city tends to host startups that are more lifestyle businesses than gazelles. And entrepreneurs who can create gazelles are more inclined to locate their companies where they will not have to struggle for the resources they need to grow. The success of such gazelles is evidence that the city that educated the entrepreneur is not doing enough to keep its talent nearby, so another city gets the benefits of that growth.

Case Scenario

This comes to mind in considering the fate of Freight Farms, a Boston-based supplier of containers for growing plants hydroponically. Freight Farms let customers "grow leafy greens, vine crops, and mushrooms hydroponically in insulated, climate-controlled containers. Its 'Leafy Green Machine' (LGM) was a complete hydroponic growing facility built entirely inside a shipping container, with environmental controls and indoor growing technology. The LGM allowed for immediate growing of a variety of crops, regardless of weather conditions, resulting in access to year-round local, fresh produce that was always in season. The farmhand suite of apps allowed for 'cloud-connected' farming, users were able to monitor their operation from any location, and purchase all of their growing supplies directly from their smartphone." Freight Farms' founders, Brad McNamara and Jonathan Friedman, were fed up with how inefficient it was to grow produce in a rooftop greenhouse. Friedman decided it would be better to use a shipping container. As they explained, McNamara graduated from Northeastern University with a degree in business and earned a masters' degree in environmental science and an MBA from Clark University. Friedman earned a BFA in Industrial Design from Massachusetts College of Art & Design. Together they started an environmental engineering consulting firm.

In 2009, they were working on the design of an urban rooftop greenhouse. According to Friedman, "I was frustrated with the technology for rooftop farming. Despite using double-walled polyvinyl chloride, it was inefficient since so much energy went for heating, cooling, and venting; you can't maintain constant internal temperature. The operating costs were too high. The numbers did not add up and it could not be done at scale." Friedman came up with the solution. As McNamara explained, "The problem was to come up with a large space but more efficient and with a smaller footprint. Jon came up with the idea—use a shipping container—it was a smack in the face. He decided that it would need to fit into a 40 foot by 8 foot space and would be efficient and profitable. And by using light emitting diodes (LEDs), annual lighting power costs are only $2,600." It took time to turn that idea into a working prototype. "In early 2010, we started working on the design, looking at components and technology. We needed money so we did a Kickstarter campaign, raising $30,000. The people who contributed money got the joy of helping us achieve our mission of taking local food global. They also got t-shirts, reusable grocery bags, and their names on the outside of our first prototype so the world would know that they were among the first to see the future of the food system." explained McNamara. After raising the money and building the prototype, they entered a local business accelerator, MassChallenge.

And their business focused on a clear market niche. "We decided to target a very specific part of the food system to start off. There are 4,400 institutional distributors of fresh fruit and produce to restaurants, hospitals, and universities. We are selling to small and medium sized distributors with revenues between $3 million and $75 million, representing an $860 million opportunity." And Freight Farms was helping these distributors who shipped to customers throughout the year to reduce their costs. That's because they bought their fresh fruit and produce from local farms during the harvest seasons. But during the rest of the year, they had to source from further away. By using Freight Farms, the customer's costs dropped. As McNamara explained, "One of our Boston customers imports basil from Mexico that is flown to California and trucked to Boston. He bought one of our containers for $60,000 and uses it to grow a third of his basil—300 pounds per week—that he sells for $120,000. He used to pay between $3.75 and $4.00 a pound for that basil and with our product it costs him much less." McNamara believed that their mission of making an impact on the broken food system was helping it attract top talent. He said, "We now have added five full-time people with great skills in technology and marketing. They are attracted to our passionate mission of taking local food global."

The continued success of Freight Farms was a lost opportunity for Worcester and a benefit for Boston. By September 2015, Freight Farms had grown fourfold and had 16 employees. As McNamara explained, "We will have about 50 Freight Farm customers across the U.S. and in Canada by the end of 2015." Moreover, investors had bought into Freight Farms' potential, writing checks for $4.9 million. Spark Capital put down $3.7 million in 2014, which followed $1.2 million from Morningside Venture Investments Ltd., LaunchCapital, and Rothenberg Ventures in 2013, according to McNamara. Freight Farms added customers around the country, from a small business farm in Davenport, Iowa to a restaurant in Boston. The Iowa farm was Friday's Fresh Market. Its owner, Andrew Freitag, said, "I decided to work with Freight Farms because their product and design have been proven to work. The business model made sense, and this was my ticket to start my own company. It's also allowed me to support my local community by supplying fresh produce year-round." The Boston restaurant was "fast food joint" b.good. As McNamara explained, "Our Freight Farmer, Scott Deluca, has paired up with one of Boston's real fast food joints, b.good, to supply their restaurants with local, fresh produce year-round. The partnership between b.good, Freight Farms, and the community is activating underused space underneath an overpass in the heart of the city." By September 2017, Freight Farms had grown even more. Its headcount increased from 20 in 2016 to 31 across all departments: Customer Support, Marketing, Sales, Engineering, and Software. Its recently hired Director of Sales came from Boston consulting firm Bain & Co.; another executive from a USA Today affiliate; teachers, government employees, and six people from Northeastern University, according to McNamara.

Case Analysis

Freight Farms is an innovative idea that seems to be making good progress in attracting customers, capital, and talent. While its CEO earned an MBA at Worcester's Clark University, the city was not his choice for a headquarters location. It is easy to see that the company gets resources that are useful for its growth, most notably, access to talent, capital, and potential customers. McNamara evidently concluded that Worcester was woefully far behind in supplying these resources and he had little difficulty locating the company where he could get what he needed. Boston's gain has been Worcester's loss.

Principles

Entrepreneurs who are educated in cities that lack pillar companies and gazelles ought to weigh the advantages and disadvantages of locating their startups there. Here are factors they should consider:

- **Advantages:**
  - Founder and team prefer to live and work in the city.
  - Real estate and salary costs are likely to be lower.
  - Mentors from the university where they studied may be more accessible.

- **Disadvantages:**
  - People with needed skills may not be available, thus limiting the company's ability to grow or forcing the company to open offices elsewhere or eventually relocate.
  - Capital providers may be limited or absent.
  - Networking opportunities that might help to find new talent or introductions to partners or customers may be limited.

Level 1: No Pillars, Some Gazelles

Success Case Study: WeLab and Aftership Overcome Hong Kong's Challenges

Introduction

A city with a long history of success in global commerce and a limited track record for high technology startups can find itself in a challenging position. After all, the capital created by those multi-generation family companies may be considerable, yet the owners of the companies might be reluctant to invest in businesses that they do not understand. This means startups could struggle to find the capital and talent they need to grow. This is the story of Hong Kong's startup scene, where old family businesses are more comfortable investing in real estate than in what looks to them to be a relatively risky app. Nevertheless, Hong Kong hosts entrepreneurs who are finding ways around these weaknesses.

Case Scenario

Hong Kong presented obstacles to ambitious entrepreneurs. These included a dearth of local startup talent and startup capital; the surge of Chinese pillar companies like Alibaba and Ten Cent Holdings, which enabled Chinese cities like Beijing to surpass Hong Kong as a startup destination; and Hong Kong's high real estate prices. In most cases, startups lacked the capital to hire people to run key functions like R&D, sales, and operations. Hong Kong's dependence on real estate and financial services drove students to study business, finance, and law instead of science, technology, engineering, and mathematics. Moreover, Hong Kong multinational regional headquarters hosted sales and marketing rather than R&D. Therefore, Hong Kong engineers and software developers lacked experience at turning a technology into a business. Hong Kong startups faced complex procedures for obtaining work visas for imported talent. What's more, most Hong Kong startup founders lacked experience managing people. Finally, mainland China, against whose increasingly tight control people were occupying the streets of Hong Kong's business district for the last four months of 2014, was becoming a more successful startup hub than Hong Kong. Instead of seeing itself as a gateway to the rest of China, thanks to its Western-style corporate governance and financial markets, Hong Kong had a tepid record of startup success.

Two Hong Kong startups, online lender WeLab and shipment tracking service AfterShip, appeared to be overcoming those obstacles. As you saw in Chapter 3, WeLab was resilient and adapted to challenges. By September 2017, it had raised over $180 million in capital and was valued at over $1 billion. CEO Simon Loong was a former Citigroup banker with a Stanford MBA who decided to step off the conventional track and start WeLab, thanks to an understanding wife and a strong sense of self-confidence, coupled with a track record of making banking more efficient. WeLab's technology made it possible to approve very quickly loans to consumers at a 15% interest rate with relatively short payback terms, and pay investors 10% yields to supply the capital. Loong offered four prescriptions for overcoming the challenges of Hong Kong's startup scene, which could be general prescriptions for the success of any leader:

- **Make other people want you to succeed.** *When you have no capital or resources to offer, the only possible way to build a company is to get other people to desire your success. You can do that if you have a mission about which you are passionate and you're an honest person who considers how your actions will benefit others. "When you start a company, you have nothing," Loong told my MBA students who visited his company in January 2015. "Your most powerful resource is the ability to inspire others with your startup's vision and to behave in a way that warrants their trust. You must be hardworking, respectful of others, and fulfill your commitments."*

- **Be honest about weaknesses.** WeLab decided that the Hong Kong market was too small to build a significant business. After surveying several countries, the company decided that the best option would be to try to enter the market of mainland China. This would pose enormous regulatory and other difficulties. But WeLab decided to tackle the biggest market opportunity despite the challenge. WeLab's management initially knew nothing about mainland China. "I do not have to know everything," Loong said. "But I do need to be able to hire talent that does know about China. So I shifted resources and hired a team there. I spend almost every day in China working with the team. It is a sacrifice but that is what needs to happen for our business to succeed."

- **Realize that failure is not the end of the world.** In Hong Kong, parents are not proud of children who fail. While meeting with people at local startup incubator StartupsHK, my students were shown a humorous picture of a Chinese mother captioned "I love you son, as long as you are doctor." Loong was not immune to this pressure but he did step away from a successful career in the banking industry. Why? Loong explains, "I was meeting with a group of Stanford students and someone said, 'We are above average and that ability should enable us to succeed at anything we put our mind and talents to solving. And if we fail, we can always go back to a corporate job.'"

- **Do your homework.** Another humorous picture I saw at StartupsHK was one of a Chinese father captioned "Facebook? Yes – face book and study." This picture emphasizes the importance of preparation and study in Hong Kong's culture. And even though Loong has left the safe career track, he has not lost that studious mindset. Before he met with my students, he studied the resume of each one in great depth and when a student asked him a question, Loong recalled details from the relevant resume during the answer.

AfterShip, which helps e-commerce sites to manage orders and online shoppers to track the status of their shipments, also overcame the challenges presented to Hong Kong startups. Founder Andrew Chan was a graduate of the University of Hong Kong with a degree in economics and finance. E-commerce companies smaller than Amazon can't afford such systems. As Chan said, "Large online marketplaces like Amazon can afford to build their own scalable tracking system, but for smaller online retailers with limited resources, our white label solution empowers them with the same sophisticated shipment tracking capability." AfterShip, which was founded in 2011 and raised a $1 million Series A round in 2014, found it difficult to hire skilled programmers. As Chan explained, "Hong Kong does not have sufficient software developers with product development experience. To tackle the hiring problem, we have turned to India and Poland to look for programmers who can be contracted to work from home. Fortunately, the results we want do not necessarily require employees to come into the office daily and technology has made communication much easier. They can work from virtually anywhere as long as they deliver the results." By August 2017, AfterShip had grown from 3 to 30 employees, partnered with 387 couriers in the world, and tracked over 20 million shipments a month. Human resource management was AfterShip's biggest challenge. "Start-ups are innately in tune with collaborating and trying to find innovative ways to work smarter. Only a creative and empowered workforce can offer innovative solutions for today's complex business environment. As a start-up owner, my challenge is how to build a team-oriented approach and create an environment in which my team members feel inspired and fulfilled," said Chan.

Case Analysis

Good entrepreneurs can find clever ways to overcome the human capital weaknesses where they locate their startups. Hong Kong presents considerable obstacles to entrepreneurs trying to attract top talent: the grass is greener in Chinese cities such as Beijing and Shenzhen; the talent in Hong Kong is not well suited to managing technology startups; and the cost of housing is very high. But WeLab and AfterShip are finding ways to overcome some of these challenges by concentrating on keeping workers engaged and inspired and by outsourcing some work to countries with more ample supplies of talent in lower-cost locations.

Less Successful Case Study: BridgeWay's Founder Basks in Glory but an Abrupt Change in Strategy Leads to Deep Regret

Introduction

Hong Kong's values shape the kind of people who start companies and their strategic decisions. As mentioned above, Hong Kong does not supply the world's best talent and capital sources for high technology startups. While some entrepreneurs seek to overcome these challenges and have made significant progress, others decide not to become high tech entrepreneurs. As a result, their ventures need different skills and sources of capital. This comes to mind in considering Hong Kong entrepreneur, Edwin Lee, who was educated and started his career on Wall Street in the U.S. to start a Hong Kong business brokerage firm. While that firm employed over 300 people, Lee decided that he was not getting where he wanted to go, which was to become a billionaire with his name on the *Forbes* list of Hong Kong 40 wealthiest people. So he fired most of his staff and tried to get into real estate. Sadly, this led to regret followed by hints of success.

Case Scenario

In January 2013, I took 26 Babson College MBA candidates to Hong Kong and our first meeting was with Edwin Lee in the headquarters of his company, BridgeWay Business Builder and Broker, which bought and sold restaurants, nail salons, and other retail stores in Hong Kong. As he explained in an interview, he was born in Hong Kong in 1975, went to the U.S. to earn a "Bachelor in Finance and Master of Accounting" from the University of Southern California. And after returning from the U.S., he earned a doctorate from Hong Kong Polytechnic University in 2011. But that was not enough formal education for Lee. As he said, "Now I am doing a three-year program (Owner/President Management Program) at the Harvard Business School." Before he got to Wall Street, Lee yearned to be "an investment banker doing IPOs and M&As," And he achieved that dream, joining Credit Suisse First Boston in the Hong Kong office in 1997 and later transferring to New York in mid-2000. But days after 9/11, Lee lost his job there. He contemplated three options and picked the one that he thought would let him learn the most. As he explained, "I had three choices: I could rejoin a mediocre investment bank (which was difficult to find back then); I could go for an MBA that would take three years to complete after my application, or I could start my own business. I asked myself, which way would I learn the most in three years and had no doubt that starting my own business would teach me the most."

To start BridgeWay, he set two goals: "spend half a million HKD [about $65,000 in today's U.S. dollars] and purchase a business, rather than start from scratch." And since there were no companies buying and selling small businesses in Hong Kong back then, he "became the first business broker in town to do those small deals." Lee targeted deals of under a million HKD and figured out that not only could he put sellers and buyers together, but he could build the acquired companies after he had invested. Moreover, Lee was targeting a substantial market. By his reckoning, "there are about 300,000 small businesses in Hong Kong. Nobody wanted to put any effort into brokering those deals because they all wanted to do bigger ones since they would get bigger fees for the same amount of effort required for smaller deals." From 2001 to 2005, Lee had the market to himself but in 2006, competitors emerged. Lee had trained his competition. Of Hong Kong's 15 business brokerage companies, "13 of them were started by our ex-employees," according to Lee.

When it came to capital, Lee appeared to have benefited from his investment banking experience. He was able to share the upside and the risk. To that end, he financed deals with three sources of capital: "myself, starting with HKD 2.5 million as seed money; commercial banks that financed business operations and mortgages; and outside investors to whom BridgeWay sold up to 30% of the property stake." By 2013, Lee had built a humming operation on what he called the "Build-Operate-Transfer model." Here is the meaning of each:

- **Build:** BridgeWay "purchases the commercial property and builds a profitable business on the site in order to enhance the business and property value."

- **Operate:** "BridgeWay operates both businesses that it starts from scratch and those that it buys and operates on behalf of buyers."

- **Transfer:** "BridgeWay sells businesses owned by the others, brokering the deals and charging a commission, and it transfers businesses that it builds itself."

While this model scaled, it was not enough for Lee. As of January 2013, BridgeWay had built 76 businesses, was operating 15, and had transferred 1,080. It had over 43,000 potential business buyers in its database. Nearly 300 employees were working in Hong Kong for the company: 70 at the office level, and over 200 at the shop level. But Lee seemed obsessed with being recognized by the media. Indeed, he said that in 2009, the Forbes 40 list changed his mind about what BridgeWay should do. As he said, "In 2009, I read the Forbes 40 list in Hong Kong, and realized that most of the richest people in Hong Kong are in either the property or finance sector. No one was in business brokerage. Therefore, I wanted to enter the property and finance sector with a hope that I can make it to the list in a few decades." In January 2015, during a return visit to Bridgeway, Lee said that in July 2013, he had cut his staff down to seven, adding his wife, a former Citicorp lawyer, as the eighth employee. Clearly very emotional, he described how he decided, based on input from his Harvard Business School program, that he needed to exit the business brokerage business and start to invest in real estate. So he fired most of his staff. At that point, it was unclear whether his goal of making it on to the Forbes 40 would ever be attainable.

By 2017, Lee had regrouped and was making some progress. He founded Bridgeway Prime Shop Fund Management, the first Hong Kong Securities and Futures Commission (SFC)-licensed fund management firm focused exclusively on shop and retail property investment. After two years, Lee obtained regulatory approval and by December 2016, it contained seven shop properties, worth between HK$7.8 million and HK$30 million. While investing in more valuable shops would get Lee to his wealth goals faster, shops valued at over HK$50 million were difficult for him due to competition from veteran retail property investors. To his credit, Lee attracted Hong Kong-listed Global Mastermind Capital as his major investor. To obtain regulatory approval for trading retail shop properties, Lee needed an SFC license and to obtain the license, a critical requirement turned out to be hiring officers who also had SFC licenses and three years' experience of trading properties. With only 11 listed companies doing this, it took Lee two years to convince two qualified candidates to join *the firm. By November 2015, his SFC license was approved. As he said in December 2016, "Finally I have now shifted all my focus purely onto specializing in trading retail shops."*

Case Analysis

Edwin Lee is a very intelligent, well-educated, and ambitious entrepreneur. He has also struggled in his career to focus on the right business idea in Hong Kong. He appears to be highly motivated to achieve the pinnacle of external recognition in educational and wealth attainment and in media approval. While Lee did not struggle to attract human capital to his business brokerage firm, he was slowed down by the shortage of licensed property traders. Moreover, in 2016, it appeared that his ambitions for building his property investment business could be limited by the level of competition he faced. While Lee partially made up for a lack of competitive advantage in his chosen field through persistence and hard work, it seemed as though he would continue to struggle to see his name on the Forbes 40 list.

Principles

Entrepreneurs who locate in cities with no pillars and some gazelles ought to weigh the advantages and disadvantages of locating their startups there. Here are factors they should consider:

- **Advantages:**
    - Founder and team prefer to live and work in the city.
    - Some capital providers may be available locally.
    - Government officials may be providing significant support to startups by creating incubators and making financing available.

- **Disadvantages:**
    - People with needed skills may not be available, thus limiting the company's ability to grow or forcing the company to open offices elsewhere or eventually relocate.
    - Capital providers may be limited.
    - Real estate prices and salaries may be higher.
    - Networking opportunities that might help to find new talent or introductions to partners or customers may be limited.

Level 2: No Pillars, Acquired Gazelles

Success Case Study: KTH Supplies Talent to Five Swedish Startups but Will That Be Enough for Them to Scale?

Introduction

If a city's gazelles are acquired, members of their founding teams could invest some of their gains into new startups. What's more, those successes could inspire talent at local universities to try their own hands at entrepreneurship. And while these startups might be able to find the talent they need from university colleagues, eventually their growth will be capped unless they can find the talent they need to manage the startup's growth.

Case Scenario

This comes to mind in considering four startups that emerged from work done at KTH, the MIT of Stockholm. These companies—Mano Motion, a maker of software that enables smartphone cameras to capture 3D hand gestures whose CEO is a serial entrepreneur; Greenely, an app that tracks home energy usage; Shortcut Labs, a maker of wireless smart buttons that offer physical shortcuts to digital functions in mobile devices; and Furhat Robotics, a maker of social robots—were all started by KTH students or professors. And most of them have been able to hire some of the staff they needed from KTH while seeking talent from the U.S.; in Mano Motion's case, opening up an office in Palo Alto in order to sell into the U.S. market.

Mano Motion's CEO, Daniel Carlman, was a ship engineer who studied Computer Information Systems and Finance at Hawaii Pacific University, developed a mobile banking application for a bank, founded a gaming company, and ended up as an executive at online gambling company Unibet. As he explained in a September 2017 interview, from there he returned to Stockholm with his daughter to start a health technology company and in 2015 joined, at the request of KTH Innovation, Mano Motion's cofounders, Dr. Shahrouz Yousefi and Professor Haibo Li, who had "started their research on hand gesture analysis" in 2010, resulting in a patent application related to how to track hand gestures accurately on a small screen. Carlman was seen by KTH Innovation as an entrepreneur who could help turn the idea into a business. When Carlman met Yousefi and Li, they said "Daniel, we want to change the world and make technology more natural and intuitive to interact with." Carlman agreed with their mission and believed that the future of human/computer interaction would combine vision, voice, and gestures that interpret human intent. Until June 2017, Mano Motion was building prototypes to get customer validation. Carlman built a team of 14 people from 10 different countries by hiring KTH students studying for a Master's or PhD in deep learning, computer vision, or human/ computer interaction. Mano Motion also recruited from National University of Singapore, Linnaeus University in Sweden, George Washington University, and UCLA.

By September 2017, Mano Motion had signed over 20 Non-Disclosure Agreements with potential partners and received over 1,000 requests from developers who want to build applications using its technology. Developers and companies can try Mano Motion's applications at no charge but were required to pay for a commercial license. Carlman intends to open a Palo Alto sales and marketing office in 2018 and will likely hire from Stanford. Mano Motion also intends to open another sales and marketing office in Asia to target Hong Kong and Shanghai. By the end of 2018, Carlman expects Mano Motion to employ over 30 people.

Tanmoy Bari, who studied civil engineering and earned a M.Sc in Sustainable Urban Planning and Design at KTH, had an idea while working on his thesis project of consulting to a smart city called the Stockholm Royal Seaport. Instead of building a computer system, which the large utilities proposed, he wanted to use data directly from the electrical grid to track household energy usage, which became the core idea behind Greenely. As Bari explained in a September 2017 interview, he officially launched Greenely in February 2014 after competing in Venture Cup, a business plan competition. In 2016, Greenely recorded about $130,000 in revenue and planned to double that to $260,000 in 2017, serving over 6,000 households and three large utilities. Greenely's 11 full-time employees had skills in energy and electricity, business development, product development and marketing. Many of its people came from KTH, and Bari also worked with headhunters in the UK and Sweden for key positions such as Product Manager and Chief Technology Officer. Bari wanted to recruit "quite a few people in the future, specifically, more administrative staff and a Human Resources manager; a psychologist and a behavioral scientist; and skilled coders and business developers from universities in Sweden (Stockholm and Gothenburg) and California (Stanford, UC Berkeley, and Caltech)."

Shortcut Labs cofounder and CEO Joacim Westlund, who in 2010 earned a M.Sc. in Design and Product Realization with Naval Architecture from KTH and then designed sailing yachts in New Zealand, could not sit still. As he said in a September 2017 interview, "I had several positions as a project management consultant and product manager. I was a consultant to larger companies such as Scania and some Swedish banks. My last employment was as a Product and Process Manager at SecMaker, a small Swedish IT security firm. I shifted jobs once a year, never quite found rest until I started my own thing." What he started was a company that made a button attached to his smartphone that would help him quit tobacco. As he explained, "I had several side projects when I was employed. One of them was an iPhone app to help people and myself to quit snus (a Swedish form of tobacco). The idea was to tap a big green button in the app when I took a snus so that I could monitor my intake. But doing that at least once every hour, it was too cumbersome to pick up the phone, unlock it, find the app and tap that single button each time. The idea grew to extract the button out of the phone into something physical, and that's how Flic was born. I kept imagining how much could be done with a wireless button. In 2012, I made a functional prototype and made it work with my snus-app, showing it around in the vivid Stockholm startup scene at different events. An advisor encouraged me to apply for innovation grants and after receiving two rounds of soft funding I decided to quit my job and engage co-founders Amir Sharifat, an extremely productive and organized executive who dropped out of production engineering studies to join as COO, and Pranav Kosuri, who complements my product design and weak social skills with an incredible charisma, networking skills, and a great stage presence to do sales." Shortcut Labs launched a crowdfunding campaign at the end of 2014. By September 2017, it had sold and shipped over 200,000 units to roughly 100,000 users around the world thanks to 20 employees, including a team of software engineers who worked on Flic as part of a software development course on KTH. Annual revenue was about $1.5 million and growing quickly. Westlund believed that Shortcut could find a designer, hardware and software engineers, and senior business development people in Stockholm and Asia from companies such as Autodesk, Salesforce, Dropbox, and ESI Group.

An artificial intelligence student moved from Damascus to Stockholm to get his PhD to build a robot that knows how to interact with people. Next thing you know, Disney called him to Pittsburgh to work with their R&D team. By September 2017, his company had 50 customers including some of the world's leading companies. As he explained in a September 2017 interview, Samer Al Moubayed studied computer science in Damascus, where he focused on artificial intelligence. Specifically, he was interested in modeling human emotion in speech, dubbed emotional speech synthesis. For example, he developed a system that would speak Arabic with varying emotions such as anger, sadness, or disgust. He went to work for a gaming company, enabling players to interact verbally with characters in the game. Al Moubayed continued his education in Belgium with an MS in speech and language technology, and then he went to Stockholm to pursue a PhD at KTH. As he said, "We spend years building technology and then ask people to use keyboards to interact with them. My vision is to create machines that know how to interact with us. I was very excited to be at KTH. I visited in June when the weather was warm and the school was the most prestigious place for speech technology. And there was also the professor's privilege, which gives researchers 100% control of their IP." Al Moubayed's pitching skills paid off when Disney saw a video of the social robot that his company built. Disney contacted Al Moubayed and expressed interest in working with him. He then went to Pittsburgh in the summer of 2014 to work with Disney, collaborating with its R&D team and getting helpful feedback on the social robot he built.

In 2014, he started Furhat Robotics; its product was a human-like robot face, which was a 3D projection that mimicked human expression and was built on a software platform, or its "brain." Furhat hoped to grow, as Apple did, by creating a developer ecosystem. To that end, Furhat was creating a platform, including an operating system and hardware, upon which developers would build applications, some of which Furhat hopes will become killer apps. By September 2017, Furhat had 13 employees and 50 customers, including Disney, Intel, Merck, KPMG, and Honda. KTH has been an excellent source of talent for Furhat. "We have four cofounders: Preben Wik, Jonas Beskow, Gabriel Skantze, and I. Three of the cofounders came from KTH and a fourth one was an old friend from Disney. Companies founded by KTH students used to leave campus, thus losing the KTH magic. But that has changed and KTH *is encouraging its startups to stay on campus. We are benefiting from that by hiring KTH talent as well as people from Disney and Yale," explained Al Moubayad. Furhat was also trying to strengthen its organization by hiring a Vice President of Product with experience developing hardware and software—and that appeared to be a challenge. Al Moubayad noted, "The kind of person we want to hire can get a $200,000 a year job at Google or Facebook. We want to find a very strong person who is excited to join a startup. We are looking for a risk-taker, someone who believes in the potential of Furhat and loves our product and vision, and who is reliable and a global citizen who can satisfy our global customers."*

Case Analysis

These four startups demonstrate that Stockholm's KTH is a source of compelling technologies with world-class potential. With varying degrees of skill, the founders of these companies have recognized that they need to complement their product development skills with other cofounders who excel in fields that the companies need in order to scale. These critical skills include sales and marketing, operations, raising capital from investors, and hiring top-tier talent. Several of these companies are extending their operations to the U.S. and Asia and certainly need to attract the right sales and marketing talent in those locations if they hope to gain significant market share in those larger markets. If these startups can hire and motivate such talent, given the global nature of their products they have the potential to become unicorns.

Failure Case Study: Housing Shortage Keeps a German Startup from Relocating to Stockholm

Introduction

If a city hosts acquired gazelles, the resulting success puts pressure on its infrastructure. Specifically, the burst in wealth resulting from the acquisitions increases demand on the city's housing stock, causing prices to rise. In addition, the well-publicized success of the city draws the attention of entrepreneurs and other talented people who may consider moving to that city with the hopes of boosting their chances for success. If city leaders anticipate the increased demand for housing and related needs for more traffic capacity, public transportation, electricity, water, and other infrastructure, then the city will be able to keep up with the growth. Otherwise, the city may lose opportunities to attract new companies from outside the region. Often, cities cannot keep up because of the political conflict created between the large number of citizens who are hurt by the gazelles' success and the small number who benefit from it.

Case Scenario

CupoNation, a Munich, Germany-based e-commerce startup that was 40% owned by Rocket Internet, wanted to move to Stockholm in 2015 but decided to stay put because of Stockholm's housing shortage. Founded in 2012, CupoNation was an online savings platform that collected data on all available coupons, discounts, and deals from online stores. It raised about $11 million in funding. In June 2016, CupoNation changed its name to Global Savings Group (GSG) to strengthen "its position as a leading global Performance Marketing Company, to reflect its growing global and multiplatform presence in the online vouchers and savings segment, [and to support its possible expansion by adding] new consumer platforms." By August 2017, GSG linked shoppers in over 20 countries with free coupons and discounts for about 20,000 online retailers such as Amazon, Zalando, and Asos in exchange for which it got a fee of 5% to 15% of the value of a shopper's purchase. GSG's gross merchandise value doubled to $546 million in 2016. Managing Director Andreas Fruth said GSG expected to grow "significantly" and "to be profitable on a group level in 2017 as well." GSG was open to buying competitors to strengthen its position in existing markets or expand into new ones.

Sadly for Stockholm, what is now GSG could have been headquartered there instead of Munich. After all, CupoNation saw Stockholm as a successful startup community enjoying the success of five unicorn companies: Spotify, Skype, Klarna, Mojang, and King. Given Stockholm's relatively small population of 1.4 million, it was ranked only behind Silicon Valley in the number of unicorns per capita. The growth of Stockholm's startup scene has attracted non-Swedish investors and entrepreneurs. However, that growth also created what CupoNation viewed as an insurmountable barrier: a severe housing crisis in Stockholm that "makes it challenging for younger people to get their first residence and almost impossible to find apartments to rent, since they mostly have been converted into housing cooperatives." Indeed, this housing shortage, coupled with a 15% increase in housing prices in 2015, put pressure on young people working in Stockholm to take on significant debt to own a home. CupoNation's 30 employees in the Nordic region wanted to move from Munich to Stockholm to be closer to retailers and other partners in the region. However, its higher cost of living and housing prices proved to be insurmountable barriers for CupoNation. What's more, these high costs were also a barrier to other talent that might otherwise have wanted to work in Stockholm. And while others, such as Klarna CEO Sebastian Siemiatkowski, recognized the difficulty this posed for companies seeking to recruit international talent, Stockholm lacked the political will to solve the problem effectively. In 2015, Stockholm city leaders claimed that to be working to alleviate the housing shortage, promising 140,000 new apartments in the center of the city to be completed by 2020 and increasing to 24 the number of floors in apartments near Stockholm. This was not enough for CupoNation.

Case Analysis

Startup success creates a difficult political problem for many cities. The financial rewards to the founders of a successful startup in the city yield big paydays for a small number of equity holders, who in turn spend that money in the city. This spending may drive up housing prices, particularly if the supply of housing is tight. Moreover, the success of those startups attracts more capital and more startups, all of which creates more demand for housing and the infrastructure needed to support a growing population. The many more local citizens who do not benefit from the success of the startups are forced to either incur a higher cost of living or to move away. What's more, those higher costs make it difficult to recruit more talent to fuel the growth of new startups and discourage companies that might otherwise want to relocate to the city.

Principles

Entrepreneurs who locate in cities with no pillars and acquired gazelles ought to weigh the advantages and disadvantages of locating their startups there. Here are factors they should consider:

- **Advantages:**
  - Founder and team prefer to live and work in the city.
  - Some capital providers may be available locally.
  - Government officials may be providing significant support to startups by creating incubators and making financing available.
  - Local universities will be a source of talent and ideas on which to base the creation of new companies.
  - Many entrepreneurs whose companies have been acquired may provide capital and advice to new startups.

- **Disadvantages:**
  - People with needed skills may not be available, thus forcing the company to open offices nearer the needed talent.
  - Capital providers may be limited.
  - Real estate prices and salaries may be higher.
  - Supply of affordable real estate and local infrastructure may be so strained that workers' commutes may be painful.

Level 3: Some Pillars in Niche Markets

Success Case Study: Boston Startups Find Local Talent to Fuel Their Growth

Introduction

A city with some pillars in niche markets may have a mixed effect on local startups seeking to hire more people to fuel their growth. The absence of significant local pillar companies could mean less local competition for local talent. That's because big pillar companies like Google, Facebook, and Amazon tend to pay the highest salaries, which makes it difficult for startups to compete. At the same time, the absence of significant local pillar companies also means that there are not enough local jobs to employ all the talent created in the region, so they move elsewhere. Another possible negative is that Silicon Valley pillar companies move into the region to hire some of the local talent, which can lead to the worst of both worlds. That's because other region's pillar companies may drive up local salaries without having the concern for the local community's well-being that they have for the places where they're headquartered.

Case Scenario

Silicon Valley pillar companies already had major outposts in Kendall Square where they could hire MIT graduates who wanted to stay in the area. But the possibility of another west coast technology leader, Amazon, opening a second headquarters (HQ2) that would employ 50,000 highly-paid people in Boston exposed some of the region's strengths and weaknesses as a source of startup talent. For one thing, Boston produced more graduates than the region could absorb. According to an analysis of 40 regions by the real estate services firm CBRE, Boston "had the largest gap between the number of technology-related degrees awarded by local schools and the number of new tech jobs created by the local economy; between 2011 and 2015, colleges in the Boston area awarded 31,400 technology-related degrees, while the region created only 11,790 jobs," according to The Boston Globe. And as a seasoned Boston technology executive pointed out, Boston lacked enough pillar companies, what Andy Palmer referred to as "a critical mass of core anchor tenants that keep people here." If Amazon chose to locate HQ2 in Boston, would it be good or bad for the region's startup scene? Nicholas Rellas, CEO of alcohol-delivery startup Drizly, which planned in September 2017 to double its workforce, concluded that Amazon's arrival would raise his company's cost of doing business. Robert Nakosteen, a University of Massachusetts Amherst professor, expected that even if Amazon could find the 50,000 people it hoped to hire in the 10 to 15 years after it opened HQ2, it would be difficult for them to find an affordable place to live and for them to commute back and forth to work without putting additional strain on the region's transportation systems.

Four Boston area startups that were hiring as of September 2017 were both enjoying the benefits of hiring in Boston and coping with some of the challenges. Cambridge-based CollegeVine uses near-peer mentors, people who had recently been admitted to college, to help high school students apply to college. Founded in 2013, it had 35 employees and 650 part-time employees in September 2017, up from 5 and 270, respectively, in September 2016, according to CEO Jon Carson. CollegeVine, which raised $6.7 million in capital, planned to triple revenues in 2018 from the $4 million to $5 million that it estimated it would generate in 2017. Carson wanted to hire more. As he said, "We are looking for people in sales (who want to achieve ambitious goals), operations (out of college who pay attention to detail), technology (with specialized skills), customer support (recent college graduates), and heads of sales and customer service. Boston has a deep talent pool and it's the region's center of gravity. We've hired from BU, Harvard, and U. Hartford. But housing is expensive and commutes are long so we try to let people work from home a day a week. We want people who are curious, coachable, driven, and likeable."

Boston-based Janeiro Digital builds systems to help companies grow. Founded in 2008, it had 80 employees in September 2017, up from 50 the year before, according to CEO Jonathan Bingham. Janeiro Digital, which planned to hire 10 more people by the end of 2017, also had offices in Charlotte, N.C. and Chicago where it could hire people with experience working for big banks and other client industries for a much lower salary than Janeiro would pay in Boston. As Bingham said, "We use social networks such as LinkedIn to show our thought leadership and attract interest from potential employees with creative and project management skills. We are competing with Amazon for talent and we used to lose out on hiring people because we took three weeks to make a decision. If everyone likes a candidate we will make an offer on the spot. Boston has lots of advantages: we hire from MIT, Northeastern, BU, BC, Harvard; it has access to capital and a great community. But housing is expensive and it's hard to afford if you don't have a $200,000 a year offer from Google. Since we are in scale-up mode, we are hiring senior people such as SVP of Marketing Dana Cordova and COO and CFO Ed Davis."

Boston-based Zerto, a provider of IT disaster recovery services, was founded in 2009 and raised $130 million in three rounds. When it launched its product in 2011, it had 50 to 60 people; as of September 2017, it employed 700. R&D, human resources, and finance operated out of its Herzliya, Israel office. Sales and marketing were located in Boston. As CEO Zev Kedem explained, "We hire experienced people from large and small companies, college graduates with energy and enthusiasm for inside sales and customer support—with a third in Boston, a third in Herzliya, and a third in Shanghai. We hire people who think big and want to win as a team. We want sales people who are not deterred by failure and we hire engineering staff mostly from the Israeli military, some big companies, and some schools."

Founded in 2004, Boston-based Motus is a vehicle management and reimbursement app. Motus was growing its staff. As CEO Craig Powell explained, "We are growing headcount at a 10% to 15% clip. We are hiring engineers, product managers,

*business development representatives and inside sales people and marketing peo-
ple who can do content-based lead generation. We recruit engineering talent from
MIT, WPI, Dartmouth, and RPI as well as more experienced engineers with mobile
app development experience at places like Amazon, Salesforce, and Fidelity. We hire
product management and product marketing people from Babson, UVM, Brown,
and Northeastern and get them oriented to our culture and software-as-a-service
through a 1.5 to 2 year training program."*

Case Analysis

Boston-based startups face some significant challenges in hiring the talent they
need to support their growth. Yet the ones discussed in the case studies seem
to be coping reasonably well with the rising salary demands, the challenges
that employees face in finding affordable housing, and the inconvenience of
commuting given Boston's strained transportation systems. Offsetting these
negatives is the high concentration of top universities which represent a compelling source of new hires that can be developed for positions in sales, marketing, customer service, and engineering. For many startups, Boston's larger
employers can supply experience managers of key functions. Other startups
cope with the high cost of talent by opening offices in locations with high quality people who earn lower salaries.

Less Successful Case Study: Facebook Leaves Cambridge for Silicon Valley

Introduction

Two companies founded by Harvard dropouts left Cambridge and moved
to the West Coast. By 2017, those two companies, Microsoft and Facebook,
accounted for $124 billion in revenue and employed 145,000. What if those
companies had stayed in Cambridge instead of moving to the other side of
the country? How much more successful would the Boston area be had they
stayed where they were started? Facebook was born in a Harvard dormitory,
moved to Palo Alto, went public in May 2012, and by September 2017 was
generating $34 billion in revenue, nearly $14 billion in profit, employed about
21,000, and sported a stock market capitalization of $477 billion.

Case Scenario

*Cambridge's loss was Silicon Valley's gain. Ironically, Zuckerberg expressed regret at
moving away in a 2012 talk. In October 2011, ahead of Facebook's May 2012 IPO,
Zuckerberg said that he would have done things differently in 2004 if he had known
what Silicon Valley was like when he moved there. As Zuckerberg explained, "If I were*

starting now, I would do things very differently. I didn't know anything. In Silicon Valley, you get this feeling that you have to be out here. But it's not the only place to be. If I were starting now, I would have stayed in Boston. [Silicon Valley] is a little short-term focused and that bothers me." In a conversation with Amazon CEO, Jeff Bezos told Zuckerberg that the average time someone stays in job at Seattle is twice as long as it is in Silicon Valley. "There's a culture out here where people don't commit to doing things, I feel like a lot of companies built outside of Silicon Valley seem to be focused on a longer term. You don't have to move out [to Silicon Valley] to do this. There's this culture in the Valley of starting a company before they know what they want to do. You decided you want to start a company, but you don't know what you are passionate about yet…you need to do stuff you are passionate about. The companies that work are the ones that people really care about and have a vision for the world, so do something you like."

Nevertheless, when Facebook tried to raise money from Waltham, Mass.-based venture capital firm Battery Ventures in 2004, Zuckerberg's cofounder Eduardo Saverin did the pitch. After two meetings, Battery passed because of Zuckerberg's brashness, the unsatisfying progress of Battery's Friendster investment, and turf battles with its Silicon Valley office but Zuckerberg did not want to raise money from a VC and accepted [a $500,000 investment] from Peter Thiel, because Thiel "could relate to us on a founder level." Zuckerberg also found it unattractive that in Silicon Valley "everyone was talking about flipping companies." He did like the fact that Donald Graham, CEO and chairman of The Washington Post, was passionate about Facebook and his recommendation that he accept funding from Jim Breyer, a partner at Palo Alto-based Accel Partners. Breyer, a Natick, Mass. native, believed that Facebook would not have succeeded had it been in Boston because of the talent coming from Silicon Valley companies like Yahoo, eBay, and Google and "a fundamentally more consumer Internet savvy than if it would've been built anywhere else on the planet."

In addition to the benefits Facebook got from raising capital there, the summer Zuckerberg spent in a Palo Alto house before he dropped out of Harvard helped him to solidify his vision. At 819 La Jennifer Way, Palo Alto, months after the 2004 launch of Facebook in his Harvard dorm room, then 20-year-old Zuckerberg found a mentor: Sean Parker, co-founder of digital music service Napster. Parker's thoughts about the future and his Silicon Valley connections helped convince Zuckerberg by that fall that he should drop out of Harvard and work on Facebook. What's more, that first investor supplied the capital Facebook needed to grow, provided connections to influential Internet thinkers in Silicon Valley, and enabled the company to lease its first data center and higher its first employees. Indeed, in August 2014, Zuckerberg said that once he got settled in Palo Alto, he never considered going back to Harvard. Parker, who also ended his formal education to go into business, influenced that decision. Parker helped Zuckerberg expand his vision for Facebook and introduced him to Thiel, who made the first substantial investment in Facebook. Moreover, Parker may have arranged for Google executive Megan Smith, then part of Google's business development team, to visit the Palo Alto house. Zuckerberg saw Google's interest in *acquiring Facebook as evidence of the value of what it was doing, but even then, he thought Facebook was better than Google.*

Case Analysis

Cambridge and Boston host a solid collection of pillar companies targeting relatively small markets. Despite Zuckerberg's ambivalence about Silicon Valley's quick-buck mentality, he stayed there. In so doing, he benefited from its relatively supportive investors and its success at producing consumer-focused technology companies that provided many of Facebook's early employees and its business strategy and culture. As Breyer pointed out, these elements are missing in other regions and therefore, Boston's relatively unsuitable human capital portfolio cost the region one of the world's most successful pillar companies.

Principles

Entrepreneurs who locate in cities with some pillars in niche markets ought to weigh the advantages and disadvantages of locating their startups there. Here are factors they should consider:

- **Advantages:**
    - Founder and team prefer to live and work in the city.
    - Many capital providers are available locally.
    - Many entrepreneurs whose companies have been acquired may provide capital and advice to new startups.
    - Local pillar companies may be a good source of talent and capital.
    - Local universities will be a source of talent and ideas on which to base the creation of new companies.

- **Disadvantages:**
    - People with needed skills may not be available, thus forcing the company to open offices nearer the needed talent.
    - Coordination with multiple offices could strain the executive team.
    - Real estate prices and salaries will be higher.

- Supply of affordable real estate and local infrastructure will be so strained that workers' commutes will be painful.

- Lack of significant pillar companies may suggest insufficient dynamism for most talented entrepreneurs.

Level 4: Many Pillars in Huge Markets

Success Case Study: Beijing ByteDance Technology Pays Up for Top Talent

Introduction

Beijing hosts many of the world's biggest technology pillar companies and is attracting billions in venture capital. The pillar companies include Baidu and Tencent Holdings; $50 billion was invested in Beijing startups in 2016. With all the capital available to invest in Beijing startups, competition for talent is fierce. And the most successful startups seek to recruit top talent by paying way more than rivals. Will this lead to an unsustainable bidding war?

Case Scenario

The startup in question is Beijing ByteDance Technology, maker of a mobile app called Jinri Toutiao, or Today's Headlines, which aggregates news and videos from hundreds of media outlets. Between 2012 and September 2017, Toutiao had grown to 120 million daily users, generating a whopping $2.5 billion in expected 2017 advertising revenue and yielding a private-market value over $20 billion. Founder and CEO Zhang Yiming, the son of civil servants, grew up in Longyan and studied microelectronics and software engineering at Nankai University. He helped out people who were having trouble with computers, repairing the PC of a girl who later invited him to dinner and ultimately married him. After graduation, he started four companies including China's first Twitter-like service and a real estate site, 99Fang. com, punctuated by a stint at the Chinese office of Microsoft. After noticing that newspapers had disappeared from subway stations, Zhang realized that people were reading news on mobile phones so he launched his mobile-native Toutiao news app in August 2012. It became popular quickly because it uses Artificial Intelligence (AI) instead of editors. In this way, it learns what each user likes to read and customizes stories to each user.

ByteDance was controversial due to the high salaries it paid and the way it aggregated news. It lured top performing people from Baidu and Tencent with 50% raises and stock options. Top performers could earn $1 million in salary and bonus a year, plus options with total compensation exceeding $3 million. The $50 billion in venture capital invested in Chinese startups in 2016, up 10-fold from 2013, was fueling talent wars. Toutiao's advertisers, like Google and Facebook, were able to target ads based on what users search for, such as Italian restaurants or Korean pop stars, fashion or financial information. Since it pulled and hosted content from hundreds of newspapers, video services, and websites on its own servers, users bypassed the original source's site, thus costing them traffic and revenues. Original sites such as newspapers in the provinces of Hubei and Jiangxi and online services such as Sohu argued in copyright lawsuits that Toutiao was stealing their stories. Zhang responded by negotiating deals with media partners to share revenue and created a platform to pay individuals who created content for Toutiao. The company was competing in a global market for AI talent, planning to hire over 200 such engineers and competing with U.S. firms that paid graduates from top PhD programs $400,000 a year and seven figures to experienced AI engineers. Would ByteDance be able to fend off rivals gunning for its advertising revenues and AI talent?

Case Analysis

ByteDance's success reflects the benefits of a successful startup scene with large pillar companies targeting huge markets. The pillar companies are sources of talent for well-funded startups that pay a premium to lure the best people from the pillar companies and give them a chance to cash out at big gains if the startups go public. As long as ByteDance can hire and deploy that talent in ways that sustain its remarkable revenue growth, it should be able to keep paying a premium for the best talent. Should Beijing's success draw in so much new capital that it helps create serious rivals to ByteDance, it is likely that there will be a shakeout as less successful competitors are squeezed for cash because they are paying such high salaries. In the meantime, Beijing's success is creating a growth fever that rewards top talent with fabulous wealth.

Failure Case Study: Theranos Overdoses on Silicon Valley Mythology

Introduction

There are many dark sides to Silicon Valley's success. Among them is the willingness to place big bets on individuals with the ability to persuade investors that they can unlock the vault to vast riches by attacking a big market with a new product. Once those investors have written their checks, they are more than willing to have their ears filled with stories about how these genius CEOs will soon make them much richer. These storytellers also excel at recruiting world-class talent who can meet a very dark fate should harsh reality collide with the CEO's beautifully rendered dreamscape.

Case Scenario

Palo Alto blood testing startup Theranos (founded in 2003) raised about $690 million and by 2014 was valued at $9 billion, making its CEO Elizabeth Holmes worth $4.5 billion. By June 2016, her net worth had declined to $0 in the wake of reporting that revealed just how much the company had overpromised and under-delivered. One of the most painful costs of that failure was the hiring in 2005 of a Cambridge-educated PhD, Ian Gibbons, as head of research. He committed suicide in 2014 after trying to persuade Theranos's board that the promises Holmes was making about the company's product could not be kept. Holmes's ruthless response to news of Gibbons's death reveals a heart of darkness still beating in Theranos's Palo Alto office.

The Theranos story had all the elements of the best-sounding Silicon Valley investments. A black turtleneck-wearing Stanford dropout said that she was afraid of needles so she started a company that would let people do over 200 blood tests with a single drop of blood. Investors, mostly outside the Silicon Valley VC mainstream, poured about $690 million into the company; Holmes received fawning cover profiles in Forbes *and* Fortune *as well as great press in* The New Yorker *and* The New York Times. *She told her Stanford chemistry engineering professor, Channing Robertson, that she was dropping out to start Theranos because she wanted to use her tuition money to "create a whole new technology, and one that is aimed at helping humanity at all levels regardless of geography or ethnicity or age or gender. The fire in Holmes' eyes convinced [Robertson] that she would succeed, and she received his blessing". What's more, Holmes planned to 'disrupt' the blood testing industry and she excelled at convincing very old men with no industry knowledge, such as Henry Kissinger and George Schultz, to sit on Theranos's board. Then in October 2015, The* Wall Street Journal *reported that Theranos was not using its own tester to do most of its blood tests, which ultimately led the world to conclude that its Edison Machine did not work. In June 2016, a string of negative news caused Forbes to slash its assessment of the value of Theranos from $9 billion to $800 million and Holmes's net worth from $4.5 billion to $0. In October 2016, Theranos fired 240 people and in January 2017, another 155 were shown the door.*

In addition to attracting capital and old men to serve on Theranos's board, Holmes hired serious scientific talent. In 2005 Robertson recruited Ian Gibbons, who had spent 30 years in the diagnostics field, to be the head scientist at Theranos. His wife, Rochelle who met Gibbons while they were studying microbiology at Berkeley, said he was initially excited by his new job. But his enthusiasm faded. After spending long hours trying to overcome the machine's apparent inaccuracies and remained loyal to Theranos even after the FBI began to look into the accuracy of the Edison tests, he realized that Holmes's idea was unworkable. But Holmes ignored Gibbons's efforts to communicate the reasons for his conclusion. Rochelle recounted that Theranos was rife with lawyers who would listen in on phone calls, and Holmes would try to break up groups of people who were talking together. She said that Gibbons was confused that a 19-year-old had been given power over hundreds of people who did not seem to be accomplishing anything. When Gibbons decided to take his concerns to the Theranos board, he was fired and then quickly reinstated so that he would not talk about what was happening inside the company. In 2013, Holmes was getting ready to launch the Edison Machines in Walgreens stores across the U.S. Gibbons stopped coming to work and was summoned to the office. On the evening of the meeting on May 16, 2013, and fearing he was about to lose his job, he took an overdose of painkillers. Gibbons, who had recently been diagnosed with cancer, died in the hospital a week later. When Rochelle called Theranos to notify the company of Gibbons's passing, the company did nothing to recognize him or his contributions to the company. Instead, Rochelle was coldly told to return any company property.

Case Analysis

The Theranos case reveals a dark side to Silicon Valley: the tendency to bet on people who its investors perceive to be geniuses. Once the bets are placed, these investors are eager to believe any reports from the CEOs that confirm the wisdom of their decision to invest. They tend to ignore any evidence that the products being developed are not working as well as reports of problems coming from those lower down in the ranks. It is perhaps common that the good news prevails over the bad in most startups, and thus the investors are rewarded for listening to the CEO. But Theranos is one of several cases where the CEO's conduct causes enormous pain to the talented people the company hires thanks to Silicon Valley's depth of talent—and later fires or worse.

Principles

Entrepreneurs who locate in cities with many pillars in huge markets ought to weigh the advantages and disadvantages of locating their startups there. Here are factors they should consider:

- **Advantages:**
  - Founder and team will want to live and work in the city.
  - Sufficient capital providers are available locally.
  - Many entrepreneurs whose companies have been acquired may provide capital and advice to new startups.
  - Local pillar companies are excellent sources of talent and capital.
  - Local universities supply talent and ideas on which to base the creation of new companies.

- **Disadvantages:**
  - People with needed skills are likely to be available but at very high salaries with very limited loyalty.
  - Surplus of capital leads to the creation of many well-financed rivals in major opportunity areas.
  - Real estate prices will be extremely high.
  - Supply of affordable real estate and local infrastructure, including roads and public transportation, will be so strained that workers' commutes will be almost unbearable.
  - Huge pillar companies will compete through higher compensation packages, with startups seeking to hire top talent.

Table 4-1 below summarizes the principles for each step in the Pillar Company Staircase.

Table 4-1. Principles by Step in Pillar Company Staircase

Pillar Company Stair	Principles
Level 0	Make the city a better place for sprinters to live, work and play.
Level 1	Encourage local sprinters to go global for revenue growth and deeper talent pools.
Level 2	Turn successful sprinters into marathoners and boost local housing and infrastructure to attract more talent.
Level 3	Keep local marathoners from leaving town and boost local housing and infrastructure to attract more talent.
Level 4	Win the battle for top talent through higher pay, better options packages, and most compelling market opportunities.

Are You Doing Enough to Deepen Your Human Capital Pool?

Here are five tests of whether a region is deepening its human capital pool:

- Are startups and larger companies moving to the city?

- Are more locally-educated university students staying to work for these companies after graduation?

- Are more professors and researchers from local universities starting companies in the city?

- Are employees of local pillar companies moving to local startups?

- Is the ratio of startup job opportunities to skilled employees who could fill those jobs growing?

Conclusion

A region's human capital is a critical factor in an entrepreneur's decision about where to headquarter his or her company. Founders who hope to lead gazelles are generally better off locating their companies in cities that have enjoyed the success reflected in a history of acquired gazelles or successful pillar companies. However, the more startup success a region has, the higher the costs of that success to startups seeking to hire talent. To adapt to those challenges, founders often choose to locate some of their key skills in cities that have similar levels of talent and lower costs. In Chapter 5, we will explore the role that investment capital plays in boosting a region's level of startup activity.

Sourcing Investment Capital

What Is Investment Capital?

Startups need different kinds of capital at different stages of their development. Moreover, the types of capital needed for a lifestyle business, often a founder's capital or funds from friends and family, are not the same as those that a gazelle requires. Gazelles ultimately seek to go public or find an acquirer and thus have ambitious growth objectives that can only be achieved with ever larger amounts of capital. Gazelles go through four predictable growth stages, each of which generally require different sources of capital:

- **Find a business model.** The first step in a startup's development is finding a business model. To accomplish this, the company must develop a product and find customers willing to pay for it. If the startup operates in a two-sided market, in which the startup attracts non-paying customers and charges advertisers to access their attention, the business may take longer to generate revenues and thus may require more capital. In either case,

© Peter S. Cohan 2018

P. S. Cohan, *Startup Cities*, https://doi.org/10.1007/978-1-4842-3393-1_5

a startup as this stage should avoid raising capital from providers who may seek control of the company. To do that, startups at this stage generally finance themselves through various methods such as bootstrapping (founders work without cash compensation), founder financing (either borrowing money on credit cards or personal funds), friends and family money, or crowdfunding (in which the public gives money to the company in exchange for early access to its product).

- **Grow locally.** Once a company has found a viable business model, it often tried to add customers within its home market; this means it seeks to sell to more people within its original target group of customers in its geographic home market. At this stage of development, entrepreneurs often seek to raise capital from wealthy individuals called angel investors, who can provide capital and advice that helps the company to grow quickly and achieve tens of millions of revenue while breaking even.

- **Expand globally.** In order to go public, startups often need to reach at least $100 million in revenue. Typically, startups cannot reach that target within their home market, so they need to expand their operations into new countries. To do that requires additional capital, both to open and staff offices in new geographies and to develop new products or modify existing ones to satisfy the needs of new customers in those locations. At this stage, startups find that they must raise funds from venture capitalists who can write big enough checks to cover the requirements of global expansion.

- **Exit.** Ultimately, entrepreneurs, though reluctant to talk about this goal in public, seek to provide an exit for their investors. in the form of an initial public offering or an acquisition by a larger company.

Takeaways for Startup Common Stakeholders

Depending on their region's level on the Pillar Company Staircase, entrepreneurs and capital providers must tackle different capital-related questions. Figure 5-1 highlights potential sources of capital by step in the Pillar Company Staircase.

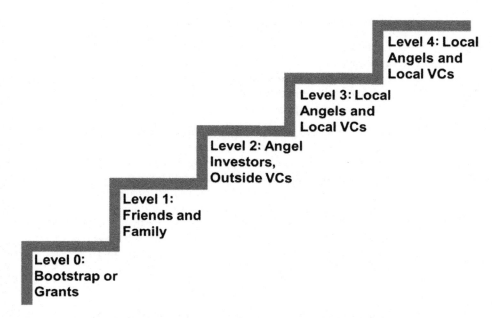

Figure 5-1. Potential sources of capital by step in the Pillar Company Staircase

- **Level 0: No Pillars, No Gazelles:**
  - *Entrepreneurs* should consider whether they should seek outside capital at all and, if so, whether they can obtain government grants and subsequently rely on profits from operations to satisfy their capital needs.
  - *Capital Providers* may wish to avoid investing in Level 0 startups because there is little likelihood of a profitable exit.
- **Level 1: No Pillars, Some Gazelles:**
  - *Entrepreneurs* may be able to obtain financing from friends and family and local government agencies that may be interested in enhancing the local startup ecosystem.
  - *Capital Providers* from outside the region may view Level 1 startups as opportunities to participate in potentially successful companies at lower valuations than they might be required to pay in Level 3 or Level 4 startups.

- **Level 2: No Pillars, Acquired Gazelles:**
  - *Entrepreneurs* should seek potential angel investors and advisors from the founding teams of local acquired gazelles who are familiar with their industries. However, the entrepreneurs may need to seek venture capital outside their regions.
  - *Capital Providers* who previously led acquired gazelles may seek to invest their capital and startup insights into local entrepreneurs while any venture investors who had supplied capital to the acquired gazelles might be interested in finding new ones locally in which to invest. Moreover, venture capitalists whose rivals enjoyed gains from investing in acquired gazelles may fear missing out on the next opportunity in that location, so they might open an office there. Stakeholders

- **Level 3: Some Pillars In Niche Markets:**
  - *Entrepreneurs* in Level 3 locations are likely to enjoy many options for raising capital at each stage of their development as long as they are building a company that is familiar to local capital providers.
  - *Capital Providers* in such locations may be happy to invest in local entrepreneurs who are developing businesses that tap into their areas of expertise. However, they may be frustrated by the limited scale of their local exits and thus may also open offices in Level 4 regions.

- **Level 4: Many Pillars in Huge Markets:**
  - *Entrepreneurs* in Level 4 regions are likely to have more than adequate access to capital for all stages of their ventures, particularly if the entrepreneurs have previously enriched those local capital providers. However, entrepreneurs must be wary of the risks of such region's excess capital; local venture firms may invest heavily in many startups targeting the same market, thus producing direct rivals.
  - *Capital Providers* in such regions may find themselves chasing after opportunities already discovered by their rivals or taking bigger risks on unproven opportunities. Stakeholders

Investment Capital Success and Failure Case Studies Stakeholders

Investing in startups is inherently risky regardless of the region in which entrepreneur and the capital provider operate. However, the potential for high investment returns tends to rise in regions with the strongest fit between the skills of the entrepreneur and the capital provider. Indeed, in such regions, the capital provider and the first-time entrepreneur have similar educational backgrounds and skills. The big difference between them is that the capital provider is one or two successful exits ahead of the first-time entrepreneur. But in such regions, both parties pull each other further up the ladder of success.

The capital provider applies her capital and expertise to a younger version of herself. If things go well, the entrepreneur gets her first successful exit and the capital provider adds to her wealth and startup insight. Indeed, over decades this process can enable a region to take a step up the Pillar Company Staircase as the founders of acquired gazelles invest in entrepreneurs who create pillar companies, which in turn invest in more local entrepreneurs.

The examples of successful and unsuccessful capital provision we explore in this chapter also reveal several risks for entrepreneurs in different regions:

- **Talent flight.** Regions whose educational institutions produce talent without startup capital support suffer talent leakage. More specifically, the best entrepreneurs leave such regions and start their companies where they can more easily obtain the capital and talent they need to realize their vision.

- **Failure to adapt to changing technologies and business models.** Regions that enjoy some initial success may become so risk averse that their capital providers are unable to adapt to changing technology and new business models, therefore they decline to invest in entrepreneurs and opportunities that may lead to higher returns in new markets. This failure to invest results in the flight of local talent to regions that are more accommodating to those opportunities.

- **Emotion-driven investment decisions.** Venture capitalists in regions that have enjoyed exceptional success may invest in entrepreneurs and business ideas without conducting sufficient due diligence because they are afraid of missing out on opportunities that they believe their peers have already captured. Investors in these regions are so eager to increase their net worth in huge increments—for example, 10-fold with each wave of investment— that they are more likely to fall victim to confirmation bias in their decision-making. As a result, they may minimize the importance of information that contradicts their conclusion they have already reached, which is to invest in the company.

Level 0: No Pillars, No Gazelles

Success Case Study: HydroGlyde Coatings Raises Government Funds to Reinvent the Condom

Introduction

A region without pillars and gazelles is also likely to lack startup capital. This makes sense because only a small number of startups are gazelles and a fraction of those become pillar companies. And a region that lacks pillar companies and acquired gazelles is unlikely to host any venture capital firms. That's because such investors look for potential pillar companies before they get big. If a region lacks pillar companies, outside venture capitalists are likely to stay away. Meanwhile, a local investor fortunate enough to have invested in the region's first pillar company could become so wealthy that she has a chance to be the region's first venture capital firm. A startup located in a region without pillars or gazelles needs to look outside to raise capital.

Case Scenario

That is what HydroGlyde Coatings did before it began operating in Worcester in June 2017. According to Karen Pelletier, Director of Higher Education-Business Partnerships at the Worcester Regional Chamber of Commerce, one of the 2017 winners is condom developer HydroGlyde Coatings LLC, which has already raised a total of $240,600. According to Ms. Pelletier, $40,000 of that came from the Massachusetts Association of Technology Transfer Offices in 2015 and the other $200,600 came from the National Institutes of Health SBIR Phase I program for 2016-2017. Stacy Chin, HydroGlyde's co-founder, hails from New Jersey and decided to attend Holy Cross because she "wanted a strong liberal arts education at a small college. After Holy Cross, where I studied chemistry, I attended Boston University to pursue my doctoral degree in chemistry under the guidance of Professor Mark Grinstaff," she said in a May 2017 interview.

The idea for the company came to her while she was getting her doctoral degree. As she said, "During my time in graduate school, we had an opportunity to collaborate on a project that was sponsored by the Bill and Melinda Gates Foundation to develop a better condom. Our angle to this was to address the problem of inadequate condom lubrication, which is a global problem pertaining to proper and consistent condom usage. This problem was also identified by the World Health Organization."

The developers say that HydroGlyde's product works better than ones currently on the market. As Chin explained, "We are a team of scientists and engineers who have developed a hydrophilic coating that stays on the condom surface. When it is in contact with water or aqueous solutions, it becomes slippery to offer longer-lasting condom lubricity. Our coating exhibits the same mechanical flexibility as natural rubber, so we do not encounter delamination or cracking with a coating, which is typically common when coating natural rubber substrates. In contrast to commercially available personal lubricants on the market, our self-lubricating coating does not wear away so that we can offer more durable condom lubricant that can last the entire duration of intercourse. We suspect by improving condom lubricity, this will promote more consistent and proper condom use among partners."

HydroGlyde is "currently working towards manufacturing and gaining FDA approval of [its] product," said Chin who viewed StartUp Worcester as "a great opportunity to bring a new venture into the Worcester area, especially with all of the resources, mentorship, and support from the community." Indeed, she hoped to use her time there to "expand [her] professional network and to learn more about how to grow [her] venture as [it moved] forward towards commercialization." By 2020, HydroGlyde hopes "to have an exit strategy in place." Specifically Chin said, "After commercializing our product and gaining FDA approval, we will begin sales of our HydroGlyde coated condoms. We will also start reaching out to seek potential partnerships."

Case Analysis

Were it not for pioneering entrepreneurs, no region would host a vibrant startup scene. Pioneer entrepreneurs are willing to take greater risks than others—or at least to think objectively about the benefits and costs of locating in a region without pillar companies or gazelles. The advantages of such a region—the lower housing and salary costs compared to more vibrant startup hubs—could outweigh the negatives—the shortage of world-class talent and local venture capital. While HydroGlyde had overcome some of these limitations by raising government funding in 2017, it was unclear whether it would be able to develop its product to the point of commercialization without additional funding, at which point it might need to seek private capital outside of Worcester. Until then, its government funding was an impressive adaptation to the weaknesses of Worcester's startup scene.

Less Successful Case Study: Worcester-Educated Serial Entrepreneur Shuns City for All His Ventures

Introduction

Universities are an essential ingredient to form a vibrant startup scene. But without local gazelles or venture capital, most locally-educated talent leaves town after graduation. This makes it difficult for the region to benefit from the advantages of hosting universities. The post-graduation talent exodus makes it less likely that successful alumni will end up reinvesting their capital into the local startup scene. And if it is relatively easy to locate their startups in regions with adequate supplies of capital, that talent exodus is likely to continue.

Case Scenario

This comes to mind in considering the career of Larry Genovesi, a Worcester Polytechnic Institute-educated entrepreneur with six informational technology start-ups in his wake. Some of them succeeded and others did not. But his views on what Worcester should do to retain more of its talent are worth considering, even though Worcester has not adopted them. Genovesi loves the thrill of turning a drawing on a restaurant napkin into a product that customers use in their business. He started his companies to capture emerging opportunities. He's learned to ask potential customers what they're willing to pay for his ideas, and to reconcile his obligation to investors with his feeling that employees are family. WPI taught him how to work well in teams and helped him acquire solid technical know-how. Born in Weymouth, Mass., Genovesi earned a bachelor's degree in computer science at WPI and went to work for Digital Equipment Corp. In 1982, he founded Digital Cable Systems, which made cables that met Federal Communications Commission radiation limits. He sold it in 1988. In 1987, he founded Egypt Beach Systems, a maker of devices that controlled computer graphics.

In 1989, he started Power Station Technologies, a consulting firm that in 1997 turned itself into a product company called Network Engines. Network Engines' computer servers were extremely popular with companies that were building out their Internet sites. This spiking demand helped Mr. Genovesi persuade venture capital firms to part with $45 million to finance the growth. That's because its servers had the best technology for what Genovesi called "phoning home;" when the server stopped working, it let a company's central office know right away. Since companies were scrambling to go online, they were buying up Network Engines servers fast. Within eight months, Network Engines' workforce grew from 50 to 200 people and its revenues climbed from zero to $45 million. Network Engines was getting orders for 500 servers a month; then IBM ordered 45,000 and slapped its name on the box to sell them to its customers. In July 2000, Genovesi took the company public and its market value peaked at $1 billion. In June 2012, the company was sold for $63 million, an 86% premium to its 72 cents a share price, as it struggled with the threat of being delisted from the NASDAQ.

In 2002, Genovesi began a string of two consecutive ventures that suffered far less profitable outcomes. The first of these was Ammasso, a maker of "network accelerators" that sped up the flow of traffic over the Internet by reducing the amount of "overhead" involved in transferring data. Ammasso's technology emerged from one of the companies that Network Engines acquired. But after raising venture capital, Genovesi had to shut down Ammasso, which raised $10 million in 2003 from Needham, Mass.-based Prism Ventures and Montreal's CDP Capital Ventures, because while customers said they would buy the product, they were not willing to pay enough to keep Ammasso going. In November 2011 Genovesi told me that realized that he should have asked potential customers how much they would be willing to pay for the product. And since potential customers were then asking him about the technology he developed for the company, he believed that he was not wrong about the opportunity for Ammasso—just too early.

With a newly acquired layer of wisdom, in 2005 Genovesi became founder, Chairman and Chief Executive Officer of Avon, Mass.-based Terascala, a developer of "high-performance, low-cost Linux cluster storage appliances." But by 2015, Terascala had burned through its venture capital and was acquired for what was probably a low price. In 2011, Genovesi was optimistic about Terascala since he had sold his product to national laboratories such as Lawrence Livermore National Laboratory and Fermi National Accelerator. He also attracted commercial customers such as Novartis, which used Terascala products to hunt for drugs, and Westinghouse, which used them to design nuclear reactors. In April 2012, Terascala raised $14 million, half from strategic partners and the rest from Boston's Ascent Venture Partners, and opened an office in downtown Boston. By October 2012, the company had 32 employees and expected to increase that by 30% through 2015. But 2015 instead witnessed the end of Terascala's independence. That July, the company was acquired for an undisclosed amount by Cray. One industry expert conjectured that the acquisition was a so-called acquihire—a bulk hiring of many, but not all, of its people—that takes a money-losing business off the hands of investors without granting them a capital gain.

While Genovesi felt he benefited from his Worcester education, he never located any of his companies there. He believed that WPI was a place for people who knew where they wanted to go and it would help them get there. It taught him to work in teams to get projects completed and exposed him to the "real world" and gave him technical knowledge. As a result, WPI students knew that big employers like DEC were sure to hire them. Genovesi never located a company near Worcester, though. Instead, he liked to set up companies on the South Shore: Terascala in Avon was closer to his Cohasset home, and he was able to recruit engineers who could save themselves an hour a day by not having to drive up Route 128 to Waltham. He thought that if Worcester wanted to attract more startups, it should keep doing more incubators, such as WPI's Life Sciences and Bioengineering Center at Gateway Park in Worcester. In Genovesi's view, Worcester could create incubators for clean technology, biopharmaceuticals and genomics. And he thought that since they have a more noble purpose to make knowledge useful than profit-seeking venture capitalists, the incubators were the best way to help academic research flow into companies that create new industries.

Case Analysis

Genovesi's entrepreneurial success was mixed, and if he was the only WPI alumnus to have chosen to start his companies outside Worcester, his story would not shed much light on the weaknesses of Worcester's startup scene. However, as you saw in Chapter 3, none of WPI's most successful entrepreneurs started their companies in Worcester. And Genovesi's successful ventures were able to raise venture capital—quite conveniently for him—from Boston-area investors. In 2011, it was clear that Genovesi had no intention of starting any companies in Worcester, and by 2017, the city appeared to have made very little progress in providing other elements such as a startup friendly climate and ample venture capital needed to overcome the magnetic pull of other cities such as Boston.

Principles

Entrepreneurs who are happy to run a lifestyle business and do not require much outside capital will likely enjoy the benefits such as lower real estate and salary costs of locating a startup in region that lacks gazelles. However, more ambitious entrepreneurs are better off moving to a region that hosts the different groups of capital providers they will need to achieve their growth goals.

Level 1: No Pillars, Some Gazelles

Success Case Study: Two Hong Kong Gazelles Take Outside Venture Capital to Become Unicorns

Introduction

Hong Kong capital providers are generally more comfortable investing in commercial real estate than in high tech startups. As a result, Hong Kong gazelles raise much of their capital from outside investors who are more comfortable with startup investing. At the same time, scions of established Hong Kong family conglomerates are being educated in the U.S., which in some cases makes them more comfortable with the process of investing in high tech startups. Indeed, the combination of generational change in control of family dynasties and the possibility of successful exits for some of Hong Kong's gazelles could boost the supply of local venture capital.

Case Scenario

In Chapter 3, you learned about two Hong Kong unicorns, Uber-for-delivery-vans GoGoVan and online consumer lender WeLab, founded by entrepreneurs educated in Silicon Valley. Not only were the founders educated outside Hong Kong, they also raised capital outside as well. GoGoVan raised $26.5 million in funding including a roughly $42,000 December 2013 seed round from Hong Kong's Cyberport, a real estate development leased out to large technology companies and some startups; an August 2014 $6.5 million Series A round led by Hong Kong private equity firm

Centurion Private Equity. At the time, GoGoVan CEO Steven Lam said the money would be used to take market share in Singapore, noting that he hoped the results there would be similar to those in Hong Kong where "within nine months of our launch in July 2013, we captured close to 50% of the independent logistics providers." In November 2014, GoGoVan raised $10 million in Series B funding from Cheoyang, China-based online social network RenRen, which GoGoVan believed would provide local expertise and connections to help it expand in China.

GoGoVan's 2016 decision to take capital from Alibaba's Hong Kong venture fund proved pivotal to its ability to reach unicorn status. In May 2016, GoGoVan raised a Series C round to be used to "improve the user experience for customers and drivers" but did not disclose the amount. Investors included Hong Kong private equity firm New Horizon Capital, Singapore Press Holdings, Taiwan-based Hotung Investment Holdings, Alibaba's $130 million Hong Kong Entrepreneurs Fund, and existing investors. In August 2017, GoGoVan merged with mainland-China based 58 Suyun, enabling GoGoVan to expand into the mainland and giving it a private market value of $1 billion. 58 Suyun, owned by online classifieds service 58.com, operated in over 100 cities in China with 1.2 million registered drivers, while GoGoVan did business in eight cities in China as well as Hong Kong, Taiwan, Singapore, Korea, and India. Both companies shared Alibaba as an investor and Lam said that GoGoVan would seek to raise at least $200 million more for expansion into two or three new markets in 2018 with the goal of moving into Australia and Europe and going public in 2019.

WeLab raised a total of $205 million. This included funding from a $20 million Series A round in January 2015 from Yuri Milner, the Russian founder of DST Global founder, Mark Zuckerberg's ICONIQ Capital, and China Post-backed ecommerce platform Ule, along with previous investors Silicon Valley's Sequoia Capital and Hong Kong tycoon Li Ka-shing's media and technology company TOM Group; a $150 million Series B round led by Malaysian sovereign wealth fund Khazanah Nasional Berhad, giving Malaysia exposure to rising Chinese consumer loan demand, and included investments from ING Bank and China-owned Guangdong Technology Financial Group (GTFG); and $25 million in debt financing in September 2016 from ING Bank. ING's supplied equity and debt capital to WeLab due to what it perceived as the growth potential of their partnership. As ING CEO Ralph Hamers said, "The stake we have taken in WeLab and the other investments prove that we are determined to transform banking to further improve the customer experience. We will look at the possibilities of starting a partnership with WeLab in ING markets."

Case Analysis

GoGoVan and WeLab successfully navigated the challenging process of raising capital in their pursuit of growth and both achieved valuations of at least $1 billion. While GoGoVan obtained more investment from Hong Kong capital providers, it also relied heavily on capital from other Asian capitals in order to benefit from their skills and connections in the cities where it wanted to expand. WeLab also obtained capital from a Hong Kong-based tycoon but relied more heavily on debt and equity from investors who could help the company to expand into China, most notably ING, which wanted to partner with WeLab to gain access to what it saw as rapidly growing untapped consumer loan demand in China. Both companies demonstrated the ability to find the capital they needed and the partnerships that would accelerate their growth in markets outside Hong Kong.

Failure Case Study: Paris's Quick Order Delivery Service Tok Tok Tok Runs Out of Cash

Introduction

Startups fail around the world with considerable frequency. How much of a difference does a startup's location make to that failure and how much of a role do local capital providers (or lack thereof) play in that outcome? One hypothesis is that startup's fail because their CEOs pick the wrong problem to solve, they build a product that offers customers enough advantages over competitors', they can't build a strong enough team to realize their vision, and they can't convince investors to give them enough money to keep the company afloat until it scales.

Location can play a role in all these sources of failure. Successful startup CEOs may gravitate to regions where they can get access to the talent, capital, and other resources they need to build a world-beating gazelle and less successful CEOs may stay where they are to start their companies. In so doing, they may struggle and ultimately lose the battle with growth challenges such as targeting a market that does not need their product; building a product that offers customers much better value (e.g., key benefits for the money) than do competitors; hiring and motivating the best people with the skills that the company needs to grow; and raising enough capital to meet its growth goals.

Case Scenario

It is hard to discern the skill of Paris serial entrepreneur Serge Alleyne. But he started 2014 on an optimistic note, raising $2 million from un-named European angel investors in his one-hour delivery service, Tok Tok Tok, but ended 2016 by selling its scraps and shutting down. Alleyne is a dropout of IUT Velizy, a technical college near Versailles, who previously founded companies that were acquired for undisclosed amounts. In 2004, he started Switzerland-based Multivea, which developed a mobile content management, delivery, and billing system that was acquired by Geneva-based mobile payments service Zong, itself a spinoff from Geneva-based mobile billing service EchoVox, in October 2005 for an undisclosed amount. In 2007, Alleyne founded Paris-based Nomao, a service to enable hotels and local businesses to track their online reputations, which was acquired in 2010 for an undisclosed price by Manhattan-based video advertising marketplace Teads. And in 2012, he founded Paris-based Tok Tok Tok, which was acquired by an undisclosed "leader of the industry" for an undisclosed price in September 2016. From there, he became a partner at the London office of La Famille, a Paris-based startup accelerator. The secrecy surrounding Alleyne's ventures suggests to me that he does not reward investors with high returns—and would certainly make me skeptical of his skills as an entrepreneur.

2014 dawned on a bright note for Tok Tok Tok, which was competing with companies like San Francisco-based Postmates, a service that shopped and delivered items for consumers within the day or hour and had raised $8 million. In January 2014, Tok Tok Tok announced it had raised $2 million from undisclosed European angel investors to expand from Paris where it had launched in April 2013 to other European cities such as London. Tok Tok Tok claimed at the time that it in Paris it was delivering 300,000 items such as groceries, electronics, office supplies, drinks, and beverages in roughly 30 minutes. Alleyne claimed that the service provided real-time tracking of the progress of its so-called runners, people Tok Tok Tok recruited, vetted and trained to deliver items via a method of their choosing such as roller-skates, motorbike, or car. Alleyne said the company had won "20,000 customers in Paris in just a few months" and those who tried it twice were using it on average four times a month. Tok Tok Tok generated revenue by taking a percentage of the extra revenue it generated for its partner retailers and from a fee it charged consumers for 30-minute delivery.

Six months later, Alleyne was out as Tok Tok Tok's CEO, replaced by the former chief financial officer of a large French department store. The new CEO was Eric Reiss, who had spent 13 years at Carrefour, the fourth-largest retail group in the world after Wal-Mart, Tesco, and Costco. At Carrefour, he did business development in Brazil and Argentina, returned to France as CFO, and then returned to Brazil to become CEO of Carrefour hypermarkets in Brazil. He then took time off, working as an independent consultant. Alleyne met Reiss and tried to convince him to join, making Reiss CEO and putting him in charge of international expansion while Alleyne became president and worked on the product. As Reiss, who speaks six languages, said, "I wanted to have fun again. Serge knows what he needs to help his business take off, and it was love at first sight when I met him. I said yes in less than 24 hours."

By September 2016 it became clear that the team of Reiss and Alleyne could not make Tok Tok Tok tick. That's when it sent an email to customers announcing that it was shutting down and that the startup's tech platform has been acquired by an unnamed "leading player" in the industry. Technology news site TechCrunch reported that the mystery acquirer was publicly-traded London-based online takeout service Just Eat, which acquired some of Tok Tok Tok's "tech assets" and planned to use them to help Just Eat's restaurant partners to manage their drivers more effectively. Alleyne did not elaborate while TechCrunch noted that Tok Tok Tok had been "on its last legs for a while." Failing food delivery services suggested that the industry was inherently unprofitable. In September 2016, Belgium-based Take Eat Easy *and Berlin-based Delivery Hero's Valk Fleet had recently closed while London-based Deliveroo had felt competition from UberEats, both of which were then suffering from driver strikes.*

Case Analysis

Tok Tok Tok ultimately did not achieve great success because its founder and the CEO who took over from the founder both lacked the skills needed to turn the concept into a growing business. Paris's limited supply of world-class entrepreneurial talent did not find its way to this company. And absent a successful exit for Alleyne's investors, it is not surprising that he was unable to raise capital from prominent investors who were willing to declare publicly that they had invested in Tok Tok Tok. Meanwhile, Reiss was too quick to jump into Tok Tok Tok and his experience at Carrefour turned out not to be a good fit for the skills that Tok Tok Tok needed to grow.

Principles

Some cities that talented people find to be attractive places to live are not necessarily great locations in which to raise startup capital. Entrepreneurs with the skills needed to run gazelles can either locate where they will have an easy time accessing capital for all stages of their company's growth or they can live where they want and must be prepared to raise capital outside their region. If these entrepreneurs ultimately exit profitably, their capital and experience may be reinvested locally in ways that benefit the pioneering founders and the new entrepreneurs in whom the pioneers invest.

Level 2: No Pillars, Acquired Gazelles

Success Case Study: KTH Professor Cofounds 10 Companies That Raise $200 million

Introduction

While Sweden does not host bona-fide pillar companies, one big telecom company acts like a pillar. In 2014, Swedish telecom company Telia Sonera invested $115 million in music streaming service Spotify. Nevertheless, some of Stockholm's gazelles have been acquired. Those acquisitions have enriched investors and founders. And that enrichment has attracted venture capitalists and other investors from outside Sweden, most notably from Silicon Valley who are hoping that lightning will strike more than once for those who bet on Stockholm-based startups. In 2016, for example, venture capital investment in Stockholm hit a record high: $1.4 billion was invested in 247 companies. The investment was distributed across many sectors: 13% were in fintech, 12% in enterprise/cloud, 11% in e-commerce, 9% in entertainment and media, 8% in health and wellness, 6% in gaming, 6% in social and communications, and 5% in Internet of Things. Stockholm's startup scene has come far in a decade. SUP46 is an incubator hosting 60 start-ups as members and more alumni which together have attracted total funding of $135 million. Its CEO and co-founder, Jessica Stark, said "Running your own company has become sexier in the last decade, but entrepreneurship has always been highly respected in Swedish society, but more associated with family-run companies. Now there is a start-up boom."

Despite considerable Swedish barriers to private capital flows, big name Silicon Valley venture capital firms—for example, Kleiner Perkins Caufield & Byers and Sequoia Capital helped fund TrueCaller, an app that finds phone numbers and blocks spam calls—have invested in Swedish startups. Sweden took steps to boost its startup scene. For example, in 1994 Stockholm built the world's largest open-fiber network and by 2015, 100% of businesses and 90% of homes were using it. At the same time, the Swedish government let people buy PCs with pre-tax dollars with employers supplementing the costs. Nevertheless, Stockholm does erect barriers to startup investment. The costs of housing and related taxes are high; landlords must obtain special permits to sublet; income taxes are high although university tuition and health care is free; stock options are taxed before and after they cash out; and if a company goes bankrupt and a person has served on its board or as the CEO, the bankruptcy becomes registered in that person's personal credit rating for life and becomes a personal liability, making it more difficult to get a mortgage or a loan for another startup.

On balance, many investors have concluded that the advantages of investing in Swedish startups outweigh the disadvantages. This is certainly true for those who bet on companies cofounded by a KTH life sciences professor who has helped start 10 companies over 20 years that have attracted about $200 million in total capital from a mixture of private investment and initial public offerings.

Case Scenario

One of Sweden's most prolific entrepreneurs is Mathias Uhlen of KTH's Science for Life Laboratory. How so? He has started 10 companies over 20 years that employ over 500 people. As he explained in a September 2017 interview, "I have co-founded 10 companies over a period of 20 years. The first one was (Affibody Medical) in 1996 and the latest (ScandiBio Therapeutics) in 2017. I own equity in all of them and in all cases, the startup involves several co-founders." Uhlen's companies focus on different parts of the health care industry. "Most of them are involved in developing pharmaceutical drugs (Alligator Bioscience, Abclon, Creative Peptides, Affibody Medical, ScandiBio Therapeutics); others are selling instruments (Nordiag and Biotage); one is selling research reagents (Atlas Antibodies); one is creating IT portals (Antibodypedia); and one is developing recombinant trees (SweTree Technologies)," he said.

He spends time with some of the companies and in others he is a shareholder. As he said, "I am chairman of the board for three companies: Atlas Antibodies, Antibodypedia, and ScandiBio Therapeutics. I am member of the board for one additional company (Affibody Medical). In the rest, I am only a shareholder." He usually hires PhD researchers from his group and often picks CEOs through an external search process. In all, his companies have raised about $200 million through private capital and IPOs and employ about 500 people. More specifically, Affibody, a developer of diagnostic imaging technology, has raised $28.5 million from Boston-based Schroder Ventures Life Sciences, Stockholm-based HealthCap, and Stockholm's Investor Growth Capital. Alligator Bioscience is a "tumor-directed immuno-oncology antibody drugs" that trades on the Nasdaq Stockholm exchange. In May 2007, it raised $4.7 million in venture capital from Norway's Home Capital and Stockholm's Malmsten Invest, which went public in November 2016 and was valued at about $250 million in October 2017. Life sciences researcher Biotage trades on the Nasdaq Stockholm exchange; its shares were valued at $540 million in October 2017.

Case Analysis

The challenges of raising capital vary depending on the startup's industry. A first-time information technology startup founder generally struggles to raise capital until the company can demonstrate rapid revenue growth. In a region that hosts acquired gazelles, such founders may be able to obtain seed funding if they can meet angel investors who understand their industry. A life sciences founder may have an easier time obtaining funding from investors outside the region if the founder has developed breakthrough science. It is quite common for companies promising life science breakthroughs to receive private funding and to go public before their products have received regulatory approval. For such companies, the lack of revenue growth does not stop them from getting funding. Uhlen has applied his technological breakthroughs to many different markets and was not limited by the relative lack of capital available in Stockholm to develop his ideas.

Less Successful Case Study: Pre-Revenue Adaptive Simulation Raises Minimal Capital As It Discovers a Business Model

Introduction

An information technology startup's long-term goals determine whether it will be able to raise significant amounts of capital. If a founder seeks to run a company that gets big quickly and ultimately goes public, venture investors are more likely to provide it with large amounts of capital. On the other hand, if a founder wants to pursue an interesting idea and is not in much of a hurry to build a large company, the startup will need to seek out other forms of capital. More specifically, government and universities may be willing to fund such companies, but private capital providers may shy away until the company has demonstrated that it is serious about generating revenue.

Case Scenario

This comes to mind in considering Sebastian Desand, a Stockholm-based lawyer fascinated with combining math and business. In October 2017, he was leading Adaptive Simulations, maker of a service that automates simulations and design optimization. As he explained in a September 2017 interview, "I went to law school in Stockholm but complemented these studies with business administration, political science, and mathematics. Just before I started the company with the other founders, I was a management consultant specialized in B2B sales and market strategy. Prior to that I worked with B2B sales, was head of trading at a bank, and started two businesses." Desand cofounded Adaptive Simulations in 2014. "We started the company three years ago. I had just met the other co-founders. They were brilliant researchers, within applied math, at KTH. Once I heard about their scientific breakthrough, I was in love. I have always dreamed of starting a business based on math. When they described how their adaptive algorithms could automate simulations and design optimization, I realized this would be a huge thing. Their scientific brilliance together with my business experience was a perfect match," he said.

By October 2017, the company had attracted considerable customer interest and had hired in anticipation of generating revenue. According to Desand, "We are now 11 people in the team. We are still pre-revenue, but launching our product in a couple of months after three years of intense work. Even before launch, and without any sales and marketing initiatives, we have received hundreds of inbound requests for our product. Out of the four founders, three are highly specialized researchers. One is a professor in numerical analysis and the two others a part of his research team. I complemented them with B2B business skills." To meet customer demand, the company has broadened its skills. As he said, "First thing we did was to recruit an experienced CTO to secure the product development and bring our complex solution to the market. Beside that we needed more engineers and developers. We want to hire not only traditional full-stack developers, but also scientific coders with a combination of coding skills and math. This is a very rare combination of skills, which is hard to find. We also needed brilliant UX/UI and product managers. We used a combination of our own network, online CV-services, and recruitment ads on LinkedIn. We want to hire people on the top percentiles of skills and abilities." And the company may need to hire from Stanford if it can't find talent locally. "We do plan to hire more people within software development, scientific coding, and of course sales and marketing. We are looking for people all over the world; we prefer that they relocate to Stockholm, but we do have employees outside Sweden working from a distance. We are currently discussing with a potential candidate within scientific coding with a research background from Stanford. We want the best in a respective area, regardless of where they have studied or where they are currently located," said Desand.

Fortunately, Adaptive Simulations has been able to attract about $1.6 million in outside capital. As Desand explained, "We were first financed by the Swedish Agency for Innovation and Growth. Then we received a small investment from KTH. We also received funding from the EU-Commission as a part of the Horizon2020-programme for disruptive innovations. Funding which is only granted to 3% of the applicants." He continued, "When we started to raise the seed round, we met a lot of different investors, mainly at startup events. But quite a few also contacted us. We met Estonia-based Karma Ventures through our incubator, STING. Later we met with Bad Homburg, Germany-based Creathor Venture at the Web Summit in Lisbon. The investment process took about six months with a rigorous due diligence process (tech, people, legal). But it was all worth it." And Creathor was eager to help Adaptive to grow. According to Dr. Gert Köhler, Managing Partner at Creathor Venture, "We are convinced of Adaptive Simulations' innovative solution and see great potential in automating flow simulations across multiple industry verticals. We see a market need for effectiveness in design processes while maintaining high accuracy and performance. The team behind Adaptive Simulations is well positioned to serve this need and to become leaders in the simulation software market. With this investment, we further strengthen our commitment to create value in European deep tech."

Case Analysis

Adaptive Simulations was on a promising course after taking three years to develop its product. It was able to raise capital from the Swedish government and KTH to develop its product, and as it approached the point where it was able to start selling the product, it raised a modest amount of private capital from investors in Estonia and Germany. Desand appeared to have a clear idea of Adaptive's mission and was able to attract talented people and investors to turn his mission into a real business. Although he was unable to raise private capital in Sweden, he met venture capitalists elsewhere in Europe who were enthusiastic about his ambitions for the company. It remains to be seen whether Desand can turn Adaptive into a fast-growing company and where he will raise the capital needed to fuel that growth.

Principles

A region with acquired gazelles represents a good opportunity for local entrepreneurs who are in the same industry as the ones in which the founder succeeded. Such local entrepreneurs will have a chance to tap into the capital and expertise of those pioneering founders. That expertise could help the local entrepreneurs to raise capital at all stages of their development and to get help with growth challenges such as finding new customers and partners, hiring skilled functional executives, and managing their growth. For local entrepreneurs who are the first in the region to build a Gazelle in their industry, they ought to seek financing from outside the region from investors who have industry-specific expertise.

Level 3: Some Pillars in Niche Markets

Success Case Study: Boston Startups Find Local Talent to Fuel Their Growth

Introduction

While the Boston region lacks large pillar companies targeting huge markets, it was formerly home to Hopkinton, Mass.-based EMC, one of the world leaders in data storage before it was acquired by Round Rock, Texas-based Dell. As we explored in Chapter 2, this company was not a pillar because it actively discouraged startups and sued former employees who attempted to compete with it. Despite efforts to squash rivals, EMC did attract considerable entrepreneurial talent, one of whom cofounded a data storage company named Diligent Technologies and sold it to IBM for $300 million. In 2011, he started Infinidat, which in October 2017 raised nearly $100 million at a $1.6 billion valuation.

Case Scenario

Infinidat CEO Moshe Yanai was an Israeli Defense Force commander who graduated in 1975 from the Technion, Israel Institute of Technology with a BSc in Electrical Engineering. He has an extensive track record of entrepreneurial success. Yanai began his career in the 1970s, building IBM-compatible mainframe storage based on minicomputer disks. He went on to develop high-end storage systems for Nixdorf, and in the late 1980s, joined EMC, leading the team that developed its Symmetrix. As Vice President of EMC's Symmetrix group, it grew during his leadership from one employee in 1987 to more than 3,500. Yanai left EMC in 2001 when Joe Tucci became CEO. In 2002, he funded and chaired Israeli startup XIV to develop the Nextra storage system. XIV grew to 50 employees and IBM bought it in January 2008 for an estimated $200 million to $300 million. Next up was another storage company, Diligent Technologies, founded by ex-IDF Special Forces commander Doron Kempel, who had to leave after an accident in which five Israeli soldiers died. He moved to the US and was VP and GM of a media solutions group at EMC from 1998 to September 2001. As we discussed in Chapter 2, Kempel quit to run SANgate, EMC sued him over a non-compete clause, and Kempel and Yanai negotiated a deal in which EMC would buy shares in Diligent and they would take over EMC's unwanted Israel R&D Center. IBM acquired Diligent later in 2008 for about $200 million. Yanai set up two helicopter service companies, one in Boston in 2010 and another in Tel Aviv in 2011. He founded Infinidat, with headquarters in Herzliya, Israel and Waltham, Mass. in 2011 which started shipping its product in 2015.

Infinidat has raised significant amounts of capital and is growing rapidly. In total, the company has raised $325 million in three rounds from three investors: Manhattan-based Goldman Sachs led a $95 million in its Series C round in October 2017 that valued the company at $1.6 billion; San Francisco-based TPG Growth provided $150 million in its April 2015 Series B round that valued Infinidat at $1.2 billion, and Manhattan-based Security Partners led its January 2013 $80 million Series A round. Infinidat says it grew 250% between the second quarters of 2016 and 2017. In so doing, Yanai surpassed rivals that went public, such as Nutanix that did its IPO in 2016 and Pure Storage (2015 IPO), both of which trade below their first-day IPO prices as of October 2017. Moreover, Yanai surpassed Kempel, who founded Westborough, Mass.-based SimpliVity, which was valued at $1 billion during its last round of private capital in 2015 before it Hewlett Packard Enterprise picked it up for a 35% discount (or $650 million) in early 2017. Infinidat believed that its strategy of selling superior technology to high-end customers with complex and critical data requirements enabled it to spend less on marketing than did those rivals.

Case Analysis

An experienced entrepreneur with a track record of enriching investors has many options for raising capital. While Yanai's work at EMC helped forge his reputation, his inability to win a power struggle there ultimately made him an entrepreneur. His successes in starting and selling two companies to IBM made it easy for him to raise large sums of capital, though for Boston it is notable that those capital providers were either in Manhattan or San Francisco. Nevertheless, Yanai chose to locate its U.S. headquarters in Waltham, which should enrich Infinidat's founders should the company scale to the point where it can go public or be acquired.

Unsuccessful Case Study: Last Minute Reservation app GoPapaya Burns Through Cash and Shuts Down

Introduction

Boston's startup scene has a well-established reputation for investing in companies that solve difficult corporate computing problems such as data storage and information security. While it has enjoyed some success with focused consumer-facing applications, such as booking travel reservations (as evidenced by the successes of TripAdvisor and Kayak), Silicon Valley hosts the most successful consumer-facing technology companies. The success of investments in corporate computing startups has conditioned Boston's venture capital community to feel comfortable investing in startups led by strong technologists who can build products and gain customer adoption. Another Israel native with a long track record of success at EMC decided to start a consumer-facing app. Less than two years later, that startup shut down after investors shunned a seed round that he hoped to raise. Perhaps he picked a problem that did not fit well with his strengths and weaknesses. And the lack of enthusiasm for his idea reinforces the idea that Boston is a difficult place to raise capital for consumer-focused startups.

Case Scenario

This comes to mind in considering the failure of GoPapaya, a Boston-based app that enabled consumers to browse and book reservations at nearby restaurants offering last-minute discounts on their empty tables. GoPapaya launched in May 2016, but by August 2017, its CEO, Marik Marshak, announced that the company had shut down. Marshak had an impressive technical background that propelled him up EMC's organization and kept him there after Dell acquired the company. He earned Bachelor's degrees in aeronautical engineering and computer science from Israel's Technion and Tel Aviv University, respectively, where he also got a Master's in computer science and holds 53 patents. In 2001, he joined EMC, where he rose from Principal Software Engineer to Director of Engineering by 2014. He started GoPapaya in January 2016. Marshak started the company because he wanted to do something that he thought would make difference for people. As he said, "I wanted to do something different, something I could put my stamp on," he said. "I wanted to make something that everybody can relate to. Everyone loves restaurants, food, and especially to save money, so I went for it. People want to get what they want, when they want it. People like to be spontaneous. Look at Uber, for example. With Uber, people want to get what they want, when they want it…If you look at all other services in our life, there's an element of time. With airlines, hotels, and retail, the price depends on demand and supply. For restaurants, the price of steak at 6 p.m. when tables are empty is the same as it is at 8 p.m. when there's a line outside. That doesn't make sense. The experience isn't the same. We give them 30 minutes to show up to the restaurant. We want to drive demand to the restaurant immediately and we don't want people to think we're a reservation system." In April 2016, GoPapaya featured about 20 restaurants and he intended to let them use the app for free and ultimately charge consumers a small fee for showing up at the tables they booked.

By the end of 2016, GoPapaya had raised some money and built a team of 10 people, but by August 2017, it was no more. To be sure, the company started 2017 on an optimistic note. In July 2016, it hired former Oliver Wyman strategy consultant Zachary Weiss as co-founder and COO; eight others joined by the end of the year. The app would give users who showed up at a table within 30 minutes a discount of as much as 50% on their bills. It raised an undisclosed pre-seed round of funding and launched an Android version of its app and was being used by 60 restaurants. GoPapaya planned to expand within the Boston area and soon thereafter to other regions. By May 2017, GoPapaya had 85 restaurants as partners and was "seeking to raise a seed round to further propel growth here in Boston and beyond," according to Marshak. That fund raising effort failed and by August 2017, GoPapaya was shut down after working with 100 restaurants. Marshak struggled with the high cost of customer acquisition and the small amount of money he had raised in the pre-seed round was not enough to grow its customer base to the size that would interest venture capitalists. He also thought that investors had been spooked by the failure of food delivery companies. As he said, "One thing that did not help us was that investors became very worried from the food tech sector, due to many food delivery companies (like Maple, Sprig, Bento, and many others) shut down. Even though we were looking for seed money, the investors were looking for traction that just a few year ago were required only from a round A funding."

Case Analysis

GoPapaya might have gotten a better reception from Silicon Valley venture capitalists than it did from those in Boston. Nevertheless, Boston investors who turned down Marshak's pleas for cash could have mustered good reasons. After all, he excelled at leading storage engineers and had no prior experience growing a startup, let alone one in a very different industry where consumer marketing skills would be critical for success. The question for Marshak is whether he should have moved to Silicon Valley to start the company where he might have found investors more willing to give him the capital he needed to expand his restaurant partnerships to the point where the business had reached critical mass and could begin charging consumers to use it. On the other hand, perhaps this experience will lead him to start a company that taps into his storage engineering skills rather than trying another consumer app where his talents may not be as helpful.

Principles

Regions that host pillars in niche markets are very comfortable investing in founders who have succeeded within those markets. This principle suggests that in some cases those founders might be able to raise capital despite their previous lack of startup success. While these bets sometime pay off, investors who ignore the fit between the entrepreneur's skills and the requirements of the market in which the startup competes are more likely to lose their investment. Aspiring entrepreneurs in such regions who are starting companies outside its most successful niche markets—Mark Zuckerberg comes to mind—ought to locate closer to capital providers who will be most comfortable investing in those markets. Sadly for Level 3 regions, growth may plateau unless local entrepreneurs discover new growth markets and can persuade local capital providers to invest in them.

Level 4: Many Pillars in Huge Markets

Success Case Study: Zoom Raises $100 million As It Grows at 300%

Introduction

An entrepreneur from overseas comes to Silicon Valley, starts a company, and sells it to a local pillar company. But from there things get complicated: the acquirer loses sight of changing technology and does not invest heavily enough in making customers happy with the service. The entrepreneur is well paid and holds a prestigious title, but he can't stand watching his employer slowly destroy his baby. So he tries to convince top management to go in what he thinks is a better direction. But his pleas are ignored and he quits so he can start a new company that better satisfies his customers. His best employees quit the pillar company to join him while local investors eagerly chip in, hoping to profit from his entrepreneurial skill.

Case Scenario

That's the story of Eric Yuan, who left Beijing in 1997 to be the founding engineering of WebEx. Cisco Systems bought the video conferencing company in 2007 for $3.2 billion and Yuan stuck around Cisco as a VP in its Collaborative Systems group. He bolted in 2011 to start video conferencing service Zoom, which grew 300% in 2016 and raised $100 million in January 2017, valuing the company at $1 billion. Yuan was not happy with the way Cisco was managing WebEx when he left in 2011. As he explained in a September 2017 interview, "I was paid very well as a VP at Cisco. But WebEx was my baby. In 2010 and 2011, I did not see happy customers. I was very embarrassed that I spent so much time on the technology. Why are the customers not happy?" He could not convince Cisco management to fix the problems. As Yuan said, "Cisco would not change its collaboration strategy. I said I had a different view and left Cisco. 35 to 40 WebEx engineers left with me. Six years later we are doing well with 750,000 customers [up 67% from 450,000 in January]. We are growing thanks to our simplicity, quality, features, and price, and we have a very high net promoter score of 69."

Zoom has 670 people in four offices and has been hiring aggressively. As he said, "We hired 114 people in the second quarter of 2017 alone. We have offices in San Jose, Denver, Santa Barbara, and Kansas City. Our customer support operation is in Kansas City where we hire young talent working under a great leader who was head of IT at Kansas State and a former WebEx customer. He said he could help us hire people there and we offer great support and our people have a lower cost of living." Zoom hire DevOps engineers, sales, and support people from Cisco and Polycom. He wants self-motivated, self-teaching people with a background in selling to small- and medium-sized businesses. As he said, "The best salespeople join us because our product is easy for them to sell and they feel like they are moving the needle here, a feeling that they do not get from working at a big company."

Zoom has attracted plenty of investor interest. According to Yuan, "We have raised $145.5 million in four rounds. Sequoia led our Series D, and we like Sequoia; they invested in Apple, Google, and Oracle. Emergence Capital is also an investor. We have raised Series A, B, and C, but have not touched the money. Sequoia is helping us with customers and connections. We were very honored that Sir Michael Moritz of Sequoia spoke at our first Zoomtopia conference. And Emergence knows Software-as-a-Service and gives us great feedback on our operational metrics." Indeed, Zoom followed a steady path of rapid growth which attracted new capital in its four rounds, boosting its private market valuation at each stage from a $24 million post-money Series A valuation in January 2013 to a $1 billion post-money Series D valuation four years later. Zoom's January 2013 Series A round raised $9 million at a $15 million pre-money valuation. Its Series B round raised $6.5 million, led by Horizons Ventures at a pre-money valuation of $42.03 million. AME Cloud Ventures, Patrick Soon-Shiong, and Former Yahoo! CEO Jerry Yang also participated in the round. Zoom raised $30 million in a February 2015 Series C funding led by Emergence Capital Partners at a pre-money valuation at $170 million. Horizons Venture, IT-Farm Corporation, Jerry Yang, Hillhouse Capital Management, TEEC Angel Fund, Qualcomm Ventures, and Soon-Shiong also invested. In its January 2017 Series D round, Zoom raised $114.96 million in a deal led by Sequoia Capital at a pre-money valuation at $885 million. AME Cloud Ventures, Emergence Capital Partners, and Qualcomm Ventures also invested. Sequoia partner Carl Eschenbach joined the firm in 2016 when he quit as President and Chief Operating Officer of VMware and is now on Zoom's board. He said that Zoom has "cracked the code for delivering effortless collaboration. They're the only enterprise startup that combines Apple-level (customer loyalty) with Slack-like usage and Facebook-caliber monetization. No other company nails all three. It's not hard to believe that in 10 years every conference room will be connected by Zoom."

How will Zoom keep growing? Companies can grow along five dimensions: current or new customers, products, geographies, capabilities, and culture. And Zoom is pursuing several such growth vectors in parallel. "We are doubling down on our U.S. productivity focus; expanding in Europe and Australia while getting organic growth in the U.S. and Canada; and we are continuing to innovate our current product by adding cool new features [it announced artificial intelligence and augmented reality features in September 2017] and making it simpler. We have a culture of happiness. We care about the community, about customers, about winning, our teammates, and ourselves," Yuan said. In September 2017, Cisco was still the leader in the videoconferencing industry but at 6.4%, it was growing far more slowly than was Zoom. In January 2017, Yuan said, "We could have gone on with the money we raised in 2016, but this was a good opportunity to bring on Sequoia's team to help us build a more scalable business. Now we can be a little more aggressive in going into international markets and innovating new products like integrating augmented reality and opening our platform to third parties. We are focused on building a long-term company. We're not ready to talk about IPO plans publicly yet. It's probably better now not to have the distraction of having to publicly report our progress every quarter." It remains to be seen whether Eschenbach's vision of a Zoom in every conference room will be realized.

Case Analysis

Zoom's success at raising capital to fuel its rapid growth follows the contours of a classic Silicon Valley success story. An entrepreneur comes to Silicon Valley from outside the country, starts a new company, and sells it for billions to a leading local pillar company. After sticking around, perhaps too long, at his new corporate home, the entrepreneur starts again. In so doing, he finds that after proving he can build his product and win customers, many of the leading Silicon Valley venture firms are happy to give him more money than he needs to keep the growing business afloat. Interestingly, along with getting capital from the VCs, he gets access to their networks of customers, partners, and talent along with skills at managing his company's growth. The hope is that his second startup enriches his investors and creates a company that gives his customers a service better than any other on the market.

Failure Case Study: Juicero, a Piñata of Silicon Valley Pretension, Burns Through $120 Million

Introduction

Silicon Valley capital providers have codified an approach to startup investing that has created a string of new pillar companies over decades. Yet some of the same decision rules that produce big successes can also lead many of the same capital providers to make big bets, the wisdom of which seem easy for an outsider to question even before they go bad. An exaggerated version of the Silicon Valley investment formula features a charismatic sales person who reminds investors of Steve Jobs, a bit of Hollywood glitz, a fancy-sounding gadget framed as a platform for "disrupting" a staid industry, and investors' fears that others have already gotten ahead of them in tapping a huge new opportunity. This can work well if customers are willing to pay a high price for the product and the charismatic CEO can attract a team that turns the platform into a fast-growing business. If the company can't build the product or the customers are not willing to pay a premium for it, then no amount of salesmanship will salvage the investment.

Case Scenario

The rise and fall of Juicero, a startup that sold a $400 machine that squeezed $5 to $8 packets of diced fruit and vegetables delivered to consumers each week to produce fresh juice, has all the elements of the Silicon Valley investment formula gone badly. Starting in 2012, a charismatic organic food entrepreneur, Doug Evans, got Juicero off the ground and by March 2016 completed its Series C round of funding, at which point it had raised a total of $118.5 million from some of Silicon Valley's leading investors including Kleiner Perkins and Google Ventures, not to mention Campbell Soup. After the Series C closed, Evans was replaced as CEO by Jeff Dunn, a former president at Coca-Cola Co who dropped the price of the Juicero machine from $700 to $400. In April 2017, a Bloomberg article pointed out that human hands were quicker than its $400 machine at squeezing out of the packets. And by August 2017, Juicero had burned through all that money and shut down. Evans is a former Army paratrooper who in 2006 became CEO of Organic Avenue, a provider of cold-pressed juices and healthy snacks which were promoted by actress Gwyneth Paltrow. With $20 million in revenue and no profits, he sold Organic Avenue to investment firm Weld North in December 2012, which in turn sold its interest in early 2015 to another investment firm, Vested Capital Partners, which shut down Organic Avenue that November.

Though not from Silicon Valley, Evans evangelized like a native, noting "Not all juice is equal. How do you measure life force? How do you measure chi? Organic cold-pressed juice is rainwater filtered through the soil and the roots and the stems and the plants. You extract the water molecules, the chlorophyll, the anthocyanin and the flavonoids and the micronutrients. You're getting this living nutrition. It's like drinking the nectar of the earth." Evans's pitch to investors featured a miniaturized industrial-strength juicer intended to let millions of households speedily liquefy fruits and vegetables. In 2016, Evans said he started the company so that everyone else could, as he did thanks to living near a market, have fresh juice all the time. "Fresh juice is something that's very powerful and something that people love. [My goal is to] make it so easy and effortless that people would choose to drink fresh juice as an option for hydration. We've built a piece of hardware that is one part iPhone and one part Tesla. It requires that level of engineering," Evans said. In introducing so-called Internet of Things elements into the product, Juicero would provide consumers "transparency about the freshness and quality of the produce through unique tracking codes. My mission really stems from being deficient in eating raw fruits and vegetables myself, so maybe I've gone a little over the top. But it's important to know."

April 2017 was the beginning of the end for Juicero. That's when two Bloomberg reporters, Ellen Huet and Olivia Zaleski, inspired by some Juicero investors, found that if they squeezed Juicero's pouches in their hands for 90 seconds; they got as much juice from the bags as the machine did after 120 seconds. A Juicero insider said that the company was aware the packs could "be squeezed by hand but that most people would prefer to use the machine because the process is more consistent and less messy. The device also reads a QR code printed on the back of each produce pack and checks the source against an online database to ensure the contents haven't expired or been recalled." In a Recode interview, Bloomberg noted that Evans compared his work to Jobs's invention of the Macintosh: "There are 400 custom parts in here. There's a scanner; there's a microprocessor; there's a wireless chip, *wireless antenna." Brian Frank, a food-tech investor, said that Juicero's subscription model appealed to VCs who had missed out on the success of Nespresso and Dollar Shave Club which had profited from similar business models. Juicero investor Doug Chertok hoped that once it hit "its sweet spot" Juicero would become a "platform" for food delivery to the home.*

By the end of August 2017, Juicero was no more. In August 2017, Juicero said it was working to cut the price further on its press and pouches. In a statement Juicero said "It became clear that creating an effective manufacturing and distribution system for a nationwide customer base requires infrastructure that we cannot achieve on our own as a stand-alone business. We are confident that to truly have the long-term impact we want to make, we need to focus on finding an acquirer with an existing national fresh food supply chain who can carry forward the Juicero mission." Within three weeks of Juicero's collapse, Evans, who became the Chairman of the company when Dunn joined as CEO, embarked on a five-day water fast in Mill Valley, California.

Case Analysis

The failure of Juicero highlights the negative parts of the Silicon Valley capital raising process. Evans was a master salesman who after his first company failed was able to move from Manhattan to San Francisco and bolt his skills at selling organic food on to a complex and expensive machine that would make money by selling weekly high-priced packets of cut vegetables. Investors who missed out on the success of other startups that had succeeded with analogous ideas were taken in, even though the product was far more expensive and worked less effectively than making fresh juice by hand or just buying it in a store. A little investor due diligence might have kept Silicon Valley's best investors from betting on Evans. But evidently they wanted to believe him and did not let facts stop them from writing him nearly $120 million worth of checks.

Principles

Entrepreneurs in Level 4 regions must compete for ample capital resources. However, founders who pass the tests required by leading venture capitalists are likely to be able to obtain ample capital for all stages of their company's development. As noted at the beginning of the chapter, Level 4 regions tend to have a surplus of capital, which leads to investment decisions that appear unwise. For example, exceptionally charismatic entrepreneurs who appear to be targeting big market opportunities can raise capital despite a lack of previous startup success. Moreover, capital providers in such regions may invest too much in me-too startups due to their fear of missing out on an opportunity that a rival has previously captured. While such investment conduct may boost the overall vitality of the region's startup scene, it can produce costly failures that seem in retrospect to have been easily avoidable.

Table 5-1 summarizes the principles for each step in the Pillar Company Staircase.

Table 5-1. Principles by Step in Pillar Company Staircase

Pillar Company Stair	Principles
Level 0	Stay local for a lifestyle startup; move if a gazelle.
Level 1	Stay and gather resources from other cities or move to higher step region with needed resources.
Level 2	Tap into local capital and mentor networks to enhance local startup scene.
Level 3	Invest in new technologies to avoid growth plateauing or leave for Level 4 region.
Level 4	Avoid risks and costs of too much local capital vying for too few great deals.

Are You Doing Enough To Source Local Investment Capital?

Here are five tests of whether a region is deepening its investment capital pool:

- Are locally-educated entrepreneurs staying near their schools to found gazelles or do they move to more developed regions to startup?

- Are local governments providing funding and tax incentives to ignite the pilot light for private startup capital provision?

- Is the region hosting gazelles that are acquired or go public and, if so, do the founders of these successful companies reinvest in the region?

- Are venture capital funds headquartered outside the region opening local offices to tap into local startup investment opportunities?

- Does the region host well-funded venture capital firms and are they continuing to invest in the region or are they investing more in regions higher on the Pillar Company Staircase?

Conclusion

A region's investment capital is a critical factor in an entrepreneur's decision about where to locate. Founders who hope to lead gazelles are generally better off locating their companies in cities that have already benefited from the capital and expertise infusion that results from hosting acquired gazelles or successful pillar companies. However, the more startup success a region has, the greater the chance that the limitations of such regions will cause negative side effects for entrepreneurs seeking to raise capital. To adapt to those challenges, founders often choose to relocate to regions whose capital providers are a better fit with the growth requirements of their company or simply seek to raise capital outside the region where they are headquartered. In Chapter 6, we will explore the role that mentor networks play in boosting a region's level of startup activity.

Building Mentor Networks

What Are Mentor Networks?

Most entrepreneurs lack the know-how to turn their idea into a billion dollar company. A well-running Startup Common fills that know-how gap through corporate and individual mentoring.

As illustrated in Figure 6-1, mentors help companies with strategy, finance, people, and product. Individual mentoring helps people with basic needs, such as housing, network building, coaching, skill building, and career growth.

© Peter S. Cohan 2018
P. S. Cohan, *Startup Cities*, https://doi.org/10.1007/978-1-4842-3393-1_6

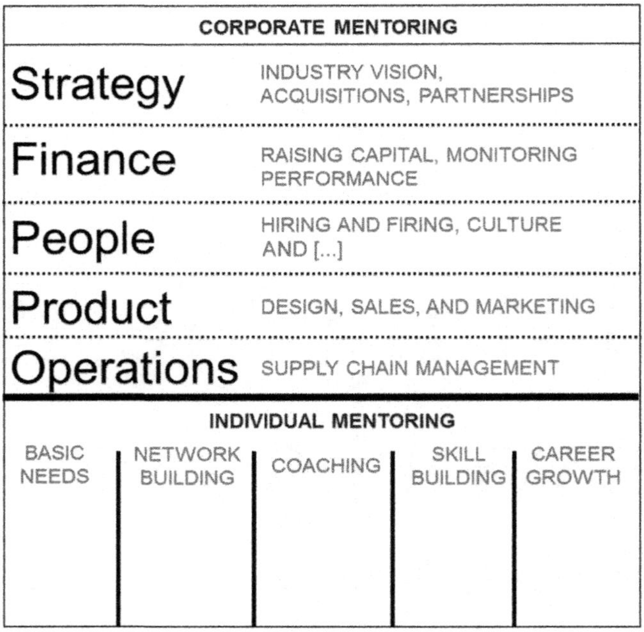

CORPORATE MENTORING				
Strategy	INDUSTRY VISION, ACQUISITIONS, PARTNERSHIPS			
Finance	RAISING CAPITAL, MONITORING PERFORMANCE			
People	HIRING AND FIRING, CULTURE AND [...]			
Product	DESIGN, SALES, AND MARKETING			
Operations	SUPPLY CHAIN MANAGEMENT			
INDIVIDUAL MENTORING				
BASIC NEEDS	NETWORK BUILDING	COACHING	SKILL BUILDING	CAREER GROWTH

Figure 6-1. Corporate and individual mentoring map

What follows is a catalog of ways that a highly developed mentor network provides advice to growing ventures.

Strategy

Often founders need help setting goals and making the right choices of target customer group, product features and benefits, pricing, distribution, marketing and sales, and service needed to achieve those goals. Mentors can help founders to make better strategic choices.

Industry Vision

Startups should anticipate the future direction of their industry and position themselves to prevail in that future state. Some corporate mentors develop an industry-specific vision so entrepreneurs can fit the startup's short-term tasks with its industry's future. LinkedIn Chairman Reid Hoffman can think about where things will be in five years and how to invest now in order to profit from that vision. Lee Hower worked with Hoffman at PayPal and LinkedIn and considers him a mentor. Hower explained that in 2003 Hoffman saw—correctly, it turned out—that social networks would be important for business. As Hower said, Hoffman "was thinking about networks of people, products, and economic activity, which is why he ended up starting LinkedIn and investing in Facebook." Mentors like Hoffman can help vision-starved entrepreneurs to target better opportunities.

Acquisitions and Partnerships

Startups often receive requests from customers for a product or service that the startup does not provide. In response, startups may choose to build the products their customers demand or acquire a company that already makes and sells those products. Acquiring is hard for most startup CEOs; doing it well requires capital and management expertise. Mentors can help. Elad Gil has helped a dozen startup CEOs to find the right acquirer, negotiate pricing, and determine the role of the founders and employees in the new organization.

Finance

First-time entrepreneurs generally lack prior experience raising capital. Unless they can run their companies with profit from customers, those founders will need to persuade other people to write them checks in the hope that those investors will earn an attractive return. Founders should find experienced mentors to help them to do this well.

Raising Capital

Most startups lack sufficient profit from selling products to pay all their bills. But entrepreneurs often lack experience in raising funds from capital providers to cover their expenses. Fortunately, mentors can help entrepreneurs to navigate the choppy waters of raising capital from angel investors and venture capitalists. For example, Gil helps startups find venture capital firms for their Series A and B rounds, assisting with negotiating key terms such as valuation and the rights of investors to appoint board members. Given the importance of raising capital without losing control of a venture, mentoring startups through the financing process is particularly vital.

Performance Monitoring

Startups must monitor the right business parameters to allocate resources for survival. They could count the number of customers, revenue per employee, progress on product timelines, or cash burn rate. Kevin Spain, a partner at

Emergence Capital Partners, helps startups in his portfolio with performance monitoring. As a former financial and corporate development executive, Spain helps design the right financial measures to manage a portfolio company's growth. Assistance with performance monitoring helps startups to make the most effective use of their limited resources so they can grow and achieve their goals.

People

Hiring people well is crucial for all startups. And quite often founders must compete with large companies and well-funded startups for the best talent. To hire well, founders should seek out mentors who can help with people.

Hiring and Firing

One of the most crucial decisions a startup CEO must make is whom to hire, whom to promote, and whom to "manage out of the company." Mentors like Gil and Spain can help. Gil found that most engineers who start companies don't have experience with hiring and firing and he helps them do both; initially, he may be asked to help with the more difficult task of firing an employee. And he helps startups establish hiring processes that include testing them for their productivity, checking their references, and finding out how they behave in an informal setting. Given the intense competition for talent in Silicon Valley and the tremendous risk to productivity of making a bad hire, making the right hiring and firing decisions are crucial to startup success. Mentors can help founders find and hire the best people who will fit within their company's culture.

Culture

The wrong culture (the shared values that determine what behavior a company rewards) can yield turnover and low productivity because it leads people to fight each other, to cut ethical corners, or to labor lazily. Mentors such as Justin Moore, CEO of Axcient, a service that helps companies protect their operations from physical interruption, helps entrepreneurs boost productivity by creating a strong company culture. He explains to them why culture is so important to achieving great results. Moore tells CEOs they must start by creating values that become the basis of what people in the company do. When Moore tried to do this the first time, he was grateful for the help of a mentor who had taken three companies public. And he tells other CEOs to develop their own values because Axcient's values are not right for other companies. What's more, a founder's actions early in a company's development can provide the foundation for a company's culture as it evolves. Early choices demonstrating integrity, passion for customers' concerns and needs, and care for employees send strong signals about the culture—and should be reinforced by what the founder says about culture. Getting the right advice on culture is important to startups because a strong culture helps them retain and motivate top talent and limits the time that the CEO must spend managing those ill-fitting people out of the company.

Organization Structure

As a startup grows, it needs to change who does what. A product visionary in a startup's early days may not want to spend his time tracking the detailed plans of six product managers. And that means the startup needs help changing its organization structure. Gil, for example, works with the founder once the company reaches about 50 employees to help analyze whether the reporting structure should be changed and, if so, how. For example, he helped a startup decide whether to hire a Vice President of Marketing first and let the VP appoint people to perform tasks such as PR, product marketing, and advertising—or whether the startup should hire those lower level people first and hire the VP later. Making the right changes to a startup's organizational structure helps it to retain existing customers and add new ones.

Product

All successful startups depend on the quality of their products. At the earliest stages, a company's most important challenge is to build a product that customers can't live without. To do that, a founder must find an important unmet customer need and apply technology in a way that meets that need. Founders should partner with mentors who can help them succeed with this important product design challenge.

Design

Most startups struggle to build a product that customers will use and ultimately pay for. Many mentors can help startup CEOs with that challenge. For example, Buckley helps startups to develop products that generate more revenue and get more "traction" in the market place. A key idea Buckley emphasizes is the need to "be data driven." This means understanding exactly how customers use a startup's product, what days they come back, and where the growth is coming from. And to that end, Buckley focuses on measurements of customer interest, including

- **Retention**: Are customers coming back after seven days, after 30 days?
- **Virality**: Are they sharing the product with their friends?
- **Monetization**: Are they spending money?

Sales and Marketing

Startups whose founders are technologists need people who can sell. And if they choose not to hire such people, they can get advice from those who excel at it. Haynie benefited from such a mentor as he tried to develop an effective sales strategy for Appcelerator. As he explained, "Todd Rulon-Miller, one of Steve Jobs' sales executives at NeXT and the head of sales at Netscape, helped me figure out how to sell the value of Appcelerator to companies." Haynie was particularly impressed by Rulon-Miller's eagerness to get into the details of building Appcelerator's sales capability as his way to give back to Silicon Valley. As Haynie explained, "He remembers when he was younger and building Netscape and NexT and this is the way he gives back. He comes in, he works, he helps us, he does sales interviews, and he sits on sales calls occasionally and helps in difficult selling situations. He does it because he cares about us individually and he cares a lot about this ecosystem and seeing success creating more success."

Operations

Once a startup wins customers, it should try to keep those customers coming back and to get new ones. In order to do this, the startup must master the details of operations: figuring out how to take orders from customers, build or buy the product they ordered, ship it to the customer's location, collect the customer's payment, and provide after-sales service. Many founders lack such operations expertise and should seek out mentors to help with this.

Supply Chain Management

One of the most fundamental aspects of operations is managing a company's supply chain. And some startup accelerators offer startups with mentoring and other resources to help them manage their supply chains effectively. One such accelerator is San Francisco-based RocketSpace's Logistics Tech Accelerator which offers startups supply chain mentoring and access to software. In 2016, one of these mentors was Ingram Micro Commerce & Fulfillment Solutions which offered mentoring to startups and gave them access to its Shipwire order fulfillment platform, a multi-channel software package for managing inventory, order, and delivery information. In 2016, startups receiving supply chain mentoring included Newport Trade Services, Eurosender, Logyc, Slick, Skuchain, Otto Motors, and Cargo Steps.

Takeaways for Startup Common Stakeholders

Mentor networks create different imperatives for a region's stakeholders. Here are three examples:

- **Entrepreneurs:** A region's entrepreneurs should address the following questions related to mentor networks:
  - What challenges must I overcome to meet my startup's goals?
  - Can I overcome these challenges or should I find a mentor who can help?
  - If I should find a mentor, is the best one already in my network or should I look outside?
  - If outside, is the mentor local or elsewhere?
  - What can I offer the best mentor in exchange for helping me overcome the challenge?
  - How should I frame the conversation with the mentor regarding how to overcome my startup's challenge?

- **Government leaders:** A region's government leaders may need to decide whether to help create local mentor networks or let them evolve without government intervention. In so doing, government leaders may address questions such as the following:
  - Does the region have sufficient private capital and entrepreneurial talent and mentor networks to spur more startup activity without external support?
  - If not, should our government supply capital and office space to attract such entrepreneurial talent?
  - Should our government seek to assemble a mentor network for these entrepreneurs or leave it to them to find their own mentors?

- **Venture investors** within a region may need to decide how they wish to help their local portfolio companies. In evaluating such options, they should address questions such as the following:

    - Should our partners mentor the CEOs of the companies in which we invest?

    - If not, should we hire operating partners who can serve as mentors to the CEOs to help them overcome the challenges that make it difficult for their companies to scale?

- **Successful startup CEOs** must decide whether they will mentor local startups and, if so, how. To that end, they might consider questions such as the following:

    - Why would I want to mentor local entrepreneurs?

    - Should I invest in startups and mentor their CEOs?

    - Should I join a more formal mentor network, such as one assembled by a local incubator?

Mentor Networks Success and Failure Case Studies

Entrepreneurs seeking to achieve ambitious growth goals for their companies ought to take responsibility for building their own mentor networks. As the cases that follow illustrate, a founder should take the following steps to achieve the best results:

- **Be coachable.** Maintain enough intellectual humility to identify key challenges with which they will need the assistance of a mentor.

- **Articulate key challenges.** Once such a challenge arises, articulate clearly the nature of the problem and why its solution is important to the company's success.

- **Identify the right potential mentors.** Search for the best people in the problem space and industry who have demonstrated through their actions that they can solve such problems.

- **Get introductions and make the pitch.** Obtain warm introductions to the best potential mentors and present the case for why those mentors should help the entrepreneur with the problem.

- **Collaborate with mentors.** If potential mentors agree to help, figure out what you can offer them to make the time worthwhile. Meet with mentors periodically, let them know how their advice worked or did not, seek out new advice, and keep the process going until the problem is solved.

- **Pay it forward.** Keep the chain of giving back alive by providing mentoring to less experienced entrepreneurs.

Level 0: No Pillars, No Gazelles

Success Case Study: StartUp Worcester Offers Space and Mentoring to Local Entrepreneurs

Introduction

A region without pillars or gazelles lacks mentor networks that might arise from successful local startups. If such a region wants to jump-start its startup scene, government and/or academia must create mentor networks. In better-developed startup cities, mentors emerge naturally from the process of creating successful startups that are acquired or go public. The leaders of such startups have the potential to offer valuable know-how to entrepreneurs who aspire to startup success and who identify business challenges and seek out mentors who can best help them overcome those challenges. Regions seeking to jump-start local entrepreneurship need to guess at the challenges that entrepreneurs might be grappling with and try to find mentors who can help address the challenges. Despite their best intentions, government or academic leaders might not always make the right guesses about the mentoring that local startups need.

Case Scenario

When Worcester's Chamber of Commerce created a startup incubator program, it offered 12 local entrepreneurs space to work and access to mentors. The program, called StartUp Worcester, began in 2015 and was still going in 2017. According to the Worcester Regional Chamber of Commerce, StartUp Worcester was an "initiative (that) helps to incubate new businesses to retain the bright young graduates of the area's college and universities. StartUp Worcester encourages them to grow their business here, where they have access to everything they need to succeed." Tim Murray, the Chamber's President and Chief Executive Officer, wants these local graduates to stay in the heart of Massachusetts. As he said, "The goal is to retain... bright, young entrepreneurs and encourage them to grow their business here, in Worcester, where they will soon learn that they have access to everything they need to succeed, including a well-educated and trained workforce." Slightly more than half the people who applied were accepted. According to Karen Pelletier, Director of Higher Education-Business Partnerships, StartUp Worcester received 23 applications from seven campuses.

Twelve companies were accepted: five from Clark University, two from Becker College, two from WPI, one each from Worcester State University and Holy Cross, and one WPI/Worcester State team. Each of StartUp Worcester's partners was represented in the group that decided on the winners: the Chamber; the startup incubator space, Running Start; Venture Forum; the sponsor's law firm, DarrowEverett; and Commerce Bank, according to Pelletier. As she explained, "The committee looked at their potential for business viability and growth, business model, potential for obtaining funding, team readiness, filling a need in marketplace, and if they would benefit from the program." The one-year StartUp Worcester membership included "space at Running Start and membership in the Chamber and The Venture Forum, affording them access to a variety of tools, events, and resources to help them succeed. They also get a mentor from SCORE [the Service Core of Retired Executives]," noted Pelletier. And Startup Worcester hoped that many of the companies would go from concept to job-creating growth. As Pelletier argued, "Many companies are in the idea stage and growing their ideas into a company. It seems likely that with that growth will come additional staff."

One of the startups accepted into the program was Petricore Games and it was still going strong in October 2017. CEO Ryan Canuel, who graduated in May 2015 from Worcester's Becker College, believed in the importance of creating a local community of game developers and finding mentors to help sustain his company. Though none of the company's team members were from Worcester, they chose to locate there because of the gaming community that already existed in the area. Worcester, Canuel said, was home to two of the best college game-design programs in the country. As Canuel said, "There are a ton of game companies in and around the Cambridge-Boston area, and they are all great studios. Right now, that doesn't exist in Worcester. There aren't any companies really making use of all the talented students that are here. We would like to foster a place in Worcester where those students can get internships and jobs."

He also encouraged collaboration, thanks to his experience at the Massachusetts Digital Games Institute (MassDiGi), a gaming and programming project hosted at Becker. Rather than compete, the three game developers at 2015's StartUp Worcester program were cooperating. For example, when Petricore had a test version of its game ready, other game developers in StartUp Worcester tried it out and gave Canuel feedback. As he said, "Within a week of showing it to people, we were getting a ton of advice. Getting our idea out there really early allowed us to change it so that it can be better. MassDiGi is the best resource in the state for that type of thing. People have different abilities and jobs that we as a team are not as advanced in. Discussing those areas with others is something that I can see being really beneficial to us, as well for others." Canuel got help learning new things to develop his company's mobile app from fellow developers and MassDiGi. As he said, "There are things we needed to do that we have never touched before. We had to go out and learn new things. For me at least, it was helpful to find a mentor, someone who has done it before. People can be afraid to admit they don't know what they are doing. We embrace the philosophy as a company that if you come across something you don't know how to do, go out and talk to as many people as you can who are better at it than you." By October 2017, Petricore was still going strong with about $300,000 in revenue from its five-person team.

Case Analysis

Petricore's experience is a good example of how a city without gazelles can create mentor networks. While it is too soon to tell whether Canuel's ultimate success will spur more successful gaming startups, his leadership created a mentor network that has helped Petricore boost its revenues. Canuel's business model of paying monthly expenses by providing consulting services and using spare cash to finance game development may make Petricore less attractive to venture investors. However, his approach helps him to achieve his goal, which seems to be to create viable and interesting careers for his employees in Worcester.

Less Successful Case Study: Worcester-Based Mentor Advises WiGo to Leave Town to Raise Capital in Boston but It Fails Soon Thereafter

Introduction

A city that educates talent but can't keep it around to start companies is squandering a valuable resource. And when that talent has enjoyed considerable success outside of the city and returns to help local startups, it is particularly sad when that mentor advises a local entrepreneur to follow in his footsteps and leave town. When that entrepreneur raises capital in a more robust startup ecosystem and appears to be on a path to success, the city that educated its founder misses an opportunity to build its startup ecosystem. But when that startup fails, the city that educated its founder does not lose as much. Yet the founder's failure could be valuable if it teaches lessons that lead to future success.

Case Scenario

A Worcester Polytechnic Institute (WPI) graduate left town and ultimately helped start a company that went public and was acquired for $1.8 billion. Rather than retire, he decided to return to WPI as a mentor to startups. In April 2014, WPI announced that one of its alums, Jim Giza, entrepreneur and former Vice President of Technology at travel price comparison service Kayak, was coming home to serve as an entrepreneur-in-residence. In so doing, he hoped to provide a good answer to his question: "Besides The Sole Proprietor restaurant, what is there to keep a 26-year-old here instead of moving east and making $110,000 a year?" A Sutton resident, Giza began working with undergraduates, MBA students, and WPI's Tech Advisors Network (TAN) to identify and help tech startups. WPI described TAN as "a virtual incubator comprising about 40 entrepreneurs, investors, and business leaders who advise and support students and faculty who hope to turn ideas and research into commercial ventures." Giza had a fascinating life story. As he recounted, "My father was in the military for 20 years, so we moved around a lot. That meant stints living in Holland, Luxembourg, and France before we landed in New Jersey. By seventh grade, we were in upstate New York and I was a terrible student, on the D-track that would qualify me for a job as a bag boy at ShopRite. Then a teacher discovered that I needed glasses, and I ended up as valedictorian." From there, Giza attended Hartwick College. "It was primarily a nursing school, but some professors from Cornell went there and started teaching computer science. The education I got there was so phenomenal that by the time I went to WPI's MS program, it was all review. I did really interesting internships, such as designing a search engine for properties for a Century 21 office so brokers could find listings based on keywords like the location or the number of bedrooms," he said.

He was miserable in a corporate job but ecstatic when working for a startup. Said Giza, "I went to work for Raytheon. I was employee number 37,068. All my colleagues were learning Italian and relocating to Italy for a project, and my boss told me to go to the library and research anything, as long as it was not comic books." He left Raytheon for a series of startups, culminating in the acquisition of online travel service Kayak by Priceline for $1.8 billion in November 2012. According to Giza, "I went to work for electronic publishing software maker Interleaf. I went with Paul English (future Kayak cofounder and Chief Technology Officer) to Boston Light Software—it made website development software—which was acquired by Intuit. After four years at Intuit, Paul and I went to venture capital firm General Catalyst and got financing to start Kayak, where I spent nine years of joy as the company grew from zero to 200 employees, a (July 2012) IPO, and acquisition by Priceline." He thought about spending the rest of his life at a farm he bought in the Berkshires, but he lost interest in that after about a week. At WPI he wants to help local students start and grow companies and create an environment that encourages these companies to stay in Worcester. Giza said, "As I see the entrepreneur-in-residence program, a large part will be getting companies into TAN. A lot of people come through here with ideas, but don't know how to implement them. I want to see more stuff happening in Worcester, and I want to see grads staying in Worcester. There are a lot of people looking for resources and don't know where to find them. I'm trying to find structure for them, and I want to help the School of Business. For me, it's great to see these companies come through here. I want to see a few successes come out of TAN."

Giza's favorite startup was founded by a [Worcester, Mass.-based] Holy Cross dropout. Giza advised him move to Boston and raise venture capital, which he did. Giza found several interesting startups in Worcester. As he said, "The No. 1 startup I've found so far is WiGo which stands for Who Is Going Out? It's an app that lets users see which friends are going out and where the hot spots are going to be on a nightly basis. It was founded by Ben Kaplan at Holy Cross, a very good-looking jock whose parents are doctors. He launched it at Holy Cross, and it gets 1,000 users a day. Venture capitalists are looking to fund it, and it's expanding to the University of Vermont and St. Michael's." The student was Burlington, Vermont native Ben Kaplan, and in December 2014, Kaplan had raised $700,000 with help from Giza and moved his startup to Boston's Fort Point Channel neighborhood. He went to Holy Cross to play hockey and in his freshman year, he got the idea for WiGo. As he said in December 2014, "I was on campus my freshman year and trying to make social plans—figure out who else was going out at night, where, and what time. There was no easy way to do it. You could text other people or put a post on Facebook, but you often wouldn't get an answer. So I came up with the idea for WiGo, and mocked up some screen shots on paper for how the mobile app would work. I found a systems developer who built the app from September to November 2013." WiGo launched in January 2014 and demand for it grew fast. As Kaplan explained, "It became very popular within three weeks. Many of the people using it were friends on sports teams at Holy Cross like volleyball, soccer, and tennis. I started getting emails and Facebook messages from people at other schools like University of Florida and University of Southern California where I had friends who wanted to use it."

Kaplan found out he was more interested in WiGo than in hockey. As he said, "I would work on WiGo until five minutes before hockey practice started. People were using it to decide to go out to local bars like Mahoney's and the Salty Dog. Then I met with Jim Giza. WPI is ahead of Holy Cross when it comes to entrepreneurship. He introduced me to Holy Cross professor David Chu, who gave me a one-on-one tutorial on how to improve the app and build a platform," said Kaplan. Giza also helped WiGo find a new home in the hub. "Jim also introduced me to Kayak co-founder Paul English, who was opening the Blade hatchery in Boston with a $20 million fund. I gave him a demo of WiGo and he immediately got it. We now have three or four employees and three to four Blade employees dedicated to WiGo," said Kaplan. WiGo also raised "about $700,000 from the founders of Kayak, Rue La La, and Tinder, and from professional athletes, including Vince Wilfork of the New England Patriots," according to the Boston Globe. As English explained to the Globe, "Boston is such a fertile place to test apps for the college market. You can test at small schools, big schools, women's schools, urban schools, suburban schools." For Kaplan, English provided a great additional benefit: he helped persuade MIT graduate Giuliano Giacaglia to join Kaplan as a WiGo cofounder. Kaplan described Giacaglia as "a really good programmer at the cutting edge."

WiGo ended up raising $1.4 million that valued the company at $14 million, yet nine months later, it was out of business. In March 2015, Kaplan told USA Today that WiGo was not about making money; it was about doing something useful. By that time, Kaplan said 1,300 universities were on "a waiting list to unlock the app." And as he explained, "We spend a lot of time trying to figure out what exactly makes a school love WiGo and we're having a hard time because it's so random. There's no one recipe for success. The unlocking feature leads to a lot of initial growth because people are wondering what's behind the door. We're 100% obsessively focused on continuing to tweak the product and making it something that every college kid can't live without. So, until we get to that point, we're rapidly—every week or two— pushing out a new build to the app store, tweaking things or adding new features." Kaplan said that the app was not bringing in any revenue. Yet, with so many features being added, he hoped that "the price of eyeballs"—or continued loyalty between WiGo and its users—would help monetize the app. "In the aggregate, nobody's making money from WiGo. It's just being a part of something cool," he said. By September 2015, it was clear that being cool was not enough to make WiGo a viable business. That was the month WiGo shut down and merged with Yeti Campus Stories, an "X-rated Snapchat clone" where the kind of sexual and violent content banned on Snapchat is acceptable. Kaplan spun the outcome with exuberance. As he said, "The majority of WiGo's backers rolled their investment into Yeti stock. Joining forces with Yeti was a strategic play for both WiGo's investors and employees. Yeti is like a Snapchat story on every campus, but it's completely moderated by the students who go there, not by us. Because of this, Yeti shows what it's really like to attend that school, showing a side of the student body not seen anywhere else." Yeti was acquired by a private investor group in July 2015 and its fate after the acquisition is unclear, which casts Kaplan's enthusiasm in a different light.

Case Analysis

The rise and fall of WiGo suggests that Worcester's mentor network was not terribly effective in helping the company to succeed. To be sure, Giza believed that he had identified a talented entrepreneur in Kaplan and helped WiGo to raise capital and locate itself in Boston where the company would be closer to more resources than it would access in Worcester. On the other hand, this move might have cost Worcester the benefit of hosting a very successful startup founded by a Holy Cross student. Yet the WiGo story ended badly; it appears that the company was burning through cash at an astonishing rate and that Kaplan was way over his head when it came to building a company and either could not admit that he needed mentoring or could not get it. Given the popularity of the app, it's possible that with a more experienced CEO or more forceful mentoring, WiGo could have grown into a real company.

Principles

A startup that locates in a region without pillars or gazelles will probably need to create its own mentor network. But before accomplishing that end, local founders will need to recognize and articulate the specific challenges their startup faces and then find and develop relationships with mentors who can help the founder overcome the challenges. As the Petricore example illustrated, those mentors could be professors or founders of companies in the same industry. Indeed, the ability to form an effective mentor network in such regions could be an important test of a local CEO's leadership skills.

Level 1: No Pillars, Some Gazelles

Success Case Study: Intelligent Parisian Entrepreneurs Cut Through the Mentor Network Thicket

Introduction

A city of gazelles without pillars may have a mismatch between the need for mentors and the supply. If that city has recently changed its attitude towards entrepreneurship—looking much more favorable on startups than it has in the past—then the supply of people calling themselves mentors might rise. After all, it is unclear what qualifies someone to be a mentor. And if it is easy to call oneself a mentor and the local government is encouraging entrepreneurship, then becoming a mentor might be seen as a great opportunity for someone who does not want to start a company but wants to go along for the ride. This leaves local entrepreneurs facing the challenge of figuring out which mentors are right for their company.

Case Scenario

This comes to mind in considering the state of mentoring in Paris, a city that once encouraged its most talented people to graduate from Sciences Po and get a job in government, banking, or consulting. In recent years, entrepreneurship has become quite popular and along with that has come the rise of startup incubators, which among other things offer mentoring. But in 2017, two directors of Parisian incubators saw an excess of mentoring often being imposed on Parisian entrepreneurs. As Antoine Lepretre, who directs the incubator for HEC, located in startup incubator Station F, explained in an August 2017 interview, "There is too much mentoring that does not work. Entrepreneurs need to find the right mentors for the specific challenges they face. I think entrepreneurship is now cool in Paris and it's alright if not all startups succeed; people will develop their skills and either do another startup or work for a large company." Roxanne Varza, who leads Station F, explained in an August 2017 interview, "We have too many mentor networks and it is easy to get lost in the noise. We have Station F but it is not efficient to figure out what is of value to an entrepreneur. It does have some high quality people. The Family has a solid network but it forces mentoring on entrepreneurs. An intelligent founder will take the initiative and build a mentor network organically. Jean at KIMA Ventures has helped create a process for required funding. And today entrepreneurship is very trendy in France."

One startup executive who has created his own Parisian mentor network is Florian Bressand, who left a partnership at McKinsey's Paris office to become chief operating officer at Mirakl, founded in 2012, which operates an e-commerce marketplace platform for retailers out of offices in Boston and Paris. In a September 2017 interview, Bressand explained that Mirakl has grand ambitions. As he said, "Mirakl's ambition is to be the catalyst of a marketplace revolution that will transform the traditional e-commerce landscape. In five years, the company has already been able to share its vision with customers in four different continents and 40 countries. Mirakl has opened subsidiaries in the United Kingdom, Germany, and the United States as it grows its staff of over 150 people, a majority located in Mirakl's headquarters in Paris. Mirakl gives retailers and brands a fast path to increase customer value by launching an online marketplace." Bressand argued that Paris has many organizations intended to help local startups to grow. As he explained, "The city of Paris promotes about 100 organizations (incubators, private, and public associations) tailored to accompany young and innovative entrepreneurs in business development, fundraising, finding the right location, and facilitating access to public procurement for startups. This promotion is part of an initiative launched by Paris' city council to support entrepreneurship in order to favor employability in the city." Mirakl has raised $23 million in capital, including from local investors who offer capital and advice. As Bressand said, "A Mirakl investor, Elaia, is also located in Paris and its co-founder, Xavier Lazarus, brings an entrepreneur's as well as an investor's perspective to the table. Mirakl's other investor, Laurel Bowden, Partner at 83North and Felix Capital, trusts Mirakl's potential, having invested in the past in renowned companies such as SAP and Farftech." Mirakl also gets mentorship from two prominent members of the Paris business community. "Mirakl is fortunate enough to count on the support and advice of influential mentors such as Xavier Niel, founder of the French Internet service provider and mobile operator Iliad, operating under the Free brand and Station F, and Laurent Dassault, CEO of the Dassault Group, both based in Paris," he said.

Case Analysis

Paris appears to be trying to supply mentoring to startups in many ways. The formalized mentor networks appear to be of limited value to entrepreneurs. This could be in part because the people who nominate themselves as mentors may be doing so to participate in a growing local trend rather than because they have the experience needed to help local startups grow. Rather than go to mentoring sessions at local accelerators, Parisian gazelles are better off first identifying the areas where they need help from mentors and then searching the world for the best people to help them answer those questions.

Less Successful Case Study: Hong Kong Keeps Trying for Local Startup Success and Mentor Networks

Introduction

Before a region can create a startup mentor network, it must first enjoy prominent local startup success. A local success story is far more compelling to the parents of potential entrepreneurs than success that happens in other regions. And parents play a very powerful role in shaping the career choices of their children. Having visited Hong Kong about a dozen times, I have always heard that parent want their children to get jobs in banking or consulting because such jobs will afford them the incomes they need to pay very high Hong Kong rents. That attitude could change if Hong Kong hosted popular startup successes. Such successes would drive envious parents to urge their children into entrepreneurship which would likely produce some more startup success. All of which would create founders with experience that would be a useful basis for building mentor networks.

Case Scenario

While Hong Kong's government seems more eager to promote entrepreneurship, prominent examples of local startup success remain elusive and mentor networks appear to fall short of the need felt by the growing number of local startups. By the end of 2015, for example, Hong Kong was home to about 7.2 million people and about 93% of its economy was driven by logistics, financial services, and real estate. Expensive real estate and a strong financial sector combined, along with parental pressure, to send young graduates to pursue a steady salary at a large bank or corporation. But in 2015, InvestHK, a government agency that helps foreign investors and entrepreneurs set up businesses in Hong Kong, reported that Hong Kong had over 1,500 startups, a 46% increase over the 2014 level, 40% of which focused on e-commerce, Internet of Things (IoT), and information technology while 5% were in fintech. Yet Hong Kong lacks important elements that a thriving flock of gazelles requires. It hosts few venture capital firms focused on seed or early-stage startups. This creates a gap in funding options for entrepreneurs that need the next round of capital soon after they have built a product that customers are willing to buy. Hong Kong is also short on mentors. Frederick Yung, a mentor at Hong Kong Business Angel Network and a lecturer on entrepreneurship at the Chinese University of Hong Kong, cited intense government efforts as one of the key drivers behind the growth. Yet Yung sees Hong Kong suffering from fierce competition from mainland cities in its bid to become the region's innovation hub. He believes that established businesses need to mentor Hong Kong startups. "Such mentoring activities now are very ad hoc and not structured. The Hong Kong government or non-profit organizations can take the lead in developing such a pool of mentors," he said.

Indeed, the absence of highly successful Hong Kong startups makes it difficult to create the cultural shift that would result in more startups and more mentors. As Blake Larson, Head of International at logistics on-demand startup Lalamove, said "Hong Kong is becoming a global innovation center, but it needs companies to look up to." By June 2017, Lalamove had raised more than $60 million from investors but Larson believed it would take time to change the banking and real-estate mindset within Hong Kong and for perceived "riskier" career options to gain mainstream attention. Traditionally, they have been the primary choice of career for fresh graduates, who have pressure to land a rewarding and established career to satisfy family and society. Added to that, here is no example of a tech company rising up to set an example for others to follow. Hong Kong doesn't have the size or scale of Shenzhen, which hosts Tencent, Alibaba, and Baidu. Hong Kong's relatively small market makes it less of a talent magnet, according to Larson. While new VCs are arriving in Hong Kong, the city lacks an obvious mentor for the next generation of startups and founders. Lalamove could go public in the coming years, according to Larson, and if it did, he said "It would be a great opportunity to be one of the first, if not the first…and be a symbol for the community to show it is possible to build a global technology company from Hong Kong."

Case Analysis

Hong Kong's gazelles face even more considerable challenges than do those in Paris. For example, Hong Kong's local market is much smaller; there are even fewer successful technology companies that can serve as local examples of startup success, despite government efforts to change this; the local culture pushes young people into jobs with high, steady salaries; and there is very little capital available for local startups. Until Hong Kong enjoys a prominent, successful exit, chances are good that the ranks of its mentor network will be thinly populated. Until then, aspiring entrepreneurs will need to rent the mentor networks of other regions.

Principles

A city of gazelles without pillars has more access to potential mentors than a city at Level 0 on the Pillar Company Staircase. After all, that city's gazelles are likely to have raised capital from venture capitalist and angels who have valuable experience that could help its startups to grow. In such regions, entrepreneurs should recognize which questions they are not well equipped to answer and to find the best mentors to help them answer those questions effectively. In the cases of both Paris and Hong Kong, entrepreneurs may also need to avoid spending too much time with mentors supplied by the government since they may take up more time than they are worth.

Level 2: No Pillars, Acquired Gazelles

Success Case Study: Three Stockholm Startups Win Local Mentors

Introduction

The more entrepreneurial success a city enjoys, the deeper its pool of local mentors. If a city has hosted many gazelles, some of which have been acquired, then the founding teams of the acquired gazelles are likely to have gained valuable experience and a significant boost to their net worth. Local entrepreneurs seeking to match or exceed the success of these fortunate individuals could benefit greatly from their advice. And in Stockholm, such mentors are busy helping those who are in the earlier stages of their entrepreneurial journey.

Case Scenario

Three companies founded by KTH affiliates have followed similar paths to build the mentor networks they need to grow. The companies, the last two of which you first saw in Chapter 3, are

- *Mano Motion, a maker of software that enables smartphone cameras to capture 3D hand gestures and whose CEO is a serial entrepreneur;*

- *Greenely, an app that tracks home energy usage; and*

- *Shortcut Labs, a maker of wireless smart buttons that offer physical shortcuts to digital functions in mobile devices.*

Mano Motion

Mano Motion's CEO, Daniel Carlman, was a ship engineer who studied Computer Information Systems and Finance at Hawaii Pacific University, developed a mobile banking application for a bank, founded a gaming company, and ended up as an executive at online gambling company Unibet. As he explained in a September 17, 2017 interview, from there he returned to Stockholm with his daughter to start a health technology company and in 2015 joined, at the request of an accelerator, KTH Innovation. In 2010, Mano Motion's cofounders, Dr. Shahrouz Yousefi and Professor Haibo Li, "started their research on hand gesture analysis" resulting in a patent application related to how to track hand gestures accurately on a small screen. Carlman was seen by KTH Innovation as an entrepreneur who could help turn the idea into a business. When Carlman met Yousefi and Li, they said "Daniel, we want to change the world and make technology more natural and intuitive to interact with." Carlman agreed with their mission and believed that the future of human/computer interaction would combine vision, voice, and gestures that interpret human intent. Until June 2017, Mano Motion was building prototypes to get customer validation. Carlman built a team of 14 people from 10 different countries by hiring KTH students studying for a Master's or PhD in deep learning, computer vision, or human/computer interaction. Mano Motion also recruited from National University of Singapore, Linnaeus University in Sweden, George Washington University, and UCLA.

Carlman tried to build a mentor network but was somewhat overwhelmed by the challenges of finding the right people. As he said in a September 2017 interview, "We had great support from our previous network, spanning both from the business side and from the University side. Early on we got an opportunity to be part of an American accelerator called founder.org based in San Francisco. This gave us very useful insights from other participating entrepreneurs and great mentors who shared their experience. We are also as a team actively looking for new knowledge as we expand and run into new challenges. In my opinion, we need a team of mentors that can help us in many different situations. I constantly find myself in new situations that require a skillset I do not yet master and there is not always time to find the right people to ask. Often you need to put the determination and persistence to push through and learn along the way. You need to be able to trust your team members and let everyone do what they do best."

By September 2017, Mano Motion had signed over 20 Non-Disclosure Agreements with potential partners and received over 1,000 requests from developers who want to build applications using its technology. Developers and companies can try Mano Motion's applications at no charge but must pay for a commercial license. Carlman intends to open a Palo Alto office in 2018 to perform the company's sales and marketing, and will likely hire from Stanford. Mano Motion also intends to open another sales and marketing office in Asia to target Hong Kong and Shanghai. By the end of 2018, he expects Mano Motion to employ over 30 people.

Greenely

Tanmoy Bari, who studied Civil Engineering and earned an M.Sc in Sustainable Urban Planning and Design at KTH, had an idea while working on his thesis project of consulting to a smart city called the Stockholm Royal Seaport. Instead of building a computer system, which the large utilities proposed, he wanted to use data directly from the electrical grid to track household energy usage, which became the core idea behind Greenely. As Bari explained in a September 2017 interview, he officially launched Greenely in February 2014 after competing in Venture Cup, a business plan competition. In 2016, Greenely recorded about $130,000 in revenue and planned to double that to $260,000 in 2017, serving over 6,000 households and three large utilities. Greenely's 11 full-time employees have skills in energy and electricity, business development, product development, and marketing. Many of its people came from KTH, and Bari also worked with headhunters in the UK and

Sweden for key positions such as Product Manager and Chief Technology Officer. Bari wants to recruit "quite a few people in the future; specifically, more administrative staff and a Human Resources manager; a psychologist and a behavioral scientist; and skilled coders and business developers from universities in Sweden (Stockholm and Gothenburg) and California (Stanford, UC Berkeley, and Caltech)." Greenely relied on KTH for mentorship. "KTH Innovation and KIC InnoEnergy, the accelerators that we were incubated under, had several mentors that were really helpful to our company. The first business coach, Donnie Lygonis from KTH, helped us through a lot. Everything between building a sustainable business model to getting the first cooperation agreements signed to getting access to VC firms in Silicon Valley. I still carry a relationship with him today," said Bari.

Shortcut Labs

Shortcut Labs cofounder and CEO Joacim Westlund, who in 2010 earned a M.Sc. in Design and Product Realization with Naval Architecture from KTH and then designed sailing yachts in New Zealand, could not sit still. As he said in a September 2017 interview, "I had several positions as a project management consultant and product manager. I was a consultant to larger companies such as Scania and some Swedish banks. My last employment was as a Product and Process Manager at SecMaker, a small Swedish IT security firm. I shifted jobs once a year, never quite found rest until I started my own thing." What he started was a company that made a button attached to his smartphone that would help him quit tobacco. As he explained, "I had several side projects when I was employed. One of them was an iPhone app to help people and myself to quit snus (a Swedish form of tobacco). The idea was to tap a big green button in the app when I took a snus so that I could monitor my intake. But doing that at least once every hour, it was too cumbersome to pick up the phone, unlock it, find the app and tap that single button each time. The idea grew to extract the button out of the phone into something physical, and that's how Flic was born. I kept imagining how much could be done with a wireless button." He continued: "In 2012, I made a functional prototype and made it work with my snus-app, showing it around in the vivid Stockholm startup scene at different events. An advisor encouraged me to apply for innovation grants, and after receiving two rounds of soft funding, I decided to quit my job and engage co-founders Amir Sharifat, an extremely productive and organized executive who dropped out of production engineering studies to join as COO, and Pranav Kosuri, who complements my product design and weak social skills with an incredible charisma, networking skills, and a great stage presence to do sales."

Shortcut Labs launched a crowdfunding campaign at the end of 2014 and since then it has sold and shipped over 200,000 units to roughly 100,000 users around the world with 20 employees, including an amazing team of software engineers who worked on Flic as part of a software development course on KTH, and annual revenue of about $1.5 million and growing quickly. Shortcut aims to hire a designer, hardware and software engineers, and senior business development people whom

Westlund believes the company can find in Stockholm and Asia from companies such as Autodesk, Salesforce, Dropbox, and ESI Group. Shortcut Labs needed mentoring in every activity except engineering and has found mentors in Stockholm and San Francisco. "Over time, we've needed mentoring in pretty much every field except engineering. Since founding, we have had support from an experienced lawyer, a business contact of Pranavs. I don't know how we would have made it without that support. But for all other fields, we always found good advice and mentoring from all the different incubators we've been through: Start-up Stockholm, KTH Incubator, Highway1, Hardware Club, EIT Digital, and 500 Startups. Perhaps Highway1 had the most applicable advice at the time, in pitching, hardware development, logistics, crowdfunding, and entrepreneurship in general. From that time in San Francisco, we've also maintained a lot of contacts; experienced mentors and business advisors that we ping from time to time," Westlund said.

Case Analysis

Sweden has had remarkable startup success given its small population. An important reason for this success is KTH's talent, which has produced start-ups that enjoyed successful exits. Most of the founders from these successful KTH startups are happy to mentor newer entrepreneurs, especially those affiliated with KTH. Moreover, the successful exits have drawn in venture investors from outside Stockholm who are eager for a chance to earn high investment returns by financing newer startups there. And along with their capital, these venture capitalists offer their expertise in helping startups to scale. These three case studies suggest that many Stockholm entrepreneurs are finding the mentors they need, and if some of those companies enjoy successful exits, those mentor networks will expand.

Principles

Entrepreneurs operating in cities with acquired gazelles are likely to enjoy a good supply of mentors from various sources. In Stockholm, those sources include outside venture capitalists, previously successful entrepreneurs, and professors and colleagues from KTH. The entrepreneurs profiled above demonstrate the intellectual humility needed to recognize the questions for which they need help to answer and the ability to seek out and build relationships with mentors who can help them get the right answers.

Level 3: Some Pillars in Niche Markets

Success Case Study: Boston Founders Pay It Forward Through Mentor Networks

Introduction

A city with some pillars in niche markets develops a culture that perpetuates itself. Locally successful entrepreneurs aspire to stay in the game—and share their know-how with founders who aspire to their own success—by mentoring the younger generation. Aspiring entrepreneurs in these regions are aided significantly by these mentors. However, they are also screened for their consistency with the region's startup values. For example, in Boston, investors tend to fund entrepreneurs who are solving relatively narrow and difficult technical problems affecting business information technology departments. The successful CEOs who provide mentoring are likely to help out entrepreneurs with similar skills and aspirations. As a result, there is a chance that the region will continue to host some pillars targeting niche markets.

Case Scenario

This comes to mind in considering two CEOs in the Boston area who achieved success—and provided and received mentoring as they sought to build their latest startups. One of these Boston mentors is Paul English, who co-founded Kayak, which he took public and sold to Priceline for $2 billion in May 2013. After selling Kayak, English started an incubator called Blade, which ran for about two years, and beginning in July 2015, has been running Lola, which operates a mobile app that "connects you instantly to a travel professional who will help you plan, book, and manage travel." He's also a senior lecturer at MIT's Sloan School of Management. As English, whose net worth The New York Times estimates at $120 million, told me in an August 2017 interview that he has passion for helping other people through mentoring, some of whom are Boston area entrepreneurs.

While English was trained as a computer scientist and started as a coder, his skills at hiring and motivating people struck me as particularly strong. And just as he now mentors younger entrepreneurs, he searched for mentors when he started founding companies. "Earlier in my career I would look for someone who was not my boss— maybe my boss's boss or a peer or someone outside the company. Scott Cook, who co-founded Intuit, continues to be my mentor," English said. He thinks mentoring helped make him a better manager. "Mentors helped me understand that when working with a co-founder, it is better to split a startup's equity 50/50 because when things get challenging you will both be highly motivated to find a solution. In managing a team, I learned that it is critical to be as transparent as possible—letting your team know what you are excited about and what worries you. Such transparency encourages your team to try to solve the CEO's problems, which leads to better ideas. In managing board members and investors, I learned that it is important to take their advice only in areas where they have expertise and to use them as a sounding board, rather than going to board meetings in fear of what they will ask you to do. Finally, mentors helped me appreciate how important it is to seize every customer interaction as a learning opportunity, so I ask Lola engineers to respond to customer support issues," he said.

English has mentored many entrepreneurs including the following four, one of whom is in San Francisco and the other three who are Boston-area entrepreneurs. Vinayak Ranade, a Buffalo, New York native who spent most of his childhood in India before returning to the U.S. to earn bachelor's and master's degrees in electrical engineering and computer science at MIT, was CEO of Drafted, a startup that helped companies hire more employees through internal and external referrals, which is far more effective, less costly, and quicker than hiring them through headhunters. As Ranade explained in an Aug 2017 interview, "I was about to accept a job at a New York hedge fund when a friend suggested I meet Paul. I contacted him by email and heard back almost immediately. Twelve hours after that, I met Paul's team at Kayak. I was not particularly interested in the travel search space, but after meeting Kayak's VPs of Technology and Engineering and its Chief Architect, I was totally hooked. I loved everyone I met; they were insanely amazing, smart, and I just wanted to be around them." English mentored Ranade through his example and coaching, teaching him the importance of hiring the best team. "I joined Kayak because of the people. The best teams—because of complementary skills, diverse backgrounds, and chemistry—win. At Kayak, I ran operations for technical recruiting and was director of mobile engineering. I started Drafted at the end of 2014 after Priceline bought Kayak. I reached out to Paul for help and found him to be way more accessible than most successful, rich, tech people," Ranade explained.

Sara Wood, in August 2017 a VP of Product Management at Gap, met English through her work with the nonprofit Partners in Health, where he is a trustee. As Wood told me in an August 2017 interview, "I have been getting authentic advice from Paul since 2005. He gave me advice on scaling companies, the legal obligations of an executive, and how to read the capitalization tables in a Series F fundraising to ask tighter questions. He's helped me raise money by serving as a reference for investors conducting due diligence. And he's helped me to give better performance reviews to build trust on both sides. He would write three words on a piece of paper and tell someone 'This is not on the record, but here is what's expected, how you're doing, and how well am I helping you get there.' He also taught me the importance of thinking and being like the customer."

Founded in 2011, Wanderu operates an app that let its four million monthly users find the best bus and train transportation options. Wanderu was growing threefold a year, had raised $8 million in venture capital, and employed 50 people—up from three in August 2013. As CEO Polina Raygorodskaya explained in an August 2017 interview, "When we started Wanderu, Paul helped me to understand why branding was important and how Kayak built its brand. He also introduced me to his VP of Engineering to find out how they integrated with their partners."

David Cancel has started five companies, including co-founding Compete, which London market research firm TNS acquired in 2008 for up to $150 million. As he said in August 2017, "Mentoring is a way for humans to simulate how they might act by using other people's 10, 20, or 30 years of experience to model where the might want to be in the future. Paul helped me to learn the importance of people, particularly recruiting experienced people in areas like sales leadership and finance. By taking a long view of how I can help them achieve their career goals, I have gotten better at overcoming the challenges of hiring such people."

CEOs who are leading larger companies face different challenges and need mentoring for addressing different challenges that stand in the way of achieving their growth goals. A case in point is Derek Langone, CEO of XebiaLabs, a maker of software that helps companies develop software more effectively. In an October 2017 interview, Langone said he was benefiting from the expertise of executives who achieved great success and are now "paying it forward" by mentoring Langone, who is himself mentoring others. XebiaLabs was in the so-called DevOps market (software that helps companies develop and test new computer applications) which IT consultant Gartner estimated would reach $2.3 billion in 2015. By October 2017, Xebia had raised $21.5 million in capital in two rounds and had produced "triple digit year-over-year growth for the past three years." Langone explained to me in a March 2017 interview that the company was spun out of a Netherlands-based software consulting firm in 2009. The company's chief technology officer, Vincent Partington, had developed tools to automate labor-intensive code writing and testing. Langone became CEO in 2015 to apply his skills in operations and scaling to XebiaLabs, thus accelerating its growth. In March, he said that there was a big opportunity for the company because the DevOps market will "accelerate five-fold in the next three years." XebiaLabs aspired to help companies in industries such as financial services, retailing, and airlines to build and get their customer-facing applications to market faster and at a lower cost.

Here are three ways that mentoring has helped Langone lead Xebia's rapid growth:

- **Avoid dead-end growth vectors.** Mentors have helped Langone avoid the mistake of interpreting what competitors are not doing as a growth opportunity. As he said, "Mentors have been through multiple cycles and they can help me avoid mistakes they've made. For example, in the past I might have looked at what competitors are not doing and think that it's an opportunity. Mentors suggested I not assume that competitors overlooked it, and instead consider that they might have done research and concluded it was a bad idea. That perspective saved me from making a multimillion dollar investment" that would have been a mistake.

- ***Manage board relationships.*** Mentors also helped him manage his board. As Langone explained, "A board of directors is made up of successful people. But I used to think that all I had to do to keep them happy was make the numbers. My mentors showed me that I should spend time explaining where we are going, why we are doing it, what our long game is. Getting their input is valuable and it makes it easier for them to see that our growth is repeatable and we are on the path together."

- ***Grow and exit.*** Mentoring is an investment in the local startup scene. As he said, "Walter Scott of [storage management companies] Imceda and Acronis scaled his companies quickly and exited. He has great advice on work ethic, growth strategy, and how to motivate a team when inevitable challenges arise. The Boston area has a huge supply of mentors who have had tremendous success and are winding down. They are willing to make time for stewardship and handing off the baton. When I interact with them, I tell them how their advice worked out before so they know the time they spend with me is worth it."

Case Analysis

The success of the Boston/Cambridge startup scene has spurred a robust mentor network that helps younger entrepreneurs to overcome the challenges they encounter on their way to achieving their growth goals. The region's mentor network is part of a self-perpetuating system, along with the values of local venture investors, that tends to support companies that solve difficult technical problems for companies. As long as these companies can grow to the point where they enjoy successful exits, local venture capitalists should benefit and local mentor networks will be refreshed. The biggest challenge facing the Boston/Cambridge startup scene is that these kinds of companies are becoming an increasingly small part of the global startup scene. Therefore, the region could be in need of a jolt of new startup energy.

Less Successful Case Study: Israel's Mentor Networks Remain a Work in Progress

Introduction

Israel has its share of pillar companies in smaller industries such as information security. And those pillars, along with acquired gazelles, have produced successful founders who in theory could provide mentoring to aspiring entrepreneurs. Yet in practice, Israel's mentor networks seem to be relatively unorganized. That could be in part because many founders do not believe that they need mentoring; they are simply seeking money from angel investors. Yet Israel also is home to founders who do see the need for mentoring, and they tend to create their own networks both from Israeli entrepreneurs and from mentors in the U.S. or Europe—or they move to the U.S. in order to get access to customers, talent, and capital, and seek our local mentors to help them navigate there.

Case Scenario

Mentor networks are not as developed in Israel as they are in the U.S. As Uri Goldberg, an expert on Israel's high tech ecosystem, told me in August 2017, "There is a growing network of angel investors in Israel. But many startup CEOs wonder what value besides capital these angels can add. The CEOs tell the angels, 'thanks for your capital; leave me be.' I know a few investors who really believe they are going to be good mentors. But it is hard to match founders with mentors [who truly add value]."

Compared to Silicon Valley, not as many Israeli entrepreneurs have built unicorn-sized companies. As Dror Berman of Israel's Innovation Endeavors said in 2015, "Over the growth stages in particular, Israeli entrepreneurs need access to mentors that can deliver contextual insights and ask tough questions about scaling up in the United States." U.S. mentors the relevant growth-stage investors and investment bankers and can help with an IPO or acquisition, The U.S. also has more companies and MBA programs that train managers. Since most Israeli entrepreneurs have not built a company from start to exit, those who have are valuable.

A Tel Aviv-based maker of software that helps control autonomous vehicles has built a global mentor network. As Igal Raichelgauz, cofounder and CEO of Cortica, explained in an October 2017 interview, before starting the company he served in the signal intelligence section of the Israel Defense Force's 8200 unit. In his last year there, he worked in a short messaging service startup that "got a lot of traffic and was an interesting experience, but not a success." From there he went to the Technion where he worked with electrical engineering professor Yehoshua Zeevi and at Intel. In 2007, he cofounded Cortica to do "deep learning and computational neuroscience. We saw a major explosion in the flat model of unsupervised learning. Now we have over 100 employees, mostly PhDs, have raised $60 million in venture capital from Li Ka-shing and Samsung among others, have 200 patents, and are licensing our technology to autonomous vehicle companies. We are the brains behind autonomous vehicles. We help sensors to recognize what is in the vehicle's environment and predict what will happen in the next few seconds. For example, a car is going forward and the sensor sees a ball on the road. Our software predicts that a child is going to be there [to retrieve the ball] and recommends that the car should stop. We will grow through development partnerships. And we have found different mentors in different domains. Professor Zeevi provides mentoring in technology and strategy. We have an advisor who was vice chair of GM who helps with automation strategy and others that help in financial strategy and building the company's value long-term. Most of the mentors are from outside Israel since most Israelis do not have business strategy expertise. Our outside mentors also help us tap global markets in the U.S. and Asia."

CyberArk, a $217 million (2016 sales) maker of information security software, has been a leader in moving to Boston and an outlier in going public (in September 2014) instead of being acquired, a common path for Israeli companies. As CEO Udi Mokady explained in August 2017, "Israelis need somebody local to get help in the first couple of steps in coming to Boston. Eyal Shavit, an angel investor, was in Boston and he helped arrange for Seed Capital Partners (part of Softbank) to invest in us. Now that we have gone public, we are well-known in Israel and help bring startups here." Now CyberArk mentors other Israeli companies that want to move to Boston. As Ukady said, the nature of that advice is "20% technical and 80% business. I provide non-commercial help to Israeli companies with technical matters like office location and providing employee healthcare, which is new for Israel since the government there provides healthcare for everyone." A common business question is how to manage Israeli R&D from Boston. "I also tell them that they may need to leave a technical founder behind in Israel to make sure the R&D team is well managed. I tell them that whoever is in charge of the Israel operations should be a person of integrity, which can be known from prior joint mileage, with the ability to lead. In our case, we appointed someone who had demonstrated leadership in the Israeli Defense Forces," said Mokady.

Being in Boston helps Cyberark in many ways. "Here we are embedded with our most strategic group of customers. We have access to talented people from the universities for our technical services and inside sales departments who come in as interns and join us full time," Mokady noted. And unlike many Israeli companies, CyberArk went public rather than being acquired. As he said, "Many Israeli companies find it too hard to scale to the point where they can go public because they do not have the sales and marketing executive talent to create a strong brand. Our customers told us that we were mission critical for their operations so that they wanted us to go public to remain independent. To do that, we were able to hire the marketing talent here and got our final round of investment from Goldman Sachs which was balance sheet money." To be sure, CyberArk still has its R&D operation in Israel; however, it is currently integrating its acquisition of Conjur, a DevOps security software developer. "The company moved to Newton, Mass. from Waltham so now we have some R&D in the U.S.," said Mokady.

Case Analysis

Israel's startup scene has expanded tremendously in the course of a few decades. In so doing, it has followed a well-established formula of designing and building products that offer customers irresistible value. While the R&D skills reside in Israel, the marketing, sales, and capital-raising talent lives in the U.S., mostly in Silicon Valley or Boston. The Israeli founders may move to the

U.S. and then seek to sell the company once it has grown large enough to provide a meaningful exit value to the founders and investors. In so doing, Israel develops talented entrepreneurs who can advise the next generation. The problem is that while Israeli entrepreneurs can build a product and scale to exit, they do not develop the skills required to run a publicly traded company. Until more Israeli entrepreneurs can start companies, take them public, and keep them growing, Israel's mentor network will keep Israel from stepping up to the top of the Pillar Company Staircase.

Principles

Cities with some pillars in niche markets host mentors from many sources. And entrepreneurs who operate in such cities generally have little difficulty finding the mentors they need to overcome the hurdles that separate their startups from a successful exit. The cases we saw in this chapter suggest that local entrepreneurs can identify the domains in which they need a mentor's help and can find the right person to help them based on the industry and the problem domain. The challenge for entrepreneurs in these locations is that the local mentor networks may not be able to help them build a huge pillar company that targets very large markets. Therefore, such entrepreneurs may be better off locating their startups in Level 4 cities.

Level 4: Many Pillars in Huge Markets
Success Case Study: Silicon Valley Turns an Engineer into a Great Startup CEO

Introduction

Mentoring is most highly developed in regions with many pillars in huge markets. Why do very successful entrepreneurs give away their time and valuable advice for free? One Silicon Valley CEO, Mike Bergelson, whose business, named Everwise, connects mentors and protégées, gave four reasons to become a mentor. As Bergelson explained in a May 2013 interview, he founded Audium, a New York City software company that Cisco acquired in 2006. Begelson then moved to California as a Cisco executive. He left Cisco and tried to come up with ideas for a company but Everwise did not gel until 2012 when Bergelson discussed these ideas with Maynard Webb, his mentor, whose Webb Investment Network (WIN) offers "young entrepreneurs seed capital, mentorship, and on-demand access to experts." Thanks to his conversations with Webb, Bergelson decided to focus solely on mentoring. As he explained, "Maynard asked questions that made me realize that I had a passion for creating a way for corporate protégés to find mentors and that addressing that need could be a big opportunity."

Bergelson knew firsthand how commonly big companies miss the opportunity to match protégés with mentors. That's because when he was working for one of those big companies, he was given the name of his mentor. That person never responded to Bergelson's email suggesting a meeting. A few weeks later, the mentor quit and the company never gave Bergelson another. Still, Bergelson believed mentoring was a great way for big companies like his former employer to develop talent. A study by a former Sun Microsystems executive found that employees who received mentoring were five times more likely to be promoted. And a study of successful people like Warren Buffett found that the second most important reason they believe they've been successful is great mentors (Buffett's was Benjamin Graham). Everwise developed an algorithm that contributed to a "96% match satisfaction rate." Assuming that's true, Bergelson should be an authority on why people agree to serve as mentors. Here are his four top reasons:

- **Give back.** Successful people I've interviewed often say that they were helped early in their career by someone who had achieved greatness. Now they believe that they should "pay it forward." But why do they feel that way? Some feel that they are repaying a debt to future generations; others believe that if their advice helps a younger person, it will make a little piece of them immortal; still others see mentoring as going back in a time machine and giving a younger version of themselves the advice that they wish they had received. This last reason highlights the importance of matching the right mentor and protégé. After all, if a mentor finds a young person with similar life experiences, such as emigrating from Chile or competing in triathlons, it will strengthen the feeling of giving back to a younger version of herself.

- **Learn from process.** Bergelson said that many mentors learn through the process of teaching others and they find that mentoring makes them better leaders. He said that 94% of mentors agree to repeat their experience because they "take away a lot from the process."

- **Meet new people.** Mentors also like the idea of meeting new people whom they can add to their "I knew when" list. After all, who doesn't like the idea of bragging to associates that they knew [currently famous person X] before they became successful? For mentors with this motive, there is also a potential financial benefit. The protégé might offer the mentor an opportunity to invest in an early-stage venture. And if that happens, the mentor may not only get bragging rights but a big slug of cash when he sells stock in the now successful venture.

- **Get exposed to new ideas.** Protégés also expose mentors to new ideas. For example, the protégé might discuss how her company is using a new approach to innovation, pricing, or customer service. Mentors may be able to apply some of these best practices to their own activities. People are willing to mentor for free because they already have, in the context of Maslow's Hierarchy of Needs, met their physiological and safety needs and now seek esteem and self-actualization. Mentoring is a way to get there.

Case Scenario

In Silicon Valley, mentors can play a role that's critical for enriching venture capital firms: helping a world-class engineer become a great CEO. A case in point is an engineer who cofounded a company, leaving it to start another company before the first one went public in 2016. That engineer was eager to learn how to become a successful CEO and worked with mentors to develop some new skills, such as hiring excellent sales people, communicating about his product's benefits (rather than its technical features), and getting introductions to potential customers. In October 2017, I spoke with the CEO-in-training Mohit Aron who cofounded San Jose, Calif.-based storage hardware maker Nutanix, which lost $458 million on revenues of $767 million in fiscal 2017, according to Morningstar. Aron left Nutanix before its October 2016 IPO to found Santa Clara, Calif.-based Cohesity, a maker of so-called hyperconverged secondary storage (HCSS). In April 2017, Cohesity received a $90 million capital injection from Silicon Valley stalwarts such as Sequoia Capital and GV (formerly known as Google Ventures). Cohesity board member and retired CEO and Executive Chairman of storage technology supplier NetApp Dan Warmenhoven (one of Aron's mentors) was far more optimistic about Cohesity than he was about Nutanix. His success so far indicates that Aron is a world-class engineer. Here are three ways that mentoring was turning him into a CEO:

- **Hire great sales people.** *An engineer like Aron might be prone to hire sales people using the same approach that helps him bring on board great engineers. But that is not a good policy; sales people need to be hired in a different way. Warmenhoven pointed out in an April 2017 interview that Cohesity's market was large ($60 billion) and its competition is fragmented, including companies like Data Domain, which EMC acquired in July 2009 by snatching it away from NetApp, and startups such as Rubrik. Warmenhoven was excited about the chance to mentor Aron, who had never been a CEO. As Warmenhoven explained, "Mohit is a world-renowned engineer. He developed Google's file system. He is brilliant and was asking for advice on how to be successful as a CEO. He has a great personality, is anxious to learn, and has a good heart; he wants to help his people develop and create products that*

improve his customers' operations. He will be a great CEO."
Indeed Aron acknowledged his opportunities to develop into
a CEO and how Warmenhoven helped him. In an October 3,
2017 interview, Aron said, "Before I started Cohesity, I was an
engineer. I don't know how to go to market. Dan has a passion
for mentoring. He gives me organizational advice on sales and
marketing. He is teaching me the job of the CEO. He was just
here yesterday for an hour and a half, and two weeks ago
as well. He asks deep questions and seems to be reliving his
NetApp experience." One specific area where Aron needed
help was in interviewing potential sales people for Cohesity. As
he said, "[Dan made me realize] that I was interviewing sales
people like engineers. He helped me interview sales people to
identify red flags early on and to test for a culture match. He
made me realize that I should not check the references that
the candidate gives me. I should check with peers and people
who reported to him to seek neutral references."

- **Win customers by framing product features as benefits.** Engineers are excited to talk about their technical achieve-
  ments. But executives don't care about technology unless it
  helps them achieve business goals. This means that an aspiring CEO must learn how to frame features in terms of their
  business benefits. Aron also respected Warmenhoven's ability
  to help him "position the company to potential customers."
  Warmenhoven explained Cohesity's competitive advantages
  as follows: "Cohesity's revenue per sales rep per year is about
  $4 million whereas for Nutanix, the comparable figure is $2.5
  million. The difference is that Cohesity has a high-volume
  product that targets the 70 percent of enterprise storage budgets
  that go to the core data centers. By contrast, Nutanix delivers
  specialized solutions to regional data centers, rather than the core."

- **Network to get in front of potential customers.** If a
  company is going to grow, the CEO must identify potential
  customers and get them to sign up. A key step in that process
  is getting introductions to decision-makers. Mentors can help
  with that task. And Aron was also grateful to another mentor, Carl Eschenbach, who cofounded Palo Alto, Calif.-based
  VMWare, "a global leader in cloud infrastructure and business
  mobility," and served as its chief operating officer between
  2011 and 2016 before joining Sequoia as a partner. Aron said
  that Eschenbach also helped Cohesity with "go to market,"
  for example, by introducing him to potential customers such
  as "a large Chicago-based financial institution."

Aron's success shows the value and scarcity of world-class engineering talent. Indeed, Silicon Valley's startup scene is set up to provide capital, talent, and mentoring to such individuals. And what makes Aron most exceptional is that he seems to have the intellectual humility needed to see his strengths and weaknesses objectively and to realize that there is no shame in getting outside help to bolster the CEO skills he needs to develop.

Case Analysis

The Cohesity case demonstrates how Silicon Valley provides crucial mentoring to engineers who can design and build world-class products that solve big problems. Such mentoring can turn engineers into CEOs and such CEOs can vastly enrich local startup investors. Of course, not all great engineers can become great CEOs. To do that, these engineers must possess reasonably strong interpersonal skills, deep intellectual humility coupled with a willingness to identify their weaknesses and a willingness to learn, and the sky-high ambition and work ethic required to overcome big obstacles to growing a startup into a public company. Silicon Valley's mentor network can help such a CEO close his or her capability gaps.

Failure Case Study: Unicorn CEO Decries Lack of Silicon Valley Mentoring and Four Years Later He's Fired for Sexual Harassment

Introduction

Not all Silicon Valley CEOs are happy with the state of its mentor networks. Indeed, one very successful founder decried the lack of mentoring in December 2012. In December 2014, I invested in his company and by March 2017, it had raised $1.9 billion from venture investors including SoftBank, Silver Lake, Temasek, GIC, GPI, Third Point, IVP, Peter Thiel, DCM, Renren, and Baseline, and was valued at $4.3 billion. Sadly it was not until August 2017 that I learned that SoFi was the plaintiff in lawsuits alleging widespread sexual harassment among other problematic conduct. About a month later, as details emerged in press, that CEO was fired from the company. This outcome leaves a big open question: Was there any connection between what the CEO perceived as a lack of mentoring in Silicon Valley and the conduct that led to his dismissal?

Case Scenario

The former CEO in question is Mike Cagney, a former Wells Fargo executive with a Master's in Management from Stanford Business School who ran a hedge fund for a decade and in June 2011 cofounded Social Finance (SoFi) with some of his Stanford classmates. SoFi's initial focus was arranging for successful alumni of top universities to help current students refinance their student loans at lower rates. In June 2017, SoFi said that it had funded $3.1 billion in loans in the quarter, generating over $134 million in revenue, having lent over $20 billion to over 350,000 borrowers between its founding and that quarter. In December 2012, Cagney raised $77 million from China's RenRen, and he pointed out that due to the large number of extremely wealthy individuals in Silicon Valley, there was ample angel capital available for a startup's seed stage, but a dearth of money for companies that had burned through their seed capital and needed the next level of funding, the so-called Series A round. The reason for the dearth of such capital is that the venture capital firms that provided it in the past had not generated spectacular investment returns for their limited partners in recent years. As a result, these venture capitalists were struggling to raise new rounds of capital from their limited partners who did not believe that the potential returns of providing that mid-level capital was worth the risk of loss. As Cagney explained, "The $5 million to $10 million dollar check just isn't out there like it used to be. However, it is not hard to raise $500,000 seed capital and ironically it is not hard to go out and get a $25 million to $30 million dollar Series B at a $100 million valuation. What is hard is getting that $5 million to $10 million Series A."

Cagney argued that angel investors did not offer first-time startup CEOs the advice they needed because they lacked prior experience making the right decisions required to build the company. Cagney argued that many start-up CEOs need mentorship to make those decisions properly but most angel investors pursued an investment strategy of placing many bets, assuming most of them would be losers and hoping that one or two would be big winners that would more than offset their losses from the losers. As Cagney explained, "There are too many startups that are seed financed and not enough people willing to give them time and focus. If you've come out of school, you've never started a business before, you go into a start-up and you don't even know what to ask someone. You don't even know you need mentorship. And by the time you've figured it out, it is too late in the process."

Indeed, Cagney believed that investors do not want to hear about the CEO's problems, they just want the CEO to multiply their money. And listening to a CEO's challenges is more likely to make investors think about replacing that CEO with one who reports ever-better results at each board meeting. Some start-up CEOs seek out others in their position for advice. But in Cagney's experience, it is rare that other CEOs are inclined or have the time to help out their peers. As Cagney explained, "The most important thing to a venture capitalist is returns. That focus often comes at the expense of developing the human capital in the companies they fund." While Cagney considered himself lucky to have engaged investors, he noted the lack of support from other entrepreneurs. "I'm guilty of this as well. I try to be responsive to requests for help, but these often get pushed down the queue as day-to-day business is all-consuming. And I feel it the other way; I have folks I can ask for help, but I can't ask them too much without becoming a burden. We're all facing similar challenges in building our businesses, and could learn from one another. At one point, this was the role of the early-stage venture capitalist: to facilitate best practices. With less 'A-round' firms out there, it just doesn't happen enough."

But Cagney's luck ran out when a former SoFi employee sued the company, alleging that he had been fired for reporting sexual harassment of female coworkers and allegations of impropriety in the handling of loans and loan applications. The lawsuit was filed by Brandon Charles who, according The New York Times, *only worked at a SoFi loan processing office for a few months. During that time, the lawsuit claimed that Charles's manager used "explicit sexual innuendo" when speaking, and made "lewd, sexualized gestures" when referring to female employees. Charles claims he was fired after reporting the behavior and was told that reporting it to his supervisors was outside of his "appropriate duties." A spokesman for SoFi told the* Times *that an internal investigation had found Charles' claims to have "no merit." However, on September 12, 2017 the* Times *reported on "accusations from more than 30 current and former employees who said he [Cagney] had treated women inappropriately and had aggressively taken on risk to accelerate the company's growth." Three days later, Cagney was fired from SoFi.*

Case Analysis

Silicon Valley leads the world in startup success. As a result, it has the most highly developed mentor networks. However, the SoFi case raises some troubling questions about these mentors. Do they care so much about rapid growth and increasing the value of their investments that they disregard whether CEOs violate social norms in the process? If Mike Cagney's rise and fall was an isolated case, it would certainly be easier to place all the blame on him. But there are many other examples of such misconduct in Silicon Valley, most notably that of Travis Kalanick, founder and former CEO of Uber. The good news is that more Silicon Valley mentors seem to act in a positive way than these prominent cases of mentor networks tolerating bad behavior.

Principles

Cities with many pillars in huge markets have the full spectrum of mentors illustrated in Figure 6-1. An entrepreneur who has raised capital in such cities is likely to have access to some of the world's most skilled mentors for helping them through the challenges of leading their startup to a successful exit. Not all such entrepreneurs will have the right personality to take full advantage of those mentor networks. For example, if such entrepreneurs are arrogant and resist being coached, then they may end up making mistakes that their more humble peers will avoid.

Table 6-1 below summarizes the principles for each step in the Pillar Company Staircase.

Table 6-1. Principles by Step in Pillar Company Staircase

Pillar Company Stair	Principles
Level 0	Use entrepreneurial leadership skills to build regional mentor network.
Level 1	Draw selectively on government-supplied mentors while building your own mentor network.
Level 2	Go global to overcome weakness of local mentor networks.
Level 3	Encourage local CEOs to mentor next generation leaders.
Level 4	Match successful entrepreneurs/investors as board members with high potential engineers.

Are You Doing Enough To Build Local Mentor Networks?

Here are four tests of whether a region is deepening its mentor networks:

- Are local entrepreneurs sufficiently humble that they recognize problems they can't solve themselves and find mentors who can help?

- Are successful entrepreneurs staying near cities where their startups were headquartered and helping out younger entrepreneurs?

- Are venture capitalists and angel investors providing mentoring to local entrepreneurs?

- Once those young entrepreneurs achieve success, do they stay in the region and mentor the next generation of entrepreneurs?

Conclusion

A region's mentor networks are an important factor in an entrepreneur's decision about where to locate a startup. Founders who hope to be geographically close to mentor networks should start their companies in cities that host many successful startups that participate in their industry. If founders can obtain the help they need from mentors who are further away, they may be best off locating their companies in the cities with sufficient capital and talent to fuel their growth. In Chapter 7, we will explore the role that a region's values play in boosting (or impeding) a region's level of startup activity.

Creating Startup-Friendly Shared Values

Different cities have different attitudes towards startups. These differing attitudes steer the conduct of the region's stakeholders. For example, if a city's professors are rewarded for moving between the classroom and helping start companies that bring their ideas to the marketplace, more professors will start companies. Conversely, if those professors are rewarded for publishing articles in academic journals that help them get tenure, they will put their efforts there instead of starting companies. Students are also influenced by a region's values. For example, if parents urge their children to try entrepreneurship, most students will start companies. And if local parents pressure their children to go into jobs, such as banking or consulting, that pay high current compensation, they will be more likely to become bankers or consultants.

If a city's values resist entrepreneurship, changing its values to make the city more startup-friendly is likely to be very difficult. As you will explore in Chapter 8, policymakers can take steps that help spur startups; however, a city's values tend to evolve slowly based on the rise and fall of industries that drive local wealth creation and destruction.

© Peter S. Cohan 2018
P. S. Cohan, *Startup Cities*, https://doi.org/10.1007/978-1-4842-3393-1_7

The most highly evolved startup city is not really a city at all. It is a region called Silicon Valley that has grown from Palo Alto, home of Stanford, to as far south as Sunnyvale and in recent decades to include San Francisco as more and more young entrepreneurs have chosen to live and work in the city. Silicon Valley values passionate founders with a strong desire to learn who want to build companies that solve big problems that represent very large market opportunities. Other regions do not spur startups as well as Silicon Valley due in part to differences in their values that tilt entrepreneurs and investors to compete over a fixed pie.

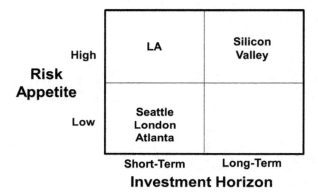

Figure 7-1. Startup Common values map

These differences become clearer through mapping cities' Startup Common values along two dimensions, as depicted in Figure 7-1:

- **Risk appetite:** Startup success in a region depends on having a high appetite for risk. Thus cities that do not value risk-taking tend to encourage fewer startups. In Hong Kong, Singapore, and Barcelona, for example, people generally view real estate rather than equity in a tech startup as a good investment and they encourage their children to take banking or consulting jobs so they can afford to own high-priced apartments. A low appetite for risk dampens the success of a Startup Common.

- **Investment horizon:** The other critical dimension of the values map is the Startup Common participants' investment horizon. A city hosting investors who have not yet enjoyed their first successful bets is likely to be in more of a hurry for a payoff. A city that hosts many investors who have already enjoyed investment success will be more willing to place bets that could take longer to pay off, but if successful will do so with a much higher return.

Interviews with venture capitalists and CEOs reveal striking difference on these two dimensions. Here are a few examples from five major cities:

- **Boston:** Boston gives back and takes risks but its investors and entrepreneurs exit early, limiting the number of pillar companies. "Many Boston area entrepreneurs have not had enough at-bats to turn down their first acquisition offer. As in other regions, we see the rusty Toyota syndrome. When an entrepreneur has been getting by with very little salary and an offer comes along to buy the company for, say, $300 million, he looks at his rusty Toyota in the company parking lot and decides he wants to swap it for a Lexus. So he takes the offer. Moreover, each time an entrepreneur starts a company, he wants to make 10 times more at the exit than the time before. Entrepreneurs on their second startups are more eager to 'go long,'" -- Bruce Sachs, General Partner, Charles River Ventures.

- **Los Angeles:** Los Angeles investors take risk and have a short-term time horizon, which manifests itself in the form of fighting fiercely over a fixed pie. "Part of the problem with Los Angeles is that the entertainment culture focuses on greed and individual success, not equity." – Scott Painter, founder and former CEO of car shopping site TrueCar.

- **Atlanta:** Atlanta places little value on expanding its Startup Common. "[In Atlanta] if you made it, you're on your boat and you're gone. Successful entrepreneurs had zero social feeling because they didn't get any help; they had to do it on their own." – Jeff Haynie, founder and former CEO of mobile app development platform Appcelerator.

- **Seattle:** Seattle's potential entrepreneurs are afraid to leave Microsoft, and its investors fight for majority control of startups. "Seattle must overcome two big challenges to realize its full potential: the adversarial relationship among angel investors, venture capitalists, and entrepreneurs, and the risk aversion of Microsoft's talent who are seeking a steady job with a good pension." – Gary Flake, founder and former CEO of content-sharing site Clipboard.

- **London:** London is highly stratified and those at the top are *short-term greedy.* "In London it is very difficult to meet with people who have capital or valuable advice, and those masters of the universe only help if they see an immediate short-term benefit for themselves. Silicon Valley was much more eager to help my startup so I moved there." – Jeff Buckley, MinoMonsters founder and CEO.

Takeaways for Startup Common Stakeholders

A region's values with respect to startups change slowly, if ever. As you will see in Chapter 8, one of the most important events that can shift a region's values is a highly-visible local entrepreneurial success story. For example, the success of Jack Ma's Alibaba inspired many young people in Hangzhou to start companies. But entrepreneurs should not decide on where to locate based on where a region's values might be in the future; they should base their choice on the region's actual startup values when they are deciding where to locate their startup. When it comes to changing a region's values towards startups, the entrepreneur is the hero and her success or failure can determine what other local stakeholders, such as government policymakers, venture capitalists, and other CEOs, will do. Here are questions that local stakeholders ought to consider in trying to shape a region's startup values:

- **Entrepreneurs:** A region's entrepreneurs should address the following questions related to mentor networks:

  - Where do I want (and not want) to live and work?

  - What product do I want to sell and to which customers?

  - How big do I want the company to become?

  - Of the regions where I could locate, which one has values that will be most supportive of my goals?

- **Government leaders:** A region's government leaders may need to change its culture and the housing, infrastructure, and transportation networks to support startup success. To that end, local leaders should address questions such as the following:

  - Does the region have sufficient private capital and entrepreneurial talent to spur more startup activity without external support?

  - If not, should we supply capital and office space to attract such entrepreneurial talent?

- Should we be planning and implementing ways to boost the region's housing stock, transportation networks, infrastructure, and schools to minimize the negative side effects of growth in our entrepreneurial ecosystem?

- **Venture investors** may need to decide how active they wish to be in boosting a region's startup scene. In evaluating such options they should address questions such as the following:

  - Should we open an office in the region?

  - Should our partners in those offices have specific skills that local portfolio companies will need to help them grow?

  - Should we hire new partners who can help build companies in new growth areas?

- **Successful startup CEOs** must decide whether they will help the region to climb the Pillar Company Staircase. To that end, they should consider questions such as the following:

  - Should I stay in the region?

  - If so, do I want to mentor local startups and/or invest in them?

  - Should I collaborate with other civic leaders to help plan the development of the region's startup scene?

Startup Common Values Success and Failure Case Studies

As noted above, a region's attitudes towards startups can change if a locally-grown startup achieves success. That success spurs a demonstration effect that attracts more capital and talent to the region and transforms the region's values. As the cases that follow illustrate, a region should take the following steps to create startup-friendly values:

- **Universities encourage professors and students to start companies.** A change in a region's attitude towards startups often takes place when parents change the career advice they give to their children. A region will become more startup friendly if its professors start successful companies and students become local entrepreneurs. These outcomes are more likely if local universities encourage them. For example, as you saw in Chapter 3, MIT and Stanford have encouraged professors to start companies for decades while WPI has put a higher value on publishing in academic journals.

- **Government helps form local startups.** Government can work with local universities and help startups in various ways, such as providing space for student startups and offering grants to cover operating costs.

- **Local startups grow and succeed, becoming local role models.** While universities and government can help local startups, the region's attitude towards startups may remain skeptical unless those startups are so successful that they become local role models. That success will create a more favorable local startup culture and will attract more talent and capital to the region.

- **Successful entrepreneurs reinvest in the region.** Successful entrepreneurs will generate wealth for the founding team. A region's values will become more startup friendly if those newly wealthy founders reinvest both their know-how and capital in the local startup scene.

- **Venture capital firms locate in the region.** Most large venture capital firms are always on the lookout for new areas of opportunity. If a region enjoys initial startup success, venture capital firms are likely to locate offices there to scout for new investments. Their presence will reinforce the region's startup friendliness.

- **Government adapts to local growth.** In order for a region to keep growing, local government must recognize when local housing stock and infrastructure are being strained by the demands of growth. And local leaders must develop and implement plans to increase housing and infrastructure before the strain of growth repels new startup activity.

Level 0: No Pillars, No Gazelles

Success Case Study: Silicon Valley's Lake Pharma Acquires Worcester Contract Researcher to Expand on East Coast

Introduction

A city with no pillars and no gazelles could still enjoy some meaningful entrepreneurial activity depending on its values. In the case of Worcester, city leaders have long touted its economic strengths in the phrase "Eds and Meds," referring to education and medicine. What this means in practice is that Worcester has long hosted a disproportionately large number of institutions of higher learning. In 1962, Worcester was chosen as the site of the University of Massachusetts Medical School, accepting its first students in 1970. U Mass Medical School has attracted a very talented group of medical educators, including a Nobel Prize winner. Worcester tried to tap into this talent by creating an incubator called Mass Biomedical Initiate that hosts mostly small contract research organizations (CROs). One such CRO attracted an outside investor who brought in a new CEO. The new CEO promptly sold the company to a Silicon Valley contract researcher who wanted to expand its operations in Worcester. However, the new owner struggled to find enough office space.

Case Scenario

The Worcester CRO in question was Blue Sky BioServices, which was cofounded by Paul Wengender and two colleagues in April 2003. By June 2013, Blue Sky had 45 employees; a month later, Wengender was replaced by a new CEO, Ted Marple, who had a track record of finding acquirers for CROs. By March 2016, Marple had done it again, selling Blue Sky to Belmont, Calif-based CRO LakePharma. While LakePharma said it would expand its operations in Worcester, by July 2017 it had not gone beyond the talking stage. Before starting Blue Sky, Wengender spent more than 15 years at Pfizer and AstraZeneca, helping run laboratories involved with pre-clinical discovery. And in response to competitive pressure to cut costs and boost the number of new products they bring to market, pharmaceutical companies have started outsourcing the service that Blue Sky provides. Wengender started Blue Sky after his boss at Pfizer told him that he would not be able to hire more people at Pfizer to build his organization. Realizing that such growth might come from being an outside service provider, Wengender, who likes "doing things for himself," started Blue Sky with two people in April 2003. By July 2012, Blue Sky had "over 40 people, 65% of whom were in laboratory operations and the other 35% in business operations."

In June 2013, Blue Sky had increased its head count 12% and more than doubled its production capacity by doing much more standardized work. As he said, "In July 2012, Blue Sky did 70% custom work and 30% crank-turning. We are moving to flip those proportions to 70% crank-turning and 30% custom." Blue Sky's strategy shift meant that it needed more capital to buy machines and hire the project managers and technicians. Fortunately for Blue Sky, Wengender was able to obtain a loan from MassDevelopment, which would be due in September 2013. Wengender was confident about his decision to locate the company in Worcester thanks to its talented employees and government leaders. As he said, "Despite all the changes in the world in the last decade, one thing that has remained constant is that we need access to talent. And Worcester definitely gives us that. New England is the hub of the biotech industry and is at the center of its vortex of talent. We have plenty of people who live in MetroWest [a group of suburban cities west of Boston] and find it easy to drive to Worcester. Blue Sky could not have achieved our 100% annual growth without the help of many people in Worcester. City Manager Mike O'Brien has been incredibly helpful. He always listens to what we need and does what he can to help. We have also gotten valuable assistance from [Worcester-based biomedical startup incubator Massachusetts Biomedical Initiatives] MBI's Kevin O'Sullivan, and WPI's Gateway Park."

About a month later, Wengender was replaced as CEO with a push from Blue Sky's biggest investor. The investor in question was Peter Glick, a partner at Blue Sky's lead investor, Ampersand Capital Partners. As Marple explained in a July 2013 interview, Glick was optimistic that with Marple as CEO, Wengender as Chief Commercial Officer, and Norm Garceau as Chief Scientific Officer, Blue Sky would have a bright future. As Marple said, "Together, our team has operations, process, strategic, scientific, and business development skills. I believe Paul is a critical part of Blue Sky's future, thanks to his understanding of the market and his ability to evangelize Blue Sky." Based on Marple's previous experience, a Harvard College graduate with an MBA from University of Virginia and two decades of life sciences experience, it was possible to guess that Blue Sky would ultimately be acquired. After all, before Blue Sky, he sold Xcellerex, a bioprocess company offering bioprocess equipment and regulatory-compliant biomanufacturing services to pharmaceutical and biotech companies, to General Electric Healthcare in May 2012. Glick instigated the process of recruiting Marple. According to Marple, "Peter was leading the conversation about Blue Sky's growth. I was familiar with the space; I knew the customers and what they need. I fit with Blue Sky's culture and got along great with Paul and Norm. Together we make a strong team of three. Blue Sky has reached a point in its growth where both Paul and its investors felt it was necessary to bring new insight, skills, and strengths on board to continue this growth and focus on execution. It's always a possibility that a company backed by a private equity or venture capital investor will sell out to a larger company in order to provide a return. But our real focus for the next few years is execution excellence. We will perform well for our customers."

And by March 2016, Blue Sky sold itself to a larger company, LakePharma, a Belmont, California-based provider of "integrated solutions in contract biologics." Mark Schmeizl, Vice President of Client Resources at LakePharma, said that the combined organization would have nearly 100 employees in four locations and would complement each other, helping these customers in their quest to discover new drugs. Hua Tu, LakePharma Chief Executive Officer and founder who became CEO of the combined organization, said, "LakePharma and Blue Sky are extremely complementary businesses that joined to create a singular company with unparalleled capabilities, broad expertise, and quality processes in biologics development and engineering. This transaction positions us to engage and meet the needs of expanding markets while better serving our customers through continued investment in innovative, complementary services." Given Marple's background, it was not surprising that Blue Sky found an acquirer. However, in the absence of details such as how much Ampersand invested and how much LakePharma paid, there was no way to know whether Marple generated an attractive return for Ampersand.

In 2017, LakePharma hoped that it would expand in Worcester but was suffering from space constraints. As Tu explained in a February 2017 interview, he had an impressive background in drug research, working in drug R&D from 1998 to 2009 and at cancer research company Tularik before starting LakePharma. As he said, "We used personal money to fund LakePharma in the early years. My wife and I had worked in the biotech industry for a long time before starting LakePharma. Much of our funds at that time originated from the stock options I received from my years at cancer researcher Tularik and Amgen. Tularik went public a year and half after I joined, and Amgen bought Tularik [paying $1.3 billion, a nearly 50% premium over its pre-deal March 2004 stock market value] and boosted its value further. I joked that Tularik funded LakePharma. We started with two people in 2009; by 2017 there were about 120 employees. Revenue growth was between 50% and 120% percent per year since 2010." He said that Blue Sky was important to LakePharma's future. As Tu said, "Blue Sky was special. It was one of the oldest biology CROs in our industry (started in 2003) and was LakePharma's closest competitor. What attracted LakePharma to Blue Sky was that we already wanted to establish a site in Massachusetts in 2015 to be close to our customers in Cambridge, and buying Blue Sky was a better option than building a site from scratch." While he was pleased with Blue Sky, the company needed more space. "The two businesses are indeed very complementary. We have been adding technical staff and upgrading equipment at the site, but we are almost out of space at 50 Prescott Street," he said. He was hoping that LakePharma would ultimately employ 1,000 people but was uncertain about whether Worcester would be a good partner to get there. "We are still learning the pros and cons of Worcester and can't comment on those yet," he concluded.

By July 2017, it was clear that LakePharma was growing and hiring in Worcester but had not resolved its space problems. As Tu said, "We expect to have a growth rate north of 50% in 2017. [This growth will come not from acquisitions but organically] driven by investments made in new product lines in the past two years, as well as strong repeat business. We have also benefited from stronger brand recognition and higher team operational efficiency. We encounter many challenges, but they are normal. One such challenge is lab space, and it is often a rate-limiting step for our expansion. We are acquiring and building up lab facilities. We just wish there are more spaces that are readily available," Tu was happy with local growth and with LakePharma's partnerships in Worcester. As he said, "Our Worcester team is doing a phenomenal job, and we expect 50% revenue growth in 2017 compared to 2016. We are very happy with the partnerships we have built with MBI and WPI." And LakePharma was hiring in Worcester. As Tu said, "We have been adding technical people and expect to continue. In addition to adding full-time staff, we have also added internship and part-time positions for college students. We hired a range of people, from community college students to experienced PhD's. It is wonderful that the Worcester area has such a diverse talent pool. We are bullish about growth in Worcester area, and have even told our European collaborators to look at Massachusetts for expansion."

Case Analysis

While Worcester lacks gazelles and venture capital, its culture, which takes pride in its local medical school, has attracted a steady, if small, stream of CROs and other medical technology startups. Blue Sky grew steadily, if slowly, over many years and made an attractive acquisition opportunity for a Silicon Valley area acquirer in the same industry. The merger of the two companies appeared by November 2017 to be going well. As a result, Worcester had the potential to help LakePharma expand its presence on the East Coast. Moreover, LakePharma offered the potential to infuse Worcester with some of Silicon Valley's startup values. While it appeared unlikely that LakePharma would grow to the point that it would become a publicly-traded CRO in Worcester, such an outcome would galvanize the local startup scene.

Less Successful Case Study: WPI Professor's Health Apps Slowly Make Their Way

Introduction

A city without gazelles is unlikely to attract private financing for the companies started there. After all, local startups are likely to grow slowly if at all. And the absence of rapid growth makes these startups unattractive for investors because there is little likelihood that a static startup will be attractive to an acquirer. What's more, if such a city hosts good technical universities, there is likely to be little pressure for professors to start companies or, once started, to set and achieve ambitious growth goals.

Case Scenario

In 2013, a WPI computer science professor partnered with U Mass Medical School to explore the possibility of introducing Sugar, an app to help diabetics, which was still being tested two years later. In 2017, he was collaborating with researchers at Brown and Boston Universities to develop another app, a drunkenness test called AlcoGait, having raised government funding to test whether it would work. By November 2017, it was unclear whether AlcoGait would be approved for sale or continue to languish. While WPI was pleased with Agu's work on these apps, he said that when WPI made tenure decisions, it was more interested in a professor's record of publishing in academic journals than on outside business activities.

The professor in question, Emmanuel Agu, certainly had an interesting life story. As he explained in a June 2013 interview, Agu's journey to this collaboration began with his emigration from Nigeria in 1994, when he decided to come to the U.S. for graduate school in computer science. He picked UMass-Amherst because a colleague of his father was a professor there. Agu was very interested in computer networking, having gained experience at a job installing computer networks at banks and other big companies in Nigeria. When Agu arrived in Amherst, he decided to write his master's thesis on creating a standard approach to wireless networking that's now known as WiFi. For his doctoral thesis, Agu focused on computer graphics, which was a topic that interested him, because as a child he liked to draw. Agu, who was involved with Internet startups in the 1990s that fizzled as the dot-com bubble burst, believes that his academic research and startups both benefited from so-called killer applications, like the Lotus 1-2-3 spreadsheets that created huge demand for PCs in the 1980s.

Agu decided that a killer app for the iPhone could track a person's health. Agu gave examples such as apps that keep track of how much a person exercises every day and apps that can calculate a person's blood pressure by analyzing a video of their face. As Agu explained, "This works due to something called PTG. When you shine a light on the human face, blood vessels absorb the light. Over time, you can see the pulsing of blood in and out of the vessels. This helps you calculate the heart rate. It was developed by the MIT Media Lab and is now the fifth most popular health and fitness app on the iPhone App Store." Such apps require FDA approval before they can be sold. In 2013, Agu was working on a diabetes app, which in 2010 attracted $1 million in government funding, through a collaboration between four faculty members at UMass Medical School's Diabetes Center of Excellence and four at WPI, including Agu. By 2013, the next step in the development process was to give the working version of the app to patients at UMass Medical School's Diabetes Center of Excellence. As he said, "We have a working version now and will start to test it in July or August. We will get feedback on what works well and what needs improvement," he said. "We will fix what needs to be fixed and deploy it six months after that. I am not sure whether we will sell it on the App Store or set up a company to develop it." About two years later, the app (named Sugar) had not launched. Instead, as of April 2015, it was headed to clinical testing at UMass Medical School, which planned to enroll 30 diabetic patients being treated for foot ulcers at the medical center's wound clinic.

In December 2016, Agu was also working on AlcoGait, which he started in 2014. It works as follows: "When you're over the limit, the phone notifies you with a text message, and also it will buzz." AlcoGait was inspired by the "walk-the-line" tests that police use to decide whether a driver is drunk. As Agu said, a breathalyzer is the most accurate test "but the next most accurate is the walk test." AlcoGait uses a smartphone's motion-detecting accelerometer and gyroscope chips. To test for intoxication, an AlcoGait user activates it, puts the smartphone in a pocket, and takes a quick walk while sober. The user would activate the app at a party and it would compare the sway of the user's upper body to the sober baseline sway. Should the user become sufficiently drunk, the sway gap would be triggered, setting off an alarm and a warning not to drive. Agu was working with researchers at BU and Brown who planned to recruit 250 volunteers to test AlcoGait's effectiveness. As Agu said, "Hopefully, it'll be ready for New Year's [2018]." Although testing was progressing, that deadline looked out of reach. By September 2017, BU School of Public Health had received a $320,000 grant to test the app, which was expected to begin by October 2017. It remained unclear whether the app was accurate.

Case Analysis

Agu's health apps are excellent vehicles for his research and teaching since they provide a way for him to work with students and researchers to potentially turn his ideas into products that can be used by people if they win regulatory approval. At the same time, his deliberate pace reflects the culture of WPI, which like many universities puts more of an emphasis on its professors' publishing in academic journals than on their entrepreneurial activities. From the perspective of an investor, Agu is a careful and curious researcher who is more interested in doing research to refine his ideas than in building fast-growing startups. WPI is comfortable with these values and sees no incentive to change them. This does not bode well for the growth of Worcester's startup scene.

Principles

A region's startup values are highly resistant to change. Indeed, my experience trying over six years to make Worcester more startup friendly has not resulted in meaningful change. The most effective force in changing a region's values is a highly visible and dramatic local success story. For example, if a WPI graduate started a company in Worcester that went public and reached a stock market capitalization of $50 billion, far more WPI graduates would stay in Worcester to start companies because of this powerful local role model. As of December 2017, such a role model was sorely lacking and there was no compelling reason to believe that one would be likely to emerge.

Here are principles that Level 0 stakeholders should consider:

- **Entrepreneurs** should decide which group of customers he hopes to serve, how big he wants his company to become, and where he wants or does not want to live. The entrepreneur should pick a location whose values are consistent with those choices. For example, an entrepreneur who wants to start a modestly-growing CRO and to live there should locate in Worcester.

- **Local governments** in such regions can boost startup activity by encouraging locally educated students to operate their companies in the region by dedicating office space to the cause and/or by providing money or tax incentives.

- **Local university leaders** can encourage more entrepreneurship by professors by rating their performance based in part on their entrepreneurial activity and by students by giving them academic credit for creating locally-based startups.

Level 1: No Pillars, Some Gazelles

Success Case Study: Paris Entrepreneurs Overcome Cultural Challenges

Introduction

Paris has a mixed attitude towards startups. While Parisians admire those who do well in the most elite schools and go on to positions in the government or banking, they also take pleasure in going on strike and defying authority, which is an entrepreneurial trait. Moreover, labor laws make the cost of hiring and firing employees very high and work laws make it easy for employees to go on strike and receive pay for the missed work time before they will return to work. On the other hand, Emmanuel Macron, who as economic minister was a vocal proponent of entrepreneurship, was elected President in 2017. Moreover, with a growing number of admired Parisian entrepreneurs, young people are increasingly seeing startups as a trendy career option. While it is unclear whether the trend will continue or evaporate, by 2017 there was some evidence that Paris was beginning to shift its culture more in favor of startups and some entrepreneurs were achieving considerable success.

Case Scenario

Paris's startup culture faced some considerable obstacles. Despite a 2009 law intended to make it easier to start a company in France, including tax breaks and an easier company registration process, two Paris-based experts on the local startup scene still noted some challenges for founders. Kathryn Baxter, a British entrepreneur living in Paris, noted that most Parisians are not comfortable speaking English, strict employment laws are difficult to navigate, taxes and social charges are high, the business culture is formal, and it takes time to be accepted. Bassières Sandrine, a Parisian with extensive knowledge of the startup scene, said, "Bureaucracy and administration mean that it's not easy to create a company. There are lots of things to pay for, far too many rules and regulations, and a reluctance to take risks among many people. Staff representation and trade unions are quite powerful and are entitled to set up bargaining units within a company."

Indeed, statistics comparing Paris's startup scene to those of other cities suggested that its culture could be made more startup friendly. Etienne Krieger, a director of the entrepreneurship program at HEC Paris, argued that Paris has an important ingredient for a successful startup scene. As he said, "The main asset in a startup company is people, and there is real entrepreneurial drive in France in these last years." Still, more work remains to foster a startup culture. France came in 29th on the World Bank's annual "Ease of doing business" ranking, well behind competitors such as the U.S. (8), the U.K. (7), and slightly behind Germany (17). The Global Entrepreneurship and Development Institute, which compiles a Global Entrepreneurship Index, ranked

France at 13, still behind the U.S., the UK, and Germany. Moreover, France had relatively little entrepreneurship with 0.03% of France's GDP invested in startups compared to 0.33% in the U.S.

Despite those barriers, Paris hosted many successful entrepreneurs. According to Forrester Research, "In the recent past, several French entrepreneurs have radically changed the business mindset. These include Loic Le Meur, Xavier Niel, Marc Simoncini, Jacques-Antoine Granjon, Pierre Kosciusko-Morizet, Gilles Babinet, and many others who have demonstrated that digital is not just a threat but also a huge business opportunity. The support of the French government with the French Tech initiative, coupled with the success stories of BlaBlaCar, Criteo, and SigFox, helped raise France's profile. There is a good reason why Facebook opened its artificial intelligence research center in Paris. France is one of the leading countries when it comes to math, physics, data science, and robotics research."

One of the more successful startups was founded by Fanny Péchiodat, creator of My Little Paris, the city's first media startup. In 2008, Péchiodat "created an email blast meant to share quirky neighborhood finds, like a flower shop that doubled as a speakeasy. Six months later her list-serve had grown to 10,000." Péchiodat recruited co-founders Anne-Flore Chapellier, Céline Orjubin, and artist Kanako Kuno, naming the company My Little Paris (MLP). They attracted four million subscribers and a business valued at $42 million with 130 employees and offices in Marseille and Lyon. As Péchiodat told Harper's Bazaar, "People underestimate the Parisian startup scene. It's growing remarkably fast, especially for women. When we launched, the startup culture was largely dominated by men, yet five out of six of MLP's founders were female. Today, 75% of our staff are women. There's a level of social engagement that comes with being an entrepreneur that I find incredibly inspiring."

Case Analysis

With the IPO of Zavier Niel's company, Iliad, has come significant funding for his projects, including Station F and his coding academy. What's more, his friendship with French President Emmanuel Macron offers hope for a strong nudge that pushes Paris's values in a more startup-friendly direction. In addition, the growing success of several Paris startups, including significant growth and capital raises, suggests that its startup scene is improving. While it appeared by 2017 that startups were increasingly considered "cool," Paris had yet to host a sufficiently strong local startup success to create a powerful local demonstration effect. Moreover, France's high taxes and social costs along with its penchant for bureaucracy had a long history that could snap back into control should the current entrepreneurship fad lose its cultural primacy.

Less Successful Case Study: Hong Kong's Startup Values Create Conflicting Cross-Currents

Introduction

In 1999, I began visiting Hong Kong to discuss the world of Internet start-ups. At the time, Hong Kong had created a section of its stock market specifically to host Internet-related initial public offerings and it was building the Cyberport, a real estate development intended to host Internet startups run by Richard Li, a Stanford graduate who was the son of Hong Kong's leading business mogul, Li Ka-shing. The Cyberport reflected Hong Kong's conflicting startup values. Hong Kong investors had achieved their wealth and status thanks to real estate investment and they viewed startup-related buildings as a way to make more money in real estate development. And not surprisingly, they did not understand the business logic of technology-based startups, a view that was confirmed when the dot-com bubble burst in 2000.

In 2012, I launched a course at Babson College for MBAs called Hong Kong/Singapore Startup Strategy Elective Abroad and by November 2017 had begun the seventh consecutive running of the course. In those seven years, it has been clear that the Hong Kong government has been trying to urge people in Hong Kong to start technology-based companies. However, a lack of local venture capital and a parental bias towards pushing their children into careers with high current salaries have kept a lid on local startup success.

As you saw in Chapter 3, the two most successful Hong Kong-based startups were founded by entrepreneurs who had been educated in Silicon Valley and those success stories are approaching the point where they might enjoy successful exits. There is little likelihood that that Hong Kong's culture will tilt strongly in favor of entrepreneurship until some of these local companies achieve visible success. Around the world, this demonstration effect is powerful. Indeed, since I began the course, the biggest change has been that Beijing, Shenzhen, and other large Chinese cities have enjoyed highly visible successes, such as Alibaba, Ten Cent, and others, that are spurring a culture of entrepreneurship. Increasingly, Hong Kong's entrepreneurial ecosystem seems to be falling behind in comparison even as China takes over greater control of Hong Kong's government.

Case Scenario

By the summer of 2017, Hong Kong's values were seen as still in a state of becoming more startup friendly. In June 2017, an event hosted in Shenzhen by TechCrunch China provided ample evidence that Hong Kong had further to go in changing its attitude towards technology startups. Blake Larson, head of international at logistics on-demand startup Lalamove told the conference, "Hong Kong is becoming a global innovation center, but it needs companies to look up to." Lalamove had raised more *than $60 million from investors but he said that it would take time for perceived "riskier" career options such as entrepreneurship to be accepted. He noted that banking and real-estate have been the primary career choices for graduates who are receiving parental pressure to land a high-paying, relatively secure career path. Eric Gnock Fah, co-founder of Klook, a travel tech company that raised $30 million from Sequoia, said "Hong Kong is still lacking a little bit. Finance and real estate [have] dominant market share in the economy and the younger generation still has that mindset. But we also see increasing interest. This summer we had 10 interns keen to learn more about the startup experience."*

Hong Kong entrepreneurs face much stronger headwinds than those in nearby Shenzhen, which has startup role models, attracts tech talent, and has a much larger local market. As Larson said, "The issue of tech talent is because there's not much of a market. The biggest opportunity we found is that if you can survive in Hong Kong with all these head winds, the opportunity, if you can get through that, the sky is limit. [That's] because you built up a tolerance to all these challenges in front of you. Nothing else is really going to intimidate you." Lalamove could be a Hong Kong role model through a local IPO. As Larson said, "It would be a great opportunity to be one of the first, if not the first...and be a symbol for the community to show it is possible to build a global technology company from Hong Kong, which is almost certainly where the IPO would happen though we might consider a dual-listing on the Nasdaq if Lalalmove deserved it."

Against these challenges, Hong Kong's government is producing reports that document local startup activity and trying to make funds available for different kinds of startups. According to the 2016 survey released by InvestHK, the investment promotion arm of Hong Kong, the number of startups in the city rose 24% from 1,558 in 2015 to 1,926 in 2016, with a focus on fintech and the Internet of Things (IoT). A survey by the Hong Kong Trade Development Council (HKTDC) found that most Hong Kong startups tend to be at later stages of development: 37% were at the market launch stage and 28% were at the growth or expansion stage with only 12% and 20% at the concept development or prototype stages, respectively. The government is offering money to promote local entrepreneurship, including $65 million towards technology to improve public services and promote "a Common Spatial Data Infrastructure (CSDI) to share geospatial data for public and private sector cooperation on different smart city applications" and a $260 million Innovation and Technology Venture Fund to invest in local innovation with private venture capital matches. And Hong Kong is working with Shenzen on a joint real estate development to convert the Lok Ma Chau Loop into the Hong Kong-Shenzhen Innovation and Technology Park.

Case Analysis

As someone who has been following Hong Kong's efforts to boost technology entrepreneurship since 1999, it appears to me that the most pronounced progress has been in the development of commercial real estate centered around technology startups. Such real estate has won as tenants more international technology giants and government-sponsored technology incubators than venture-backed startups. Meanwhile, Hong Kong is home to many startups, some of which have succeeded in raising venture capital (mostly from outside Hong Kong) and a handful of which were valued at over $1 billion, dubbed unicorns, as of November 2017. Meanwhile, without Hong Kong-based startup heroes to rival those of Shenzen, there is little force to pressure a cultural change away from parent's traditional preference that their children win coveted jobs in banking or commercial real estate.

Principles

Level 1 regions are changing their values towards startups. In general, local governments are pushing those regions towards startups. If local entrepreneurs build successful companies there, then the momentum for cultural change is likely to be stronger. Without such a pairing between government efforts and entrepreneurial success, the local push in favor of entrepreneurship is likely to fail.

Here are principles that Level 1 stakeholders should consider to make their region more startup friendly:

- **Entrepreneurs** should bolster their teams and raise sufficient capital to scale to the point where their companies can either be acquired or go public. And if these entrepreneurs succeed, they should give back to the local community, providing mentoring and capital to local startups.

- **Local governments** in such regions should help local startups by removing obstacles to their growth, such as simplifying the process of hiring and firing staff, easing their move to larger offices, and making it more attractive for them to give stock options to employees and raise capital.

- **Local university leaders** should help students get internships and full-time positions with local startups and help professors who have started companies to build teams, find customers, and raise capital.

- **Venture capitalists** are generally based outside such regions; however, if their portfolio companies in these cities begin to grow, the VCs should consider opening a local office to mentor the founders and to seek out new investment opportunities.

Level 2: No Pillars, Acquired Gazelles

Success Case Study: Stockholm Becomes Startup Friendly

Introduction

When it comes to startups, cities are not stuck with the same values forever. Indeed, the fall of big, old companies can change peoples' attitudes towards entrepreneurship. After all, if a big employer sheds jobs, the community will be much happier if local companies reemploy those who lost their jobs rather than supporting them through social welfare programs. And should some of those local startups grow and create new wealth, values are likely to change from viewing startups with suspicion to welcoming the benefits they provide the community.

Case Scenario

This is the story behind the rise of Stockholm's startup scene starting in the 1990s. That improvement in Stockholm's startup culture yielded dramatic results. Indeed by 2016, 375 Swedish startups had attracted $1.6 billion in growth capital. That was more than twice the $787.6 million of venture and growth capital invested into Swedish companies in 2014. While Stockholm enjoyed some IPOs—38 Swedish tech companies raised $160 million in capital that way—the biggest names in Stockholm's startup firmament had either been acquired or were hoping to go public. These included Skype, the Internet phone service founded in 2003 that eBay bought for $2.5 billion in October 2005 and sold to Microsoft for $8.5 billion in May 2011; King Digital, maker of Candy Crush, which was founded in Sweden in 2003 and migrated to Dublin before its March 2014 IPO that raised $500 million but in February 2016, Activision Blizzard bought it for $5.9 billion; and Mojang, the creator of Minecraft, which was also sold to Microsoft, in this case in November 2014 for $2.5 billion. Stockholm also had a few unicorns. Indeed, in 2015 investment firm Atomico found that at 6.3, Sweden had the second largest concentration of unicorns per capita, behind Silicon Valley's 8.1. At the top of that list were streaming music service Spotify, valued in May 2017 at $13 billion in anticipation of a possible IPO, and online payments service Klarna, worth $2.5 billion.

Hjalmar Windbladh, a serial entrepreneur who in 1999 sold mobile app developer Sendit to Microsoft for $130 million, is founding partner of €556 million EQT Ventures and is excited about the future of the city's startup scene, which is due, in part, to a cultural change that took decades. "The attitude towards entrepreneurship in Sweden has changed dramatically since the 1980s, when it was considered bad; it was highly likely that a startup would go bankrupt and not pay its taxes. But in the 1990s, that began to change as venture capital came here and a lot of people got a taste for entrepreneurship. We decided that you were not a crook if a startup failed, and we gave people a second chance," Windbladh said in an August 2017 interview. That turned out to be very important because "when Ericsson got into *trouble, it spit out engineers who had a nice severance package and no hope for a new steady job. So they started companies. The founder of King came out of Spray Networks, and Spotify was also founded at that time. Now entrepreneurship here is a great test bed for startups in gaming, fintech, and music streaming because we have a mature consumer market, thanks to high broadband penetration and high GDP per capita. Startups can get their services working here and expand to larger markets around the world," he said. Now entrepreneurship is what undergraduates want to do. "We are seeing the Bjorn Borg model—Borg's success at tennis made it much more popular in Sweden—for entrepreneurship. Before, young people wanted to go into banks or Ericsson, but now they want to take a risk to realize their dreams by starting a company or going to work for a startup. And our educational system—which encourages collaboration and questioning others using data—gives people [helpful skills for startup success]," Windbladh said.*

One of the strengths of Stockholm's startup culture is that it encourages successful entrepreneurs to give back. As Olle Zetterberg, CEO of Stockholm Business Region, explained in an August 2017 interview, "Niklas Zennstrom, who founded Skype, made an exit twice, and he reinvested in Stockholm startups, which drew capital from U.K. and U.S. investors. He did not buy a Beverly Hills mansion [as did the founder of Mojang], which is important for developing the startup community. Another thing that helped build our gaming startups was an investment in black fiber 25 years ago to deliver high-speed urban cable connections." The Swedish financial services industry has traditionally been eager to use technology. "The OMX was our auto-mated stock exchange that NASDAQ acquired and our banks supported the use of the smartphone payments service iZettle. Swedes are not using cash much anymore; I can pay my bills with a cellphone in two seconds," he said.

But Sweden has a tradition of letting great engineering speak for itself, which means that sales and marketing are "not traditionally highly regarded. After World War II, our industrial companies were the only ones left standing in Europe, so we didn't need a sales force," said Zetterberg. But with the success of companies like King, Klarna, and Spotify he sees that changing. Sweden's universities are helping out to some extent. As Invest Stockholm's Joseph Michael explained in an August 2017 interview, "We have Stockholm School of Economics and Royal Institute of Technology. They are sources of talent for startups, particularly in software engineering and human interface design, and they all have incubators." Meanwhile, if the culture of entrepre-neurship remains strong in Sweden, the tax system makes it attractive to take a low salary and make a big capital gain on a startup. "We have high income taxes, which go into single-payer health care and other government programs that make people trust the authorities. Our value-added-tax is lower if you buy a computer, and we have low capital gains taxes and lower cost of living," Windbladh said.

Case Analysis

Sweden culture seems ideally suited for creating a growing startup scene. It hosts considerable technical talent and puts a strong cultural emphasis on excellent engineering, personal modesty, and giving back to the community. With the acquisitions of some of its startups, considerable wealth has flowed into the hands of successful founders, many of whom are investing their funds in a younger generation of startups. While Stockholm does not have a strong sales culture, which is often an important element to building a pillar company, some of its gazelles seem headed to possible initial public offerings. While it is not yet clear whether they will reach this destination, its startup scene has considerable positive momentum.

Less Successful Case Study: Stockholm Gaming Founder Sells Out for $2.5 Billion and Skips Town, Buying a $70 Million Beverly Hills Mansion

Introduction

In the 1960s TV show called the Beverly Hillbillies, a family in Arkansas discovers oil in a swamp on their property and they are offered millions of dollars to sell the property. Instead of staying in the neighborhood and giving back to the local community, the Clampetts take their wealth and move to Beverly Hills. While viewers of the program never knew how their former neighbors felt about their departure, Zetterberg's thinly-disguised contempt for Mojang CEO Markus Persson's decision to leave Stockholm, after receiving his 71% share of the $2.5 billion Microsoft paid to acquire the company, for Beverly Hills gives a hint of how the Clampett's neighbors might have felt. Stockholm wants its successful entrepreneurs to stay and reinvest in the local startup scene, but Persson did the opposite.

Case Scenario

Persson is an exceptionally talented individual who created a very valuable company. However, when he sold Mojang to Microsoft, he did the opposite of what Stockholm's leaders wanted him to do. Instead of quietly accepting his newfound wealth and reinvesting his wisdom and capital in the local startup community, he bought the most expensive house in one of the flashiest neighborhoods in the world. Mojang, started in 2009, made an online game called Minecraft that required its players to build a house every day that would allow them to survive a night of marauding monsters. Persson grew up far from Stockholm and his father was a railroad engineer who abused alcohol, divorced his mother when he was 12, and committed suicide. While Persson was intelligent, he was very introverted and preferred to spend time with his computer and with other video gamers than to attend school. Fortunately, Persson's mother forced him to take an online course that taught him how to write video games. He got a series of jobs writing such games and ultimately started work on Minecraft which by March 2015 had over 100 million users. In 2012, Minecraft, with about 30 employees and no outside owners, generated $230 million in sales and $150 million in gross profit, $101 million of which went into Persson's pocket.

While Minecraft continued to grow in popularity, Persson was getting increasingly frustrated by user demands to improve the game. In June 2014, he put out a plaintive Tweet for a buyer and by September 2014, he had one; Microsoft paid $2.5 billion in cash for the company—of which Persson got 71%.

Persson was quite conscious of what he was expected to do with his money, but he did the opposite. As he told the New Yorker in a 2013 interview, "The money is a strange one. I'm slowly getting used to it, but it's a Swedish trait that we're not supposed to be proud of what we've done. We're supposed to be modest. So at first, I had a really hard time spending any of the profits. Also, what if the game stopped selling? But after a while, I thought about all of the things I'd wanted to do before I had money. So I introduced a rule: I'm allowed to spend half of anything I make. That way I will never be broke. Even if I spend extravagant amounts of money, I will still have extravagant amounts of money." In December 2014, Persson decided to buy a $70 million, 23,000-square-foot mega-mansion, the most expensive home ever in Beverly Hills. He spent over $180,000 a night at Las Vegas nightclubs. He and Mojang cofounder Jakob Porsér started a company called Rubberbrain in case they thought of a new game idea, but they spent most of their time just looking at social media in expensive Stockholm offices (In a 2015 Forbes interview, Persson was refreshing Twitter and Reddit, while Porsér played an online clicking game that exploded bugs and critters for coins.) And by October 2017, they were still partying on in Beverly Hills. As The Blast wrote, Persson turned his "Hillcrest Road mansion into 'Hellcrest,' a spooky 1800s mansion complete with a freakin' swamp, mummies, taxidermy and just about every other creepy haunted thing, for the night. Guests, including Avicii and Taylor Lautner, were tended to by undead butlers."

Case Analysis

Markus Persson took the winnings from the sale of his company and knowingly violated the norms of Stockholm's startup scene. On the one hand his success, especially with such a small staff and the absence of outside capital, was one of the most spectacular startup stories in Sweden from a financial perspective. On the other hand, Persson truly did the opposite of what Stockholm's norms would prescribe. Instead of remaining personally modest and humble, he flaunted his success by purchasing the most expensive house in Beverly Hills. Based on his history, it is possible that he now sees himself as enjoying the childhood and adolescence that he spent writing computer games. Perhaps he will mature out of his bacchanalia and someday return to Stockholm and invest the proceeds of his success in the local startup scene. But for now, his decision to flaunt its norms is a loss for Stockholm.

Principles

Level 2 regions have more clearly defined startup-friendly values. In general, those regions are eager to make the transition from places that start companies that get acquired to regions that host pillar companies. In order to do that, such regions recognize that they must enhance the skills of local entrepreneurs, helping them develop the skills required to take a company public and operate it under the quarterly scrutiny of public shareholders.

Here are principles that Level 2 stakeholders should consider to make their region more startup friendly:

- **Entrepreneurs** should seek out mentors who can help them identify the skills they need to add to their teams in order to operate a public company. They should also find investors with prior experience taking companies in their industry public and guiding their founders in that pursuit.

- **Local governments** in such regions should plan to build out local housing and infrastructure to support the increase in the number of professionals and other workers coming to the region to work in the startups.

- **Local university leaders** should bring local entrepreneurs into classes to meet with students and should encourage internships at the local startups.

- **Venture capitalists** should locate new offices in the city in order to support the local startups in their efforts to go public and to scout out new startups.

Level 3: Some Pillars in Niche Markets

Success Case Study: Israel Makes Bigger Bets

Introduction

Israel has made remarkable strides as a nation of startups. However, with few exceptions, its most successful companies have located their engineering operations in Israel and their sales, marketing, and top executive teams in the U.S. This trend has allowed the companies to grow to the point where a few could go public and many more could be acquired for hundreds of millions of dollars. But Israel was concerned that this model limited the development of Israeli management talent, capped the number of local pillar companies, and damped the potential of those local pillars to scale. In recent years, Israeli investors and entrepreneurs have been stepping up on the Pillar Company Staircase.

Case Scenario

Israeli venture investors noted that recent successful exits had enriched investors and made them eager to invest more to finance the longer-term growth of Israeli startups. Moreover, Israeli CEOs were learning how to staff their companies almost *entirely from people in Israel. Danny Cohen was a partner at Viola Ventures. As he explained in a November 2017 interview, the 48-year-old was originally from Haifa, but he lived in Palo Alto and attended junior high school there. He earned a degree in computer science and psychology, and he worked in R&D and product management before earning an MBA at INSEAD. After joining an Israeli dot-com in 2000, Cohen joined Israeli venture capital firm Gemini in 2001 and became a partner in 2005. He spent three years in Silicon Valley, joined Carmel Ventures, and in 2012 helped start Viola, which was "trying to build billion dollar companies in Israel." Cohen believed that Israeli investors were more willing to take risks than those in Europe but were more conservative than those in Silicon Valley. As he said, "Israeli startups tend to exit at $200 million to $500 million. Our investors tend to look for companies that have technological differentiation. We have every type of flower in the garden. Our venture capitalists like a little bit of everything, but they like cybersecurity. We have a few unicorns, such as Lightricks, a consumer-facing selfie editing service that has sophisticated image processing technology behind it."*

Cohen saw significant changes in the Israeli venture capital market between 2012 and 2017. As he said, "Five years ago, total venture capital invested in Israeli startups was about $2 billion to $3 billion. In 2017, the number had risen to $6 billion, which was going for growth money. The number of companies getting $50 million investments had increased along with the appetite for large exits. More companies in Israel were able to sell to businesses over the Internet. While in the 2000s, Israeli companies would go to the U.S. to hire a VP of Sales to reach U.S. companies, by 2017, Israeli companies could sell software as a service using low-touch sales, marketing on Facebook and Google without sales people. An example was Redis Labs, an Israeli company that used GitHub and Facebook to market an open source database to developers. Israel had also created consumer brands like website development service Wix and soda machine maker SodaStream. So investors and entrepreneurs were less afraid of consumer brands."

Amit Karp was a partner at Bessemer Venture Partners. As he explained in a November 2017 interview, Karp was an officer in the Israeli Defense Force before earning a degree in computer science from Haifa's Technion, worked as a software developer and product manager, and then earned an MBA from MIT's Sloan School of Management. From there he joined McKinsey in New York and in 2011 took at position at Bessemer in New York before moving to its Israeli office in 2014. Karp saw a growing appetite for Israeli investors to take risks. As he said, "Three years ago there was much less risk tolerance and growth capital available in Israel than there is today. In 2014, there was capital available for the seed stage and for Series A and B. But there were no growth rounds of $30 million to $50 million. To find investors for that, who had longer time horizons, Israeli entrepreneurs had to go overseas. There is emerging a new generation of Israeli venture capitalist as the older school VCs are winding down. There is still less risk appetite in Israel since the growth rounds are for companies whose markets are in the U.S. There has also been the concern that U.S. companies compete by raising more money so they can cut their prices to grow fast [with the hope that they will be able to grow fast enough to exit before they burn *through their cash]. In Israel, it is hard to buy your way to success. In Israel, we want to invest in a company that is clearly number one in its market and it should have an underlying technical core, which helps it to fend off competition and makes it more attractive to a potential acquirer."*

Israel still lacked enough executives who could scale a startup. As Karp explained, "In Israeli startups, we are very careful about which founders we invest in. One reason is that Israel does not have a lot of people who can scale a business from $10 million in revenue to $100 million. So there is not enough talent with which to replace a founder. We tend to invest in technology companies such as those in semiconductors or autonomous vehicles. But we do have companies like Wix where the team is in Israel and is talented at performance marketing, freemium business models, and conversion of customers from free to paying versions of the service. But for businesses that require a sales force to sell to enterprises, the sales and marketing are still typically in the U.S. What's changed is that there is a bigger risk appetite than there was before. Many investors have a better track record. When a company like Mobileye is acquired for $15 billion to $16 billion, it changes the mindset of entrepreneurs and investors. Four years ago, A rounds were $2 million to $4 million; today we have bigger A rounds in the $6 million to $8 million range."

Lior Prosor, a partner at Manhattan's Elevator Fund, echoed many of these comments. As he explained in a November 2017 interview, he was the son of an Israeli diplomat who lived in Bonn and London before going to school in Washington. From there, he was an Israeli paratrooper who went to law school in Israel and did investment banking at Rothschild before joining Israeli venture capital firm Pitango. He moved to the U.S. to set up Elevator Fund, a multifamily office, and said he was in the middle of raising $100 million. He saw three significant changes to Israeli's startup culture. As he explained, "Most of the established venture capital firms in Israel are run by 60-year-olds who have no succession plan. A new generation of venture capitalists is starting their own funds. Second, we realize that the biggest companies have consumer touchpoints—companies like shared workspace supplier WeWork, Wix, ride sharing app Via, and Gett, an on-demand ride service. Older VCs are less comfortable funding such companies than the new generation. Finally, the nature of exits is changing. When VCs were trying to sell their startups for $100 million to $300 million, they were more concerned with valuations so they could get a big share of the upside and they demanded preferred participating shares with 2x liquidation preferences [which in the event of the startup's acquisition or IPO gave these investors the right to two times their investment before other investors received their proceeds]. But consumer-focused startups expect Israeli VCs to give more founder-friendly terms, not participating preferred. Finally, as more Israeli entrepreneurs get the experience of scaling a company above $10 million in annual recurring revenue and consumer-focused companies—like consumer review site Yotpo and renters and homeowners insurance app Lemonade Insurance—have successful exits, Israel will host more consumer pillar companies."

Case Analysis

Israel became famous as a startup nation. Yet it recognized that it was too dependent on American executives to turn its world-beating products into companies making technology for enterprise customers that could scale to the point where they would make attractive acquisition candidates. To be sure, these exits enriched many local investors and gave the management teams of the acquired startups some experience working in successful Silicon Valley companies after being acquired by the likes of Microsoft, Facebook, Google, Intel, and Cisco. In recent years, Israel has been trying to build companies in Israel that target consumers using online marketing techniques so they can grow without shifting control to a U.S. headquarters. As more of these companies grow and go public, Israel could rival Silicon Valley as host to large pillar companies in huge markets.

Less Successful Case Study: Boston Leaks Talent as It Sticks with What Worked Before

Introduction

A city with some pillars in niche markets values entrepreneurs who have demonstrated their ability to do a few things well. In so doing, such a city is good at identifying quickly a founder who fits with one who does not. In the Boston/Cambridge startup scene, for example, investors are eager to invest in startups that pass two tests: they are developing better solutions to the technical problems facing companies (as opposed to developing services for consumers) and their founding team has a track record of prior success solving similar problems. New York and Boston are in distant second and third places, respectively, relative to San Francisco, which when combined with Silicon Valley dwarfs all other regions in terms of capital. According to the PWC MoneyTree report for the second quarter of 2017, San Francisco ($4.1 billion invested in Q2 2017) and Silicon Valley ($3.6 billion) overshadowed New York ($2.8 billion) and New England ($1.4 billion).

Boston was in strong second place from the 1980s to about 2001 and then went into a slow period. In a July 2017 interview, Jeff Fagnan, a partner at Boston-based venture capital firm Accomplice, explained, "During those years, Boston had a lot of momentum. It had the best DNA for hardware technology in areas such as networking, telecommunications, virtualization, storage, and security. But Boston missed the first phase of the Internet; the center of gravity was in Silicon Valley and younger Boston-based venture capital firm partners from places like Greylock, Charles River Ventures, and Matrix opened offices in Silicon Valley." Stanford professor Chuck Eesley, who earned his doctorate at MIT, thinks that Silicon Valley has broader technological skills that have weathered waves of new technologies better than Boston with its "narrower focus." As Eesley explained in an August 2017 interview, "Boston VCs generally don't believe in consumer Internet; they favor startups in computer and network hardware and life sciences. Silicon Valley keeps catching the next wave; it was early on the Internet, the social web, machine learning, and artificial intelligence."

After the dot-com crash, Boston's share of startup activity began to plunge. Fagnan said from 2001 to 2008, Boston was "in the dark ages because the older general partners lost their way. I was at Atlas Ventures and in 2014, our IT investing group rebranded itself as Accomplice so we could operate with a clean sheet of paper. Today we are the leading early stage firm with three times more seed stage investments than any other firm." Fagnan believes that Boston's heritage puts it at a disadvantage to Silicon Valley. As he said, "Boston's puritan mindset is afraid of big visions, putting Boston at a disadvantage when it comes to marketing, branding, and messaging. It had the best technology but it was in non-sexy infrastructure. It did not get attention because it lacked a bigger, broader story. Boston does not have the West Coast pixie dust." A more experienced general partner, Paul Maeder, co-founder and Chair of Highland Capital Partners, with offices near MIT and in Palo Alto, Calif., explained, "Culturally, people in Boston stay with hard problems longer; whereas in Silicon Valley, there is much more movement. Boston has much better public transportation while Silicon Valley is all spread out. [To MIT and Harvard students, my question is] 'Why would you leave?'"

Case Scenario

Larry Bohn was an English teacher in the Boston area whose career took off when he got into business both as a CEO and a venture capitalist, where he helped generate about $6.9 billion in value for investors. He progressed from a local minicomputer company, Data General, to become CEO of a startup that he took public and sold, then became a venture capitalist and made several successful investments in Boston-based (and other) companies. As he said in a November 2017 interview, "I grew up in the Boston area and my father died when I was 16. I got a scholarship to the University of Massachusetts and was an English major in the late 1960s and early 1970s. From there I got a Master's in English Linguistics at Clark University in Worcester and then got a job teaching at a Boston junior college. I was disheartened because I realized that I could not make a living as a professor. But in addition to writing, I liked computer programming (having taken a college course in FORTRAN). So I got a job as a technical writer at Data General and rose up the management ranks. I went on to be head of product at electronic workstation publishing company Interleaf."

After this, Bohn became a CEO and venture capitalist. As he said, "From there I ran PC Docs, a maker of software to handle word processing documents and email that went public on the Toronto Stock Exchange, later got a U.S. listing, and was sold [in 1999 for $155 million to Canadian software company] Hummingbird. After that I wanted to get into the Internet so I took over as CEO at Netgenesis, a website analysis service founded by some MIT graduates. We took it public in [February 2000] and its market capitalization peaked at $1 billion before sinking to $10 million after the dot-com crash. We sold Netgenesis to SPSS [in December 2001 for $44 million]." From there Bohn became a venture partner at Boston venture capital firm General Catalyst, which was just getting started. He led General Catalyst's investments in marketing software provider HubSpot, which went public in October 2014 and by November 3, 2017 was valued at $3.1 billion; e-commerce services provider DemandWare, which went public in March 2012 and was acquired by Salesforce for $2.8 billion in July 2016; San Francisco-based merchant finder Locu, which GoDaddy acquired for $70 million in August 2013; mobile payment service provider Paydiant, which PayPal acquired for $280 million in March 2015; and Burlington, Mass.-based cybersecurity software maker Black Duck, which announced in November 2017 that it would be acquired by California-based chip design software maker Synposys for $565 million.

From this experience, Bohn distilled important insights about Boston's startup culture. He liked to invest in entrepreneurs who had talent, optimism, and resilience. And he reflected the common Boston preference for funding founders with a prior track record of successfully solving technical challenges facing businesses. As he said, "America is a place where dreamers can do great. Someone with talent who is driven, resilient, and ambitious can do a lot. We back people with two characteristics. They focus on the enterprise market and have domain expertise, over-the-horizon radar, and the vision and charisma to attract and motivate a great team. Second, they are resilient because startups never have a straight path. I want people who can recover from failure and pivot. To test an entrepreneur's domain expertise I ask 'Why did you come up with this idea? Why do you think it is big? Did you talk with people about it? Are competitors doing it?' To test their resilience, I ask challenging questions. If they react sharply when challenged, I am concerned that this is how they'll be in front of investors, customers, and employees. It can be ideal to have two cofounders who complement each other and act as one person. That's what happened at Hubspot. Brian Halligan is a great sales person. He smiles, shakes your hand, he's warm, he sees the future and is engaged in making it happen, Dharmesh Shah is a brilliant technologist who is a good tinkerer. He talks about technology in a facile way. They work together very well."

Boston is leaking talent to Silicon Valley and New York. "Boston is different because we want to invest in people who know business technology and have experience. With a Snapchat, you have a really interesting kid who loves his iPhone with a great idea. He has no precedent baggage, people want to follow him, and [Snapchat] has virality. Boston is a tough place to do consumer-oriented startups and I have struggled when I went away from my enterprise focus. Boston is losing talent to New York, which has emerged in the last eight to 10 years. Young people want to be in New York and some of them start companies here and move there. It's also a center for new media and fashion e-commerce. Boston is the center for biotechnology and health technology," Bohn explained.

Case Analysis

Boston has been very successful in creating companies that could be acquired or go public. The problem is that its culture supports startups with limited potential. Many brilliant students educated in Boston and Cambridge migrate to Silicon Valley if they have greater ambitions. To be sure, it is possible that a new generation of venture capitalists in Boston may be willing to bet on consumer-focused startups; however, for many decades its culture of risk avoidance by investing in seasoned enterprise technology entrepreneurs remained in place.

Principles

Level 3 regions should consider whether their established startup values are becoming too rigid. As you saw in the cases in this section, the success that comes with creating small pillar companies in niche markets can either reinforce the old way of doing things or spur the region on to new values in order to achieve even greater success. The danger of complacency is that a region loses ground to more ambitious rivals and is unable to stop the leakage of its best talent to more ambitious regions. The danger of setting more ambitious goals is that the region is unable to enhance its skills enough to reach Level 4.

Here are principles that Level 3 stakeholders should consider to make their region even more startup friendly:

- **Entrepreneurs** should mentor young entrepreneurs and push efforts to reach Level 4. To that end, successful local entrepreneurs should study the skills that enable Level 4 regions to succeed, identify their region's capability gaps, and help find way to close those gaps.

- **Local governments** in such regions should build out local housing and infrastructure to support the increase in the number of professionals and other workers who will keep coming to the region to work in the startups. Such governments should also participate in discussions about reaching Level 4 in order to plan for future expansion of housing and infrastructure to support bigger local pillar companies.

- **Local university leaders** should bring local entrepreneurs into classes to meet with students and should encourage internships at the local startups. They should also consider hiring faculty who can help bolster the local skills needed to reach Level 4.

- **Venture capitalists** should consider adding to the skills among their partners in these cities as the local ecosystem augments its skills to support a move to Level 4.

Level 4: Many Pillars in Huge Markets

Success Case Study: Emergence Capital Creates $100 Billion in Value

Introduction

Silicon Valley places a great emphasis on betting on youth and opportunity, and on giving back to the community. Consider how Silicon Valley's values emerged. Mike Maples, Jr., founding partner of venture capital firm Floodgate, believed that Silicon Valley's culture originated in the gold rush of the 1850s. As Maples explained, "The gold rush happened in Northern California primarily. If you think about the gold rush for a second, you say, 'Okay, I'm in a river next to you and we're both panning for gold, and then you fish out this huge rock of gold and you're rich.'" Maples argued that someone nearby would see that happen and conclude that he should keep panning because the other fellow is no smarter. Maples continued, "I look at you and I'm sitting there in the river away from you. How do I interpret that? Well, I probably don't come away thinking, 'Oh, he's so much smarter than I am.' I might instead conclude, 'Wow. First of all, there really is gold in these rivers; second of all, if I stay in the river and keep panning for gold, I'm liable to get me some too.'"

Maples argued that the roots of Silicon Valley came from Leland and James Stanford and the gold rush. "The default assumption should be idealism. Everybody knows somebody who struck it rich, and it could happen for you at any time. Don't over-think it, just get in the game. Those roots were well in place even before [Stanford professor] Frederick Terman encouraged [William] Hewlett and [David] Packard to start HP out of the garage." A philosophy of expanding opportunity propelled Silicon Valley in the 1970s and 1980s. As Maples explained, "A lot of the early founders of these companies were very free market-oriented and wanted to grow the pie. They understood that it didn't make sense to fight over the current map, because the map hadn't even been drawn yet." He believed that American explorers shared that philosophy. Maples said, "You know, when you're Lewis and Clark and you're discovering the Louisiana territory, you're not worried about fighting over a tiny little municipality that's already been discovered. You're like, 'Holy crap, look at all this undiscovered land, let's go!'" Maples concluded, "I just think that a mindset of abundance and idealism drove people to conclude that you don't have to lose for me to win, so we might as well help each other."

Eesley agreed with Maples and emphasized that community building was a key part of Silicon Valley's value system. As he explained, "These settlers and frontiersmen and women were also community builders. When you're out at the frontier, you know that you have to help one another so that everyone can get ahead and do better. Silicon Valley and Stanford especially is a strong community where people recognize that the more you put into it, the more you get out of it. Also, if you engage in bad behavior in the community, then there are consequences. So I think the Western frontier contributed to that dynamic, which doesn't exist as much in places like New York."

Case Scenario

These values played out in the success of a Silicon Valley venture capitalist whose career began in New York. Jason Green, founder and General Partner of Emergence Capital, laid claim to investing in companies worth $100 billion. Green is an East Coaster. He graduated cum laude with a B.A. in Economics from Dartmouth College and an M.B.A. from Harvard with Distinction. He worked as a Kauffman Fellow with Manhattan-based Venrock. Yet Green had achieved the Silicon Valley version of the American dream. Green enjoyed a spot on Forbes's 2017 Top 100 Venture Capitalists Midas List. Here's why: "A string of exits propels Green onto the Midas List, capped off by ServiceMax's acquisition by GE in November 2016 for about $1 billion. In December 2015, Salesforce acquired Steelbrick for $360 million; Green was also an investor in TouchCommerce (acquired in August 2016 for $215 million) and Yammer (acquired in July 2012 by Microsoft for $1.2 billion). An investor in Aaron Levie's enterprise company Box before it went public, Green's portfolio currently includes HR software company Gusto, performance management startup BetterWorks, and marketing software company Groundtruth. The founding chairman of the Kauffman Fellows Program, Green is also a twin married to a twin."

It was the excitement of the dot-com boom that drew Green to Silicon Valley. As he said in a November 2017 interview, "When I was at HBS, professor Jeff Timmons urged me to apply for the Kauffman Fellows program one week before the deadline. I applied and got in and went to work for Venrock with legendary partners like Peter Crisp and Roy Rothrock. In 1997, the Internet started taking off and I went to US Venture Partners." The dot-com bust was not pleasant for Green but it contributed to his decision to start his own firm. According to Green, "In 2002/2003, I decided to bet on myself. Emergence's vision was [about the growing opportunity in] the enterprise cloud. My cofounders shared this vision and we have now raised $1 billion in four funds. When we started Emergence, we saw that the consumer Internet, with e-commerce companies like Amazon, was creating a demand for software that would affect the quality of the way consumers would spend their day. On the East Coast, investors thought that it was enterprise customers that were at the cutting edge. But we realized that consumers would be the early adopters of the cloud; they were two to three years ahead of the enterprise."

An early test of this thesis was Marc Benioff's Salesforce.com. "Salesforce was a dotcom at a time when nobody was interested. But we saw it as a big space with tons of innovation. Everyone else was retrenching and we thought there was not much to lose. Salesforce was creating real value for real businesses and would deliver recurring revenue from a big market. And as a leader Marc was beyond extraordinary. We did not expect that 15 years later it would be producing $10 billion in annual revenue and a $75 billion market capitalization," he said. With Salesforce, Emergence discovered a formula that has worked for other investments. As Green said, "We look at the unit economics of a business, comparing the cost to acquire a customer with the customer's lifetime value. Once you understand how that works, you can achieve success over 10 to 15 years. We saw that with SuccessFactors, Box, and ServiceMax. A great team plus great opportunity plus a product that customers like can yield great value."

Emergence preferred to work with its portfolio companies to build their value over time. As he said, "With ServiceMax, we made a Series A investment in 2008. We recruited the CEO from SuccessFactors and the VP of Sales. We invested in five rounds of financing. We helped them form partnerships with Salesforce and GE. And it was acquired by GE for $1 billion," he said. Another successful Emergence portfolio company was life sciences cloud service provider Veeva, which was founded in 2008. "Peter Gassner started the company and it was profitable from the beginning and never used the first $4 million we invested. It went public in October 2013 [making Emergence 300 times its investment, according to Bloomberg] and by November 2017 had an $8.5 billion market capitalization. We've made 12 investments in companies like that."

Green saw some important differences in culture between the East and West Coast venture capital firms. "Here we focus more on the size of the pie instead of our slice. We offer more founder-friendly terms. The East Coast is more conservative. On the West Coast we think that if founders are smart, ambitious, passionate, intense, and driven, they can learn a lot. The biggest risk is losing all your investment. We lose money on 20% to 30% of our investments. But we look at what the upside is if we're right."

As Green approached 50, he had legacy on his mind, moving from "success to significance," he said. "I love what I do. I love the people I work with. And I am involved with two non-profits that help entrepreneurs. Success breeds success. You don't have to hold your cards close to your chest. Our companies have created a million jobs and I feel good about that. We have a responsibility to give back to the community. Rockefeller University is one of our investors, which has 23 Nobel laureates and is working on a cure for cancer. We've hired young people and are passing along the wisdom, process, approach, and philosophy. It is fulfilling to see people succeed."

Case Analysis

Emergence Capital epitomizes the best things about Silicon Valley's startup culture. Like many of Silicon Valley's leading lights, its founder was educated on the East Coast and decided to go west in pursuit of excitement in the Internet boom. In the aftermath of the dot-com bust, he saw an opportunity to turn his vision of the enterprise cloud into a series of profitable investments that came from putting capital into great leaders who were targeting huge opportunities with attractive "unit economics." He also believes in giving back to the community through mentoring and building the next generation of leaders.

Failure Case Study: Jawbone Shuts Down after 18 Years and $900 Million in Investment

Introduction

Silicon Valley likes to make big bets on passionate young entrepreneurs. Sometimes those bets attract outsiders under the spell of the fear of missing out (FOMO). FOMO can compound a bad bet and ultimately lead to a bigger failure. FOMO tends to attract capital providers who are eager to get in on what looks to them like a more attractive investment opportunity than the ones that they generally review. Such capital providers tend not to be venture capitalists; instead, they are relative outsiders with large amounts of capital such as mutual funds, sovereign wealth funds, private equity firms, and even banks. FOMO blinds these investors to basic problems with the business such as a weak CEO or a company's inability to build and sell a product that customers are willing to buy. Ultimately, FOMO is replaced by fear of losing everything (FOLE) —and the money-losing company is abruptly unable to raise new capital so it fails.

Events in 2014 through 2016 illustrated the phenomenon of outside money being punished by purchasing a ticket to the party after the fun is over. In 2014, there were 273 IPOs, the largest number since 2000. The next year, venture capital investment rose 23% from the year before, reaching $58.8 billion. And 2015 was also the year that mutual funds poured into startups, accounting for about 45% of the funding rounds of startups valued at over $1 billion. Sovereign wealth funds piled into startups as well, investing $12.7 billion into tech startups in 2016, up from $2.2 billion in 2015. Unfortunately for these investors, it was too late. In 2015, the number of IPOs fell 38% to 170. What's worse, the number of venture-backed companies going public fell from 30 in 2014 to 16 in 2015. And by February 2016, not a single venture-backed technology company had gone public.

Case Scenario

San Francisco-based Jawbone, a maker of portable fitness devices, was among the biggest recipients of this capital, raising $900 million in equity and debt during its 18-year life only to shut down in July 2017. While it created some successful products including a Jambox wireless speaker, wireless Bluetooth headsets, and the Up *fitness band, Jawbone could not get products to market on time; was unable to main-tain a stable executive team; could not fend off competition from Apple and Fitbit; filed costly lawsuits with its supplier and Fitbit; and suffered a final round of financing that halved its value before it shut down.*

The valuation of Jawbone, which launched in 1999 under the name AliphCom, peaked at $3.2 billion in 2014, fell 55% when it borrowed money in January 2016, and hit zero in July 2017, evaporating nearly $900 million in equity and debt capi-tal. Silicon Valley venture capitalists including Sequoia, Andreessen Horowitz, Khosla Ventures, and Kleiner Perkins invested in Jawbone, including a September 2014 round that raised $147 million at a valuation of $3.2 billion. In February 2015, it raised $400 million in debt, of which $300 million came from Manhattan-based money manager BlackRock. By November 2015, Jawbone realized that its prospects were bleak and laid off 15% of its workforce. Two months later, Jawbone's presi-dent, who had joined from Google in June 2015, returned from whence he came. That same month, Jawbone borrowed—since venture capitalists would not provide more equity—a whopping $165 million from a sovereign wealth fund, the Kuwait Investment Authority, at a 55% lower valuation of $1.5 billion. Jawbone tried to sell itself in 2016 to rival Fitbit, which offered a small fraction of its then $1.5 billion valuation, but was unable to find a buyer and it was "sued by vendors who allege the company owes them hundreds of thousands of dollars," according to Reuters.

Case Analysis

A dark side of Silicon Valley is the fierce competition for wealth. People who have achieved a net worth of $100 million are in a hurry to reach $1 billion and those with $1 billion are in aggressive pursuit of even more. The combina-tion of fierce competition, enormous wealth, and unquenchable yearning for more means that as soon as a new market space is ripe for investment, it is quickly populated by many well-funded companies seeking to dominate the market. This often means to there are too many very well-funded companies going after the same opportunity. If their founders can make a compelling enough case, they can raise ever-greater amounts of capital despite the lack of market share gains. Ultimately even the deepest-pocketed investors will stop writing checks for these money-losing companies and they will fail. Jawbone is among the biggest examples of this process.

Principles

Level 4 regions are the most startup friendly. However, that friendliness has considerable negative side effects. These include excessively high hous-ing costs, too much traffic, lack of employee loyalty, and intense competition among over-funded local startups. Level 4 regions should seek to minimize these negative side effects and to guard against the dangers of complacency.

Here are principles that Level 4 stakeholders should consider to make their region even more startup friendly:

- **Entrepreneurs** should mentor young entrepreneurs and work with local leaders to create and implement policies that minimize the negative side effects of the region's startup success. These policies could include allowing employees to work from home more frequently, helping with housing and childcare, and providing other benefits to boost employee loyalty and minimize their exposure to the negative side effects of the region

- **Local governments** in such regions should take the lead in policies that can ease the strain on local housing and infrastructure by building more affordable housing, strengthening infrastructure, and expanding public transportation.

- **Local university leaders** should hire and promote professors and researchers who can create new technologies and intellectual property that creates new opportunities for startup growth.

- **Venture capitalists** should give back to the community by mentoring and should seek out and invest in startups with the potential to create new opportunity areas that will enable the region to keep growing as older technologies mature.

Table 7-1 below summarizes the principles for each step in the Pillar Company Staircase.

Table 7-1. Principles by Step in Pillar Company Staircase

Pillar Company Stair	Principles
Level 0	Build on local strengths while encouraging amblers to become sprinters.
Level 1	Unleash local entrepreneurship by eliminating regulatory and cultural impediments.
Level 2	Use local startup successes to encourage entrepreneurship and local reinvestment of capital and talent.
Level 3	Use experience of talent from acquired gazelles to turn local sprinters into marathoners.
Level 4	Build on successful operating experience to provide capital and advice to next generation of pillar company CEOs.

Are You Doing Enough To Nurture Local Startup-Friendly Shared Values?

Here are five tests of whether a region has startup-friendly values:

- Are local entrepreneurs achieving sufficient startup success to make startups a more viable career option for students?

- Are successful entrepreneurs staying near cities where their startups were headquartered and helping out younger entrepreneurs through mentoring and investing?

- Are venture capitalists from other regions opening local offices to find and invest in local opportunities that will make the region even more startup friendly?

- Are local universities encouraging professors to start companies and giving students academic credit for working with local entrepreneurs?

- Are local government leaders creating the infrastructure needed to support startup growth?

Conclusion

A region's values are an important factor in an entrepreneur's decision about where to locate a startup. Founders must choose where they should locate their startups based in part on the fit between their goals and the local startup values. For example, if a founder seeks to start and grow a consumer-focused technology startup, she should locate in a region that values such ventures. If a founder aspires to help build the local startup ecosystem, he should locate where such giving back to the community is expected. In Chapter 8, I will conclude the book by providing guidance to regions that lack vital startup scenes. To that end, I will present case studies and principles to help such cities identify and build on their strengths to initiate a process that jump-starts the region's startup ecosystem.

Implications for Cities

Boosting Your Startup Common

Startup Common Insights

The case studies in the first seven chapters of the book suggest that many cities suffer from Silicon Valley envy, fueling a desire to build their own startup hubs. City leaders realize that they do not know where to begin but they often bring in people from Silicon Valley to advise them. And from there, such cities often use government resources to lure entrepreneurs from outside the region and/or to encourage local entrepreneurs to start companies in the city rather than moving to a more well-established city.

As illustrated in Figure 8-1, the path to building a successful Startup Common can take decades and depends heavily on outcomes that are difficult to plan and fraught with uncertainty.

© Peter S. Cohan 2018
P. S. Cohan, *Startup Cities*, https://doi.org/10.1007/978-1-4842-3393-1_8

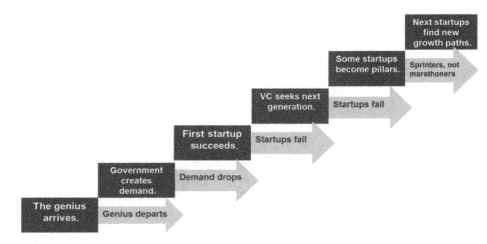

Figure 8-1. How cities climb the Pillar Company Staircase

Let's take a look at the meaning of each of these steps:

- **The genius arrives.** To set a region's startup scene afire, a match must spark a combustible material. In practice, this means that a very talented entrepreneur arrives in a region at the time it needs rapid growth. This "genius" could be a talented inventor, a professor with a startup-friendly mindset, or a charismatic individual who can build local enthusiasm for entrepreneurship. This individual could be living in the city but more often arrives from somewhere else.

- **Government creates demand.** Sometimes government can help turn an idea into a growing business. Government can create demand for a startup's products by purchasing them, as it did when HP was getting started. Or government can make an entrepreneur attractive tax incentives, as New Hampshire did when Cabletron's founder was trying to decide where to locate his company.

- **First startup succeeds.** Every region that ultimately becomes a thriving startup hub hosts its first highly-visible startup success, often after the startup is acquired. Such success provides meaningful rewards such as money and startup know-how to the startup's founders and investors.

- **Venture capital seeks next generation.** The region's initial success creates wealthy individuals who can invest in new startups and it sends a signal to successful capital providers in other locations that they should seek out startups in this newly enriched city.

- **Some startups become pillars.** By attracting new capital to the city, the initial success leads investors to fund many other people who are inspired by that success to take a chance on becoming entrepreneurs. Some of the founders of the first successful startup develop from *sprinters* (leaders who can build and sell a company quickly) to *marathoners* (who can turn an idea into a large public company growing at over 20% a year). While many of these companies do not succeed, after enough tries, one or two of them are led by newly formed marathoners who build pillar companies.

- **Next generation of startups finds new growth paths.** Eventually the investors who enriched themselves in these waves of startups lose their ability to identify the next wave of opportunity. If these investors retire and a new generation comes along that can continue to envision new growth curves, then the region's startup scene will remain vital. Otherwise, the region will stagnate and its Startup Common will wither.

Here are some examples of how this process has played out in the case studies we examined earlier in the book. For example, government can help boost a city's startup scene in meaningful ways but only when it partners with exceptional entrepreneurial talent. What's more, the arrival of such talent in a city is often due to factors beyond the government's control. For example, was it not for William Shockley's decision to move from AT&T in New Jersey to Palo Alto to take care of his mother who lived there, Silicon Valley might not have become the world's leading place to design and build semiconductors. Had MIT not declined to offer tenure to Frederick Terman, he might not have decamped to Stanford, where he applied many of the same principles that were the basis of MIT's success, such as encouraging professors to consult with businesses and start their own companies. Moreover, was it not for Terman's encouraging his students William Hewlett and David Packard to start HP, many other Silicon Valley successes might not have happened.

Another example is Israel's emergence as a startup hub through a combination of the arrival in Israel during the early 1980s of a million Russian immigrants, many with PhDs, coupled with its creation of Yozma, using Israeli government money to co-invest with 10 foreign VCs, matching every $1 in investment from a U.S. venture capital firm with $2 from this fund. When the VC sold its shares, Israel required it to repay the $2, leaving most of the gains to the VCs. The combination of the startup talent and government-abetted venture capital helped Israel to transform itself from a socialist society to a startup nation. Moreover, requiring all citizens to serve in the Israeli Defense Forces serves as a training ground for entrepreneurs in two ways: giving them the experience of taking on heavy responsibilities for the lives of others at a young age and giving them valuable technical skills such as in cybersecurity.

What seems to work less well is for government to open incubators and provide small grants for startups to use if they locate their startups in a city. This approach has been used in cities like Santiago, Chile (its Startup Chile program offers grants to startups that stay there for six months) and to a lesser extent in Worcester, Hong Kong, and Lisbon, Portugal (which tends not to provide capital for startups). These programs raise many questions:

- *On what basis should their success or failure be judged?* I think the best way to measure their success is whether they produce successful exits for investors, either by building companies that are acquired or go public. While local leaders may enjoy positive media coverage for taking action to try to encourage startups, these programs will ultimately have no long-term reason to continue unless they result in successful startups.

- *Is there a better way for local governments to encourage startup activity?* Cities that host good universities and colleges can help encourage more local startup activity by making the city a more attractive place for recent graduates to live, work, and play. For example, if a city is lacking attractive neighborhoods in which to rent apartments, to shop, and to recreate, locally educated students will find it far more pleasant to move to a city that is already known for these amenities and is seen as a great place for a startup.

In addition to government, local universities can also help determine whether local startup activity increases or plateaus. The case studies we explored demonstrate that the right university culture can improve a region's startup scene dramatically. For example, MIT and Stanford encourage faculty to consult with businesses as a way to test the value of their ideas. When these professors start companies, they employ talented students and act as role models for entrepreneurship. Indeed, these local examples of startup success create a demonstration effect that can change the local culture. In Israel, for example, the success of local startups has made parents far more comfortable urging their children to become entrepreneurs than in the past when parents might have wanted them to become doctors or lawyers. Conversely, the absence of local role models keeps parents in Hong Kong pushing their children to seek careers in banking or consulting instead of entrepreneurship.

Ultimately, what propels a region's startup scene to the top of the Pillar Company Staircase is an ample supply of talented entrepreneurs who have the ability to scale a company to $100 million or more in revenue. Indeed, of all the critical resources that make the difference between a region's startup success and failure, nothing is more important than an adequate supply of entrepreneurs who can scale a company. Regions that attract and develop such talent over generations of companies sustain their leadership, and regions that repel such talent face overwhelming hurdles to creating local startup success. There is a very small number of individuals who can turn an idea into a company with over $50 billion in stock market value—Jeff Bezos (Amazon), Mark Zuckerberg (Facebook), Sergei Brin and Larry Page (Google), and Reed Hastings (Netflix) come to mind—and keep it growing at over 20% a year. Such leaders are essential for a region's startup success. But there are many more individuals, such as Cohesity's Mohit Aron, who start off their careers as successful product developers (he developed Google's file system before cofounding Nutanix) and grow into excellent CEOs through a combination of starting a company that is acquired by the likes of Amazon or Facebook and staying there long enough to learn more about how to manage growth and mentoring from people who have scaled companies successfully. Regions that host the first or second kinds of entrepreneurs exert a magnetic pull that attracts talent from around the world, which in most cases is a loss for the cities where they grew up and were educated.

The reason for this is simple to describe: the economy values certain skills more than others. What's more, the people who are the world's best in those skill areas are many times more valuable than those who have just average ability. Furthermore, the skills that the world valued 10 or 300 years ago are likely to become stale in the future. Therefore, a region that seeks to be in the lead when it comes to starting companies must be thinking about what skills will be needed 10 or 100 years from now and make sure that it is attracting the best people with those skills. Often a generation of investors that succeeds by investing in a specific set of skills can't see to the next wave of opportunity and must rely on the next generation of investors to find the skills needed to tap into new opportunities.

For example, in the 1880s the ability to manufacture ceramics for grinding was a very valuable skill. A potter named John Jeppson immigrated from Sweden to Worcester and bought its Norton pottery company, ultimately transforming it into a publicly-traded abrasives maker that was Worcester's largest employer; in the 1980s it was acquired by a French company, Saint Gobain. These days pottery skills are not so highly valued, but people with doctorates in artificial intelligence can command compensation packages in the tens of millions of dollars. In all likelihood, a hundred years from now society will put a much higher premium on other skills. But for now, regions that attract the best people in the most highly valued skill sets and teach them how to turn ideas into huge companies will enjoy the most startup success.

How to Build Your Startup Common

This leads to a question that is easy to ask and difficult to answer: What should a city do to build up its Startup Common? Two Harvard Business School (HBS) professors offered their views. Josh Lerner, in his book *Boulevard of Broken Dreams*, highlights the most common errors that cities make in trying to create effective startup ecosystems. As Lerner explained in a July 2017 interview, "I have been intrigued by the foolish things that states and cities have done and thought there ought to be a better way. Europe split billions into 27 equal pieces [divided equally among the EU's 27 member countries]; it was spread so thin that it had no impact anywhere." Lerner's prescription advocates overcoming local barriers to entrepreneurship. "I recommend a different approach. Government leaders should examine local impediments to entrepreneurship and develop a plan to address them; they should get the private sector involved as a reality check; and they should recognize that it will take decades, not three or four years to make progress," he said.

How exactly should cities approach these challenges? Karen Gordon Mills, HBS Senior Fellow, proposed a logical process. As she said in a July 2017 interview, "First, assemble a group of local leaders: people from government, business, research, academia, labor, philanthropy, and other key groups and decide what specific outcome they want to achieve." She continued, "With that outcome in mind, the group should analyze local assets [using local industry-specific employment and other data from the Cluster Mapping Project] and try to figure out which ones are world-class. Next, they should create a local competition backed by significant funding to encourage the emergence of startups that will build new businesses around these world-class assets. A non-political third party should select the winner of the competition."

Another approach from MIT focuses on cities outside the U.S. As MIT Sloan School professor Michael Cusumano explained in a July 2017 interview, "We created the Regional Entrepreneurship Acceleration Program (REAP) which admits eight regions annually to participate in a two-year learning engagement with MIT." REAP is based on a stakeholder and systems approach. As Sloan School professor Scott Stern explained in a July 2017 interview, "REAP uses a series of mechanisms to translate, convene, and educate teams of regional leaders through a full five-stakeholder approach, including entrepreneurs, risk capital, government, big corporations, and universities. The teams address the existing system by setting a strategy to deploy new interventions to improve it."

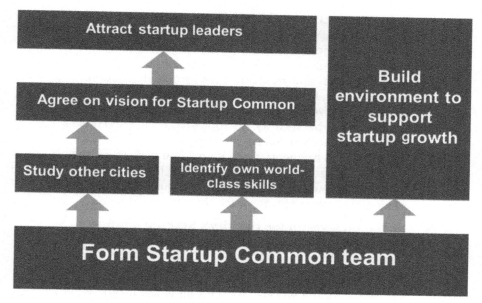

Figure 8-2. How to build a Startup Common

Based on their ideas and my own thinking, here is a six-step methodology, illustrated in Figure 8-2, for boosting a city's startup scene:

- **Form a Startup Common team.** Local government leaders should assemble a team of local entrepreneurs, capital providers, government leaders, universities, selected corporation, and philanthropists and charge them with creating a process that will boost the city's startup scene.

- **Study what worked in buildingsuccessful Startup Commons and what did not work for less successful ones.** The team's first step should be to learn about how other cities have tried to create Startup Commons. The team should identify cities that have achieved successful outcomes and those that have tried and fallen short. Specifically, the team should study research on what these cities did to boost local startups and the number of successful startups that were built and exited, either through acquisitions or going public. The team should interview the key local leaders to understand what worked, what did not work, the reasons behind these outcomes, and the lessons they learned.

- **Assess objectively the city's world-beating skills.**
  The next challenge the team must face is to identify
  objectively whether the city has or could have specific
  skills that would be both valuable ingredients for successful startups and would be seen by outside observers
  as world-class. In the cases you've examined in previous
  chapters, you've seen some examples, such as Israel's
  strengths in cybersecurity, Boston's abilities in enterprise
  technology, and Sweden's skills in gaming, music streaming, and online payments. Since it could be difficult for the
  team to look at this question objectively, it might be useful to hire an outside consultant to help guide the process
  of identifying the skills on which the city would focus.

- **Agree on a vision for the city's Startup Common.**
  The Startup Common team should agree on a shared
  vision for the city's startup scene. The shared vision
  would answer questions such as the following:

  - What are the world-class skills on which local
    startups will build?

  - What talent and capital will they need to turn ideas
    into fast-growing companies?

  - What skills will be available in the mentor networks
    to help these companies to grow?

  - How many local startups will be acquired and how
    many will become public companies?

- **Attract talented leaders who can turn those skills
  into fast-growing companies.** The team should next
  turn its attention to bringing talented leaders to the city
  that can turn its skills into fast-growing companies. Such
  individuals could be professors or students at local universities, be working in local companies, or be living and
  working elsewhere. The team would need to develop
  specific strategies for each leader to encourage them to
  build companies that apply local world-beating skills and
  offer to help these leaders to gather the resources they
  need to start and build the companies.

- **Build the housing, infrastructure, and cultural
  elements needed to support the growth of these
  companies.** Finally, the team should develop a plan, raise
  financing, and complete the construction of housing, infrastructure (such as roads, sewer, power, startup incubator

space, and high speed Internet), as well as cultural locations such as restaurants, museums, shopping areas, parks, and entertainment venues to attract talented people to work in the startups.

How Cities Apply the Startup Common Building Methodology

There is an important difference between how cities climb the Pillar Company Staircase and the six-step Startup Common Building Methodology described above. The former always gets started by pioneering entrepreneurs operating in a context that may eventually help them succeed. The latter begins with government officials leading a process intended to jumpstart local entrepreneurship. Sadly, there are no examples of cities that have used this methodology to build a Startup Common that hosts many pillar companies. This is not to say that government can't help in the process; it certainly helped in Silicon Valley, Tel Aviv, and Stockholm. However, in all these cases, government was a supporting actor rather than the start of the startup show.

Nevertheless, it is easy to see why local governments would want to do something to attract startups. Most notably, there are many cities that are heavily dependent on industries that were formerly growing robustly and creating job opportunities and tax revenue for their host regions. Many such cities have suffered along with those now-declining companies. And they see Silicon Valley as a model of a region that keeps growing, thus creating many jobs, boosting housing prices, and adding to tax revenue. These moribund regions would like to turn themselves around and begin the journey that produces the benefits of growth. And without some *deus ex machina*, those cities are likely to keep falling further behind. So it makes some sense for government leaders to try to be that outside force that reboots the local economy.

Here are two cases that demonstrate the strengths and limits of such a government-led effort.

Chattanooga, Tennessee

In 2009, Chattanooga was suffering the negative effects of the financial crisis; it had lost jobs in government, construction, and finance. That year, local government officials obtained federal financing to turn the rights of way controlled by a local utility into a high-speed fiber optic network that attracted startups to the city. While none of these startups have become pillar companies, at least one of them grew large enough that it was acquired for a modest amount. Moreover, by 2017, these startups had created enough jobs to meaningfully offset some of the jobs that had been lost during the economic downturn.

Case Scenario

By 2014, there was evidence of success resulting from the Chattanooga government's initiative. According to a February 2104 New York Times report, "In 2009, a $111 million federal stimulus grant offered the opportunity to expedite construction of a long-planned fiber optic network," said David Wade, Chief Operating Officer for Electric Power Board of Chattanooga (EPB). Wade said it quickly became apparent that customers would be willing to pay [55 businesses and 3,640 residences] for the one-gigabyte connection offered over the network. Chattanooga, by 2014 known as "Gig City, had the first, fastest, and among the least expensive (less than $70 a month) high-speed Internet services in the United States," noted the Times. This attracted some new businesses, but not enough to make up for the ones that closed. As the Times reported, "Gig created about 1,000 jobs in the last three years. The Department of Labor reported that Chattanooga still had a net loss of 3,000 jobs in that period, mostly in government, construction, and finance."

Mayor Andy Berke told the Times, "We don't need to be the next Silicon Valley. That's not who we're going to be, and we shouldn't try to be that. But we are making our own place in the innovation economy." That place included two startups that prove the power of Chattanooga's one-gigabyte-per-second network. One of them moved from Florida after winning a $100,000 prize offered by a local incubator, and another local startup was acquired for nearly $12 million. Toni Gemayel is a Florida native who started Banyan, a software company working on a way for researchers in different locations to share real-time editing of huge data files. In 2013, he moved Banyan from Tampa to Chattanooga because of the Internet speed. As he said, "This is a small city that I had never heard of. It beat Seattle, New York, San Francisco in building the Gig. People here are thinking big." Gemayel first came to Chattanooga in 2012 when he heard about a startup contest sponsored by The Company Lab with a $100,000 prize, which Banyan won. Gemayel took that money to Tampa but he could not get the bandwidth he needed there so he moved to Chattanooga.

Another local startup, Quickcue, which built a tablet-based guest-management system for restaurants, began working in Chattanooga in 2011, raised $3 million in capital over two years, and was acquired in December 2013 for $11.5 million to Open Table. Chattanooga took a chance—betting millions on a city-wide Wi-Fi network—that did not pay off since it is mostly unused. And the Gig is only partially useful because as Miller Welborn, a partner at business incubator Lamp Post Group, said, "The Gig is not fully useful to Chattanooga unless a hundred other cities are doing the same thing. To date, the best thing it's done for us is it put us on the map." Nevertheless, by May 2017 the Gig's benefits were showing up in Chattanooga's 3.3% unemployment rate, which was well below the Tennessee average, according to Times Free Press, which quoted a July 19 Paychex report "that Tennessee led the nation in small business job growth during June 2017 with employment gains of 1.31%."

Case Analysis

After supplying the city with a one-gigabyte-per-second fiber optic network, Chattanooga has made considerable progress in building a startup community. Since its network was faster than those in many other cities, Chattanooga attracted entrepreneurs from different regions and kept them there. Moreover, the city created an entrepreneurship competition that helped finance some of the startups that located there. One of the startups raised outside venture capital and sold the company to Open Table. While the jobs created by the startups were not enough to offset the losses in the wake of the financial crisis, by 2017 Chattanooga was enjoying one of the lowest unemployment rates in the state. Nevertheless, Chattanooga has much further to go if it hopes to build a booming local startup scene, most notably to attract or create more local capital for startups and reward those investors with gains.

Santiago, Chile

In August 2013, I presented the Startup Common idea to an audience at the University of Chile in Santiago. What I found most striking was learning that business failure is considered illegal in Chile. It is hard to imagine a greater disincentive to starting a company than the fear of being labeled a criminal should your enterprise run out of money. I thought surely there must be a legal distinction between someone who failed despite earnest efforts and someone who took capital from others, siphoned it into a bank account in another country, and left the county before his theft was discovered. As far as I know, that law has not changed. Therefore, it does not surprise me that despite government efforts, startup success in Santiago is hard to spot in the sense of successful companies that enrich capital providers despite a program that gives cash to entrepreneurs who locate and operate their startups in Chile.

Case Scenario

Chile's government is trying to encourage more startup activity. It has plenty of cash thanks to its heavy economic dependence on copper, which increased in price due to strong demand from China. However, Chile realizes that it does not want to risk its entire economy on the notion that copper prices will remain high. Moreover, it sees the benefits to a region of hosting a vibrant startup scene. To that end, Chile has created various programs to draw in startups, mostly to Santiago. Beginning in 2010, Chile's state-backed accelerator, Start-Up Chile, began offering a $35,000 grant in exchange for which a startup would work in Chile for six months and a one-year visa. In 2015, the organization launched a follow-fund called Start-Up Chile SCALE to give certain graduates even more support. Ten of the roughly 100 companies in each class receive an additional $100,000 grant if they meet certain requirements and agree to keep their business in Chile for at least a year. The results of all this were considerable; between 2010 and October 2016, Chile had distributed over $40 million to 1,300 startups from almost 80 countries, which by the summer of 2016 had generated roughly 1,600 jobs in Chile and raised $100 million outside capital.

Chile's economic development policies are formulated by the Corporación de Fomento de la Producción de Chile (CORFO), which has been around since 1939. In the past, CORFO helped developed Chile's banking and telecommunications industries and in the last decade has focused on startup innovation, although its 2016 budget was a mere $45 million. In 2010, Chile benefited when Groupon paid $30 million to acquire ClanDescuento. In 2010, Start-Up Chile hosted 20 companies from 14 countries and by 2012, 500 companies from 37 countries had graduated from the program. In 2011, an early stage VC fund called NXTP Labs opened in Santiago, and Nazca Ventures raised $15 million to invest in Chilean countries. That year, PayPal acquired Multicaja for an undisclosed amount. In December 2011, Microsoft announced it would open an innovation center in Chile to serve 2,000 companies and 6,000 entrepreneurs by 2017; thanks to a law passed in 2010, CORFO was allowed to invest in it. Sadly, most of the companies that participated in Start-Up Chile—68% to be specific—ended up leaving Chile after the program. To remedy that, Chile began offering Start-Up Chile SCALE in 2015. Meanwhile, Chile has many startups, but of 11 highlighted in May 2017, only one, an apartment investment site called BRICKOP, reported revenue: $4 million in 2016.

Case Analysis

Chile has tried to establish a lively startup scene in Santiago. While there has been some money going into startups and many people coming from around the world to spend it, there has been very little coming out, such as gazelles that are approaching substantial exits through acquisition or initial public offerings. Instead, Chile looks as though it has given money in hopes of luring entrepreneurs who will stay there and build a local startup ecosystem, but two-thirds of them leave. To be sure, Chile has gotten substantial attention from the global media as a result of Start-Up Chile but it has not attracted substantial inflows of venture capital that can come after creating a pillar company. And absent that, it will be difficult for Chile to change its culture, most notably its laws related to business failure.

Lessons Learned From Applying the Startup Common Building Methodology

These two case studies reveal that the Startup Common Building Methodology could be useful, but factors that that determine whether a city achieves its goals are outside of the team's control. For example,

- Will the team's efforts attract pioneering entrepreneurs to the city?

- Will the pioneers decide to stay once they get started or will they move elsewhere?

- Will the pioneers achieve a highly visible success that draws more talent and capital to the city?

- Will the founding teams of these successful startups start new companies in the city or invest in new startups there?

- Will the next generation of entrepreneurs and capital create a pillar company?

- Will the pillar company help spur more local entrepreneurship?

- Will a new generation of entrepreneurs and capital keep the city at the forefront of technology?

The ways a city uses the Startup Common Building Methodology can help increase the chances of positive outcomes in many of these factors. By asking and answering the right questions at each step, the process yields better results. Here are some of the steps and questions:

- **Form a Startup Common team.** The team should include leaders of all the key local stakeholders and the individuals selected should possess wide-ranging networks of people who can help. At this stage, the following questions should be answered:

    - Who are the key stakeholders of the city's Startup Common?

    - Which representatives of these stakeholders would be willing to participate on the team and do these individuals have the skills and talent network to contribute to the success of the process?

    - What incentives does each of the team members need to remain engaged with the process?

    - Are other team members available in case the original ones leave?

- **Study what worked in building successful Startup Commons and what did not work for less successful ones.** The team should recognize that other cities have tried to build Startup Commons and that valuable lessons can be learned from what worked for them and what did not. To find these insights, the team should answer questions such as the following:

  - Which cities have had the most success trying to build a Startup Common?

  - Which ones have suffered the most failure in trying to build a Startup Common?

  - Which cities most like ours have tried to build a Startup Common?

  - From these three groups of cities, which ones should we study further?

  - For each of the cities we choose to study,

    - What were the city's goals in trying to create a Startup Common?

    - Who participated in the city's Startup Common team and what strengths and weaknesses did they bring to the process?

    - What proposals did the team develop and how did it choose the ones to implement?

    - What resources were gathered, such as capital, facilities, and talent, to turn the proposals into reality?

    - How long did the city take to implement the proposals?

    - What outcomes did the proposals achieve?

    - Were the outcomes better or worse than expected and why?

    - What lessons did the city learn from the process and the outcomes?

    - What principles did the city develop based on this learning?

    - Based on the answers to these questions, which are the most important insights the team should apply?

- **Assess objectively the city's world-beating skills.**
  The team must next decide which skills it needs to host
  in order to spur the growth of its Startup Common. To
  pick the right one, the team should answer the following
  questions:

  - Are there skills that enabled the city to prosper
    in the past that could be used to tap future
    opportunities? If so, which ones?

  - For these skills, are other cities using those skills
    to create new companies? If so, which cities and
    companies?

  - How successful are these companies and what
    factors contribute to their success?

  - How well does the city perform key skills compared
    to these other cities?

  - If the city is at a competitive disadvantage, does
    the city have other skills, perhaps being taught at
    its universities, which could be the basis of new
    companies and industries?

  - If so, are these skills currently or potentially strong
    enough to be the basis for the city's Startup
    Common?

  - Would these skills give the city's startups the ability
    to gain a significant share of a large, rapidly-growing
    market?

  - For these skills, what resources would the city need
    to add in order to achieve these market share gains?

- **Agree on a vision for the city's Startup Common.**
  The Startup Common team should agree on a shared
  vision for the city's startup scene. To make the right
  choices, the team should answer specific questions about
  each:

  - *Skills focus:* Are the skills in question targeted at a
    large market? Compared to rivals, is the city strong
    enough in these skills to attract world-class talent?

  - *Added resources:* Has the city identified specific
    talented entrepreneurs and investors who it would
    like to attract to the city?

- *Mentor network*: Has the city identified specific individuals with various skills who could mentor the entrepreneurs?

- *Startup success*: Are goals for the number and timing of successful startup exits realistic in light of the city's strengths and the performance of other cities?

- **Attract talented leaders who can turn those skills into fast-growing companies.** The team should next turn its attention to bringing talented leaders to the city who can turn their skills into fast-growing companies. To do this effectively, the team should answer these questions:

  - Do the team members have professional colleagues who can provide introductions to these talented individuals?

  - If so, what would be the most effective way to invite the talented individuals to consider moving to the city to start a company or teach at the local university?

  - What incentives could the city provide these individuals to help them overcome objections to moving?

  - Who from the team would be responsible for efforts to attract each of the talented individuals to the city?

- **Build the housing, infrastructure, and cultural elements needed to support the growth of these companies.** To do this well, the team should answer the following questions:

  - What are the most important aspects of a city's architecture for attracting and keeping top talent?

  - How does this talent perceive the city's housing, cultural elements, roads, commuting patterns, shopping, and entertainment facilities compared to those of the most desirable cities?

  - Which of these elements needs the most improvement first in order to convince talented individuals to live and work in the city?

  - How can the city obtain the financing and other resources it needs to make these improvements?

Despite attempting to answer all these questions, the history of successful and unsuccessful Startup Commons makes it clear that the most important participants in the rise or fall of a city's startup scene are the entrepreneurs and investors who put their careers and capital on the line. Their actions are unlikely to bend to the will of government and others who hope to benefit from their success.

Conclusion

In today's global economy, location matters. Start your company in one city and it has access to the world's best technical and marketing people and an ample supply of capital and mentoring to help an entrepreneur turn her idea into a $100 million company. Another city 40 miles away sees its best talent is fleeing its universities after graduation to make their fortune elsewhere and venture capitalists will not even deign to set foot there. Why does this 40-mile distance matter? As reflected in the relative vitality of the two cities' startup scenes, they place a different value on entrepreneurship. One location's startup scene hums because so many talented people start companies, take them public, and stay around to help the next generation of entrepreneurs. In the other, successful startups can't be found so people educated there conclude that the risks of pioneering a startup in the city exceed the potential benefits.

But cities are not static; they are either getting further ahead or falling further behind. Cities with the most active startup scenes now can only maintain their lead if they take steps to offset the high costs that their growth imposes on residents and seek out and invest in new opportunities for growth. Cities in decline must decide whether to do nothing—and thus fall further behind—or to do something, as Chattanooga and many others have, to help make their cities more compelling to talented entrepreneurs.

I hope this book helps both kinds of cities overcome their challenges.

Notes

Introduction

[i] Thomas Friedman, *The World is Flat: A Brief History of the Twenty-First Century* (New York, NY: Farrar, Straus and Giroux, 2005).

[ii] "Cabletron Systems," *Crunchbase*, accessed July 27, 2017, www.crunchbase.com/organization/cabletron-systems#/entity

[iii] "Oracle buys Acme Packet," *Oracle*, accessed February 4, 2013, www.oracle.com/corporate/acquisitions/acmepacket/index.html

[iv] Peter Cohan, "Mulling the Worcester Startup Common," *Telegram & Gazette*, May 12, 2013, www.telegram.com/article/20130512/column70/305129983

[v] Peter Cohan, "Oxford Historian Creates Silicon Valley's Future," *Forbes*, December 30, 2011, www.forbes.com/sites/petercohan/2011/12/30/oxford-historian-creates-silicon-valleys-future/

[vi] Peter Cohan and Srini Rangan, *Capital Rising: How Global Capital Flows Are Changing Business Systems All Around the World*, (Basingstoke, United Kingdom: Palgrave Macmillan, 2010).

[vii] Peter Cohan, *Hungry Startup Strategy: Creating New Ventures With Limited Resources and Unlimited Vision*, (Oakland, CA: Berrett-Koehler Publishers, 2012).

© Peter S. Cohan 2018
P. S. Cohan, *Startup Cities*, https://doi.org/10.1007/978-1-4842-3393-1

Chapter 1: What Is the Startup Common?

[i] The term startup refers to a company that starts small and intends to get big quickly—what The Kauffman Foundation refers to as a Gazelle. While so-called lifestyle startups with more modest ambitions are more widely dispersed geographically, Gazelles are concentrated in regions such as Silicon Valley and Boston/Cambridge.

[ii] Garrett Hardin, "The Tragedy of the Commons," *Science*, December 13, 1968, http://pages.mtu.edu/~asmayer/rural_sustain/governance/Hardin%20 1968.pdf

[iii] "PWC/CB Insights Money Tree Report Q2 2017," PWC, accessed July 23. 2017, https://www.pwc.com/us/en/moneytree-report/assets/MoneyTree_ Report_Q2_2017_Final_F.pdf

[iv] In Northern California, for example, consumer-focused Internet companies prefer to locate in San Francisco's South of Market area; database companies put their headquarters near Oracle's in Redwood City. Similarly, Boston is a popular location for its consumer-focused startups while enterprise software companies might locate in Route 495 communities such as Littleton and Chelmsford.

[v] P.S. Cohan and U. S. Rangan, "Capital Rising: How Global Capital Flows Are Changing Business Systems All Around the World," Palgrave Macmillan, 2010.

[vi] P.S. Cohan interview with co-head of Stanford D-School's Launchpad, Michael Dearing, May 25, 2011.

[vii] Peter Cohan, "How Silicon Valley Helped PlanGrid Lay its Foundation," *Forbes*, January 4, 2013, https://www.forbes.com/sites/petercohan/2013/01/ 04/how-silicon-valley-helped-plangrid-lay-its-foundation/

[viii] Chuck Eesley email to Peter Cohan, "Comments regions/startups," August 24, 2013.

[ix] *Hungry Startup Strategy*, Ibid.

[x] "Silicon Valley Investing Slump Continues, Fewer Startups Get Funded," *San Jose Mercury News*, April 4, 2017, http://www.mercurynews.com/2017/04/04/ silicon-valley-investing-slump-continues-fewer-startups-get-funded/

[xi] Peter Cohan, "Why Elad Gil Gives Back To Silicon Valley," *Forbes*, July 23, 2012, https://www.forbes.com/sites/petercohan/2012/07/23/ why-elad-gil-gives-back-to-silicon-valley/. As Gil said, If an entrepreneur fails due to unethical conduct, he is ostracized; however failing due to bad luck, taking a risk that does not pan out, or other ethical sources of failure is worn as a badge of honor.

xii Peter Cohan, "How Cambridge and Silicon Valley Became Startup Hubs," *Forbes*, July 18, 2017, https://www.forbes.com/sites/petercohan/2017/07/18/how-cambridge-and-silicon-valley-became-startup-hubs/

xiii Peter Cohan, "Wayfair sheds light on path for startups," *Worcester Telegram & Gazette*, March 18, 2013, http://www.telegram.com/article/20130318/COLUMN70/103189921

xiv Kasey Wehrum, "Special Report: Wayfair's Road to $1 Billion," *Inc.*, April 3, 2012, https://www.inc.com/magazine/201204/kasey-wehrum/the-road-to-1-billion-growth-special-report.html

xv Adam L. Penenberg, "Wayfair: Your Online Mega-Pivot Megastore," *Fast Company*, June 19, 2012, https://www.fastcompany.com/1840173/wayfair-your-online-mega-pivot-megastore

xvi Wehrum, Ibid.

xvii Penenberg, Ibid.

xviii Wehrum, Ibid.

xix "Can Boston compete with Silicon Valley?," *Boston Globe*, June 10, 2012, https://www.bostonglobe.com/business/2012/06/09/shawn-harris-nyopoly-com-and-niraj-shah-wayfair-entrepreneurship/0cQH7GKvHeyga6JIfIIhSJ/story.html

xx Justine Hofherr, "How Wayfair's CEO hires employees, builds office culture and unwinds at home," *Boston Globe*, May 6, 2016, https://www.boston.com/jobs/jobs-news/2016/05/06/wayfair-ceo-niraj-shah

xxi "Wayfair sheds light on path for startups," Ibid.

xxii Peter Cohan, "With $201 Million Of Capital And $1 Billion In Sales, Wayfair's IPO Can Wait," July 15, 2013, https://www.forbes.com/sites/petercohan/2013/07/15/with-201-million-in-capital-and-1-billion-in-sales-wayfairs-ipo-can-wait/

xxiii Ancient writings attributed to the Greek geographer Strabo's Geographika were compiled roughly 2,000 years ago according to "Strabo's Geographica," *BBC Radio 4*, accessed July 27, 2017, http://www.bbc.co.uk/programmes/b03zr11t

xxiv Alfred Marshall, "Principles of Economics," 1890, http://eet.pixel-online.org/files/etranslation/original/Marshall,%20Principles%20of%20Economics.pdf

xxv Peter Cohan, "Why Do Fast-Growing Startups Gather In A Few Cities?," *Forbes*, July 17, 2017, https://www.forbes.com/sites/petercohan/2017/07/17/why-do-fast-growing-startups-gather-in-a-few-cities/

xxvi "Why Do Fast-Growing Startups Gather In A Few Cities?," Ibid.

xxvii "Why Do Fast-Growing Startups Gather In A Few Cities?," Ibid.

xxviii "Why Do Fast-Growing Startups Gather In A Few Cities?," Ibid.

xxix Peter Cohan, "Buy Stock In Pillar Companies Like HubSpot, Wayfair, iRobot," *Forbes*, July 7, 2017, https://www.forbes.com/sites/petercohan/2017/07/12/buy-stock-in-pillar-companies-like-hubspot-wayfair-irobot/

xxx "How Cambridge and Silicon Valley Became Startup Hubs," Ibid.

xxxi "How Cambridge and Silicon Valley Became Startup Hubs," Ibid.

xxxii "How Cambridge and Silicon Valley Became Startup Hubs," Ibid.

xxxiii "How Cambridge and Silicon Valley Became Startup Hubs," Ibid.

Chapter 2: Creating Pillar Companies

i For example, in the 1990s network equipment maker Cisco Systems acquired as many as 60 startups a year that had developed a product their customers wanted to buy but lacked a powerful salesforce. In this way, Cisco outsourced some new product development to these startups.

ii Peter Cohan, "Can Boston Catch Up With Silicon Valley?," *Forbes*, August 14, 2017, https://www.forbes.com/sites/petercohan/2017/08/14/can-boston-catch-up-with-silicon-valley/

iii "IPG Photonics Corp. Quote," *Morningstar*, accessed November 24, 2017, http://www.morningstar.com/stocks/xnas/ipgp/quote.html

iv "IPG Photonics Corp. Income Statement," *Morningstar*, accessed November 24, 2017, http://financials.morningstar.com/income-statement/is.html?t=IPGP&region=USA&culture=en_US

v "Valentin Gapontsev & family," *Forbes*, accessed November 24, 2017, https://www.forbes.com/profile/valentin-gapontsev/

vi An April 2014 survey by The Research Bureau distributed to nine area colleges and universities, and completed by more than 260 graduating students, found that just 18 percent planned to locate in Worcester after graduation. Walter Bird Jr., "Worcester ponders how to keep college grads from leaving town," *Worcester Magazine*, October 30, 2014, https://worcestermag.com/2014/10/30/worcester-ponders-keep-college-grads-leaving-town/28650

vii Peter Cohan, "Zephyr Workshop showcases Becker's gaming skills," *Worcester Telegram & Gazette*, June 21, 2015, http://www.telegram.com/article/20150621/NEWS/150629972

viii Peter Cohan, "Zephyr Workshop showcases Becker's gaming skills," *Worcester Telegram & Gazette*, June 21, 2015, http://www.telegram.com/article/20150621/NEWS/150629972

ix Peter Cohan, "Zephyr Workshop showcases Becker's gaming skills," *Worcester Telegram & Gazette*, June 21, 2015, http://www.telegram.com/article/20150621/NEWS/150629972

x Peter Cohan, "Two gaming companies win StartUp Worcester berths," *Worcester Telegram & Gazette*, May 16, 2016, http://telegram_com.g53-wtstage.newscyclecloud.com/article/20160516/NEWS/160519546

xi Peter Cohan, "Wall & Main: Local gaming company wins at Kickstarter," *Worcester Telegram & Gazette*, June 12, 2017, http://www.telegram.com/news/20170612/wall-amp-main-local-gaming-company-wins-at-kickstarter

xii Peter Cohan, "Startups led by Worcester-educated executives," *Worcester Telegram & Gazette*, April 14, 2013, http://www.telegram.com/article/20130414/column70/304149979

xiii Peter Cohan, "Can Boston Catch Up With Silicon Valley?," *Forbes*, August 14, 2017, https://www.forbes.com/sites/petercohan/2017/08/14/can-boston-catch-up-with-silicon-valley/

xiv Jo Maitland, "EMC Sues Another Ex," *Byte and Switch*, October 11, 2001, http://www.networkcomputing.com/careers/emc-sues-another-ex/223647501/

xv Barnaby Feder, "Private Sector; Dismissed and Sued, but Nothing Personal," *New York Times*, December 1, 2002, http://www.nytimes.com/2002/12/01/business/private-sector-dismissed-and-sued-but-nothing-personal.html

xvi Maitland, Ibid.

xvii Feder, Ibid.

xviii Maitland, Ibid.

xix Eynav Ben Yehuda, "SANgate Closes Shop in Israel, Dismisses Most Staff," *Haaretz*, July 1, 2003, http://www.haaretz.com/print-edition/business/sangate-closes-shop-in-israel-dismisses-most-staff-1.22995

xx "SANgate," *Crunchbase*, accessed August 22, 2017, https://www.crunchbase.com/organization/sangate#/entity

xxi Spencer Hamer, "Non-Compete Clauses In California," *Law Journal Newsletters*, January 2017, http://www.lawjournalnewsletters.com/sites/lawjournalnewsletters/2017/01/01/non-compete-clauses-in-california/?slreturn=20170731091155

xxii "Check Point Software Technologies, Quote," *Morningstar*, accessed August 23, 2017, http://www.morningstar.com/stocks/xnas/chkp/quote.html

xxiii "Gil Shwed net worth," *Forbes*, accessed August 23, 2017, https://www.forbes.com/profile/gil-shwed/

xxiv John Leyden, "Firewall tech pioneer Gil Shwed: Former teen sysadmin on today's infosec biz," *The Register*, April 23, 2013, https://www.theregister.co.uk/2013/04/23/check_point_profile/

xxv "Imperva. Quote," *Morningstar*, accessed August 23, 2017, http://www.morningstar.com/stocks/xnas/impv/quote.html

xxvi "Palo Alto Networks. Quote," *Morningstar*, accessed August 23, 2017, http://www.morningstar.com/stocks/xnys/panw/quote.html

xxvii Guy Grimland, "Together They Built Check Point, Separately They've Gone Even Further," *Haaretz*, February 10, 2012, http://www.haaretz.com/israel-news/business/together-they-built-check-point-separately-they-ve-gone-even-further-1.412072

xxviii Peter Cohan, "IBM's 'Close To $1 Billion' Trusteer Buy Extends Shlomo Kramer's Winning Streak," *Forbes*, September 12, 2013, https://www.forbes.com/sites/petercohan/2013/09/12/ibms-close-to-1-billion-trusteer-buy-extends-shlomo-kramers-winning-streak/

xxix Peter Cohan, "After Imperva And Mobileye, Here's What's Next For Israeli Startups," *Forbes*, August 21, 2017, https://www.forbes.com/sites/petercohan/2017/08/21/after-imperva-and-mobileye-heres-whats-next-for-israeli-startups/

xxx Vikram Rupani, *LinkedIn profile*, accessed August 23, 2017, https://www.linkedin.com/in/vrupani/?ppe=1

xxxi Terence Lee, "These former investment bankers are changing grocery shopping in Singapore," *TechInAsia*, January 14, 2012, https://www.techinasia.com/these-former-investment-bankers-are-changing-grocery-shopping-in-singapore

xxxii Lee, Ibid.

xxxiii RedMart, *Crunchbase*, accessed August 23, 2017, https://www.crunchbase.com/organization/redmart

xxxiv Michael Tegos, "Redmart is still losing money. But its revenue is growing fast," *TechInAsia*, July 8, 2016, https://www.techinasia.com/redmart-financial-reports-2016

xxxv Lee, Ibid.

xxxvi Victoria Ho, "Online Grocery Store Redmart Raises Series A Round To Stay Put In Singapore," *TechCrunch*, July 17, 2013, https://techcrunch.com/2013/07/17/online-grocery-store-redmart-raises-series-a-round-to-stay-put-in-singapore/

xxxvii Catherine Shu, "Singapore Online Grocer RedMart Raises $5.4M From Investors Including Facebook Co-founder," *TechCrunch*, January 22, 2014, https://techcrunch.com/2014/01/22/singapore-online-grocer-redmart-raises-5-4m-from-investors-including-facebook-co-founder/

xxxviii Jon Russell, "Singapore Online Grocer RedMart Raises $26.7M Ahead Of Southeast Asia Expansion," *TechCrunch*, August 20, 2015, https://techcrunch.com/2015/08/20/singapore-online-grocer-redmart-raises-26-7m-ahead-of-southeast-asia-expansion/

xxxix Tegos, Ibid.

xl Jon Russell, "Singapore-based online grocery company RedMart is close to raising a massive $100 million Series C round to expand its service across Asia," *TechCrunch*, January 29, 2016, https://techcrunch.com/2016/01/29/redmart-100-million/

xli Jon Russell, "Alibaba's Lazada confirms acquisition of Singapore web grocery startup RedMart," *TechCrunch*, November 1, 2016, https://techcrunch.com/2016/11/01/alibaba-lazada-redmart-confirmed/

xlii Jane Peterson, "A Showdown Brews Between Amazon and Alibaba, Far From Home," *New York Times*, October 22, 2017, https://www.nytimes.com/2017/10/22/business/alibaba-amazon-southeast-asia-lazada.html

xliii Peter Cohan, "After Skype, King, Mojang And Spotify; Here's What's Next From Stockholm," *Forbes*, August 17, 2017, https://www.forbes.com/sites/petercohan/2017/08/17/after-skype-king-mojang-and-spotify-heres-whats-next-from-stockholm/

xliv Dan Mitchell, "Skype's long history of owners and also-rans: At an end?," *Fortune*, May 11, 2011, http://fortune.com/2011/05/11/skypes-long-history-of-owners-and-also-rans-at-an-end/

xlv "After Skype, King, Mojang And Spotify; Here's What's Next From Stockholm," Ibid.

xlvi Stefan Lundell, "Niklas Zennström is raising $1B for new fund," *Swedish Startup Space*, January 19, 2016, http://swedishstartupspace.com/2016/01/19/niklas-zennstrom-is-raising-hundreds-of-millions-for-new-super-fund/

xlvii "Swedish payments firm Klarna taps debt market for the first time," *Reuters*, June 26, 2016, www.reuters.com/article/us-sweden-klarna-idUSKCNOZ DOH9

xlviii "Klarna," *Atomico*, accessed August 24, 2017, http://www.atomico.com/portfolio/klarna

[xlix]"Klarna," *Crunchbase*, accessed August 24, 2017, https://www.crunchbase.com/organization/klarna#/entity

[l] "Truecaller," *Crunchbase*, accessed August 24, 2017, https://www.crunchbase.com/organization/true-software-scandinavia#/entity

[li] "Zennström invests in Truecaller," *Swedish Wire*, December 23, 2014, http://www.swedishwire.com/business/19592-zennstroem-invests-in-truecaller

[lii] Tom Turula, "The 10 Swedish startups that received the most funding in 2017," *Business Insider*, July 6, 2017, http://nordic.businessinsider.com/the-10-swedish-startups-that-received-the-most-funding-in-2017-2017-7/

[liii] Zoë Henry, "How a Country the Size of North Carolina Became a Global Startup Hub," *Inc.*, Mar 13, 2017, https://www.inc.com/zoe-henry/stockholm-sweden-hub-fast-growing-private-companies-2017-inc5000-europe.html

[liv] Michael Carney, "Failure report: Dissecting the biggest flameouts in venture history," *Pando*, January 31, 2014, https://pando.com/2014/01/31/failure-report-dissecting-the-biggest-flameouts-in-venture-history/

[lv] Ben Gilbert, "24 of the biggest failed products from the world's biggest companies," *Business Insider*, December 29, 2016, http://www.businessinsider.com/biggest-product-flops-in-history-2016-12/#1957-ford-edsel-1

[lvi] Robin Wauters, "Joost Is Now Officially Dead – Assets Acquired By Adconion Media Group," *TechCrunch*, November 24, 2009, https://techcrunch.com/2009/11/24/joost-acquired-adconion/

[lvii] "Iliad's warrior," *The Economist*, September 10, 2009, http://www.economist.com/node/14402214

[lviii] Simon Kuper, "Lunch with the FT: Xavier Niel," *FT*, May 3, 2013, https://www.ft.com/content/22167134-b24a-11e2-8540-00144feabdc0

[lix] "Xavier Niel Real Time Net Worth," *Forbes*, accessed August 20, 2017, https://www.forbes.com/profile/xavier-niel/Xavier Niel

[lx] Arthur Scheuer, "Xavier Niel explains 42: the coding university without teachers, books, or tuition," *VentureBeat*, June 16, 2016, https://venturebeat.com/2016/06/16/xavier-niel-explains-42-the-coding-university-without-teachers-books-or-tuition/

[lxi] Scheuer, Ibid.

[lxii] Mathieu Rosemain and Gwénaëlle Barzic, "French tycoon Niel sees Paris overtaking London as startup leader," *Reuters*, June 29, 2017, http://www. reuters.com/article/us-france-start-ups-macron-idUSKBN19K2RR

[lxiii] David Jegen, "Where Are They Now – Exploring Boston's Iconic Startup Stories. Introducing Founders Diaries," *LinkedIn*, March 28, 2017 https:// www.linkedin.com/pulse/where-now-exploring-bostons-iconic-startup-stories-founders-jegen

[lxiv] "EXACT Sciences Corp.," *MarketWatch*, accessed August 27, 2017, http:// www.marketwatch.com/investing/stock/exas

[lxv] Peter Cohan, "Boston Pillars Analysis," August 27, 2017.

[lxvi] Jeanne Whalen and Mimosa Spencer,"Sanofi Buys Genzyme for Over $20 Billion," *Wall Street Journal*, February 11, 2011, www.wsj.com/articles/SB10 001424052748703373404576147483489656732

[lxvii] George Slefo, "Salesforce Buys Krux, the Data-Management Platform, for $700 Million," *Adage*, October 3, 2016, http://adage.com/article/digital/salesforce-buys-krux-data-management-platform-700-million/306139/

[lxviii] Jordan Novet,"CenturyLink is acquiring cloud-database startup Orchestrate," *VentureBeat*, April 20, 2015, https://venturebeat.com/2015/04/20/centurylink-is-acquiring-cloud-database-startup-orchestrate

[lxix] Janelle Nanos,"ThriveHive was acquired for $11.8 million by Propel Business Solutions on Tuesday," *BetaBoston*, March 22, 2016, http://www.betaboston. com/news/2016/03/22/thrivehive-is-acquired-by-propel-business-solutions-for-11-8-million/

[lxx] Leslie Berlin, *Troublemakers*, (New York, NY: Simon & Schuster, November 2017), p. 51.

[lxxi] Lora Kolodny, "How Google parent Alphabet exercises massive influence over start-ups in Silicon Valley," *CNBC*, August 17, 2017, https://www.cnbc. com/2017/08/17/alphabet-google-start-up-investment-vehicles.html

[lxxii] Kolodny, Ibid.

[lxxiii] "The Global Unicorn Club," *CB Insights*, accessed August 26, 2017, https:// www.cbinsights.com/research-unicorn-companies

[lxxiv] Ingrid Lunden, "GV's Tom Hulme on AI, life sciences and the Alphabet VC's future in Europe," *TechCrunch*, March 31, 2017, https://techcrunch. com/2017/03/31/gvs-tom-hulme-on-ai-life-sciences-and-alphabet-vcs-future-in-europe/

lxxv "Rideshare Company SideCar Experiences Explosive Growth Raises Series A Financing of $10 Million From Lightspeed Venture Partners and Google Ventures," *Marketwire*, October 10, 2012, http://www.marketwired.com/press-release/rideshare-company-sidecar-experiences-explosive-growth-raises-series-a-financing-10-1711061.htm

lxxvi Alex Wilhelm and Alexia Tsotsis, "Google Ventures Puts $258M Into Uber, Its Largest Deal Ever," *TechCrunch*, August 22, 2013, https://techcrunch.com/2013/08/22/google-ventures-puts-258m-into-uber-its-largest-deal-ever/

lxxvii Brian Solomon, "Ride-Share Pioneer Sidecar Shuts Down, Outmuscled By Uber And Lyft," *Forbes*, December 29, 2015, https://www.forbes.com/sites/briansolomon/2015/12/29/ride-share-pioneer-sidecar-shuts-down-outmuscled-by-uber-and-lyft/

lxxviii Solomon, Ibid.

lxxix Biz Carson, "IN THEIR OWN WORDS: 13 startups explain why they failed," *BusinessInsider*, May 5, 2016, http://www.businessinsider.com/founders-explain-startup-failures-2016-4/

lxxx Ken Yeung, "Sidecar: 'We failed because Uber is willing to win at any cost'," *Venturebeat*, January 20, 2016, https://venturebeat.com/2016/01/20/sidecar-we-failed-because-uber-is-willing-to-win-at-any-cost/

lxxxi Julia Love and Heather Somerville, "Alphabet's lawsuit against Uber marks the end of a relationship that was tense from the start," *Reuters*, March 6, 2017, http://www.businessinsider.com/r-alphabet-lawsuit-against-uber-marks-end-of-uneasy-marriage-2017-3

lxxxii Kia Kokalitcheva, "Where things stand on the Waymo-Uber lawsuit," *Axios*, July 28, 2017, https://www.axios.com/current-status-of-the-waymo-uber-lawsuit-2466532911.html

lxxxiii "Mutual funds reportedly mark down investments in Uber by up to 15%," *Reuters*, August 23, 2017, https://www.cnbc.com/2017/08/23/mutual-funds-mark-down-investments-in-uber-by-up-to-15-percent-wsj-reports.html

Chapter 3: Launching Startups from Universities

i Peter Cohan, "How Clark and UMass Medical School help Worcester's startup scene," *Worcester Telegram & Gazette*, September 10, 2017

ii "How Clark and UMass Medical School help Worcester's startup scene," Ibid.

iii "How Clark and UMass Medical School help Worcester's startup scene," Ibid.

iv "How Clark and UMass Medical School help Worcester's startup scene," Ibid.

v "How Clark and UMass Medical School help Worcester's startup scene," Ibid.

vi "How Clark and UMass Medical School help Worcester's startup scene," Ibid.

vii Peter Cohan, "Grow Produce Anywhere In Freight Farms' $60,000 Shipping Container," *Forbes*, June 27, 2013, https://www.forbes.com/sites/petercohan/2013/06/27/grow-produce-anywhere-in-freight-farms-60000-truck/

viii "Grow Produce Anywhere In Freight Farms' $60,000 Shipping Container," Ibid.

ix Jade Scipioni, "The Future of Farming May Live Inside This Box," *FOXBusiness*, March 10, 2016, http://www.foxbusiness.com/features/2016/03/10/future-farming-may-live-inside-this-box.html

x "Grow Produce Anywhere In Freight Farms' $60,000 Shipping Container," Ibid.

xi "Philippe Foriel-Destezet," *Forbes*, September 12, 2017, https://www.forbes.com/profile/philippe-foriel-destezet/

xii "Pierre Bellon & family," *Forbes*, September 12, 2017, https://www.forbes.com/profile/pierre-bellon/

xiii Pierre Kosciusko-Morizet, *Crunchbase*, accessed September 12, 2017, https://www.crunchbase.com/person/pierre-kosciusko-morizet#/entity

xiv Ingrid Lunden, "Groupon is buying LivingSocial, plans to downsize business to 15 markets from 27," *TechCrunch*, October 26, 2016, https://techcrunch.com/2016/10/26/groupon-is-buying-livingsocial-plans-to-downsize-business-to-15-markets-from-27/

xv "Crédit Mutuel Arkéa / Leetchi," *Crunchbase*, September 22, 2015, https://www.crunchbase.com/acquisition/c5255ffbb25b6b7682263329162e4310

xvi "Spartoo," *Crunchbase*, accessed September 12, 2017, https://www.crunchbase.com/organization/spartoo#/entity

xvii "Adobe Systems / Fotolia," *Crunchbase*, December 22, 2014, https://www.crunchbase.com/acquisition/9765e92585f0b1644d3f59fbecc49708

xviii "Made.com," *Crunchbase*, September 12, 2017, https://www.crunchbase.com/organization/made-com#/entity

xix Zen Soo and Yujing Liu, "How a high-school dropout with big ideas founded GoGoVan, Hong Kong's first US$1bn start-up," *South China Morning Post*, September 1, 2017, http://www.scmp.com/tech/leaders-founders/article/2109032/how-high-school-dropout-big-ideas-founded-gogovan-hong-kongs xx Jon Russell, "GoGoVan becomes Hong Kong's first $1 billion startup following merger deal," *TechCrunch*, September 1, 2017, https://techcrunch.com/2017/09/01/gogovan-becomes-hong-kongs-first-1-billion-startup-following-merger-deal/

xxi Simon Loong Chief Executive Officer and Co-Founder, WeLab, accessed September 9, 2017, https://www.welab.co/team?locale=en

xxii "Hong Kong: Incubator for success," *BBC*, accessed September 9, 2017, http://www.bbc.com/storyworks/capital/city-of-inspiration/stories

xxiii Catherine Shu, "Online Lending Platform WeLab Gets $160M Series B To Expand In China," *TechCrunch*, January 21, 2016, https://techcrunch.com/2016/01/21/welab/

xxiv "WeLab," *Crunchbase*, accessed January 17, 2018, https://www.crunchbase.com/organization/welab

xxv "Snapask," *Crunchbase*, accessed September 10, 2017, https://www.crunchbase.com/organization/appedu#/entity

xxvi "9GAG," *Crunchbase*, accessed September 10, 2017, https://www.crunchbase.com/organization/9gag#/entity

xxvii "Innopage," *Crunchbase*, accessed September 10, 2017, https://www.crunchbase.com/organization/innopage-limited#/entity

xxviii Frank Vinluan," Athenex IPO Raises $66M to Fund Clinical Trials for Cancer Drugs XConomy," June 14, 2017, http://www.xconomy.com/new-york/2017/06/14/athenex-ipo-raises-66m-to-fund-clinical-trials-for-cancer-drugs/

xxix "Athenex," *GoogleFinance*, accessed September 10, 2017, http://www.google.com/finance?q=NASDAQ%3AATNX&ei=ppC1WZC-L9W5mQGC_oLgBQ

xxx "An innovative European technical university," *KTH*, accessed September 8, 2017, https://www.kth.se/en/om/fakta

xxxi "About KTH Innovation," *KTH*, accessed September 8, 2017, https://www.kth.se/en/innovation/vi-erbjuder/om-kth-innovation-1.504834

xxxii "Lisa Ericsson, Head of KTH Innovation," *KTH*, accessed September 8, 2017, https://www.kth.se/polopoly_fs/1.347369!/Menu/general/column-content/attachment/Bakgrund%20och%20kompetens%20LE_ENG.pdf

xxxiii "The Global Unicorn Club: Spotify," *CB Insights*, accessed September 8, 2017, https://www.cbinsights.com/research-unicorn-companies

xxxiv Peter Cohan, "Sorry Investors, MIT Can't Save IBM From Secular Decline," Forbes, September 7, 2017, https://www.forbes.com/sites/petercohan/2017/09/07/sorry-investors-mit-cant-save-ibm-from-secular-decline/

xxxv "Sorry Investors, MIT Can't Save IBM From Secular Decline," Ibid.

xxxvi "Sorry Investors, MIT Can't Save IBM From Secular Decline," Ibid.

xxxvii Scott Thurm and Ben Fox Rubin, "Sycamore Networks: From $45 Billion to Zilch," *Wall Street Journal*, February 1, 2013, https://www.wsj.com/articles/SB10001424127887323926104578278350413288348

xxxviii "Desh Deshpande," *Deshpande Foundation*, accessed September 8, 2017, http://www.deshpandefoundation.org/about-us/founders/desh-deshpande/

xxxix Steven Syre, "Internet-era boom icon's quiet bust," *Boston Globe*, October 26. 2012, https://www.bostonglobe.com/business/2012/10/25/quiet-end-for-sycamore-networks-brief-star-internet-era/7GA6JOLQ1bz6NMrms4osoN/story.html

xl Peter Cohan, "Huh? This Startup Couldn't Raise Venture Capital So It Went Public," *Inc.*, September 1, 2017, https://www.inc.com/peter-cohan/huh-this-startup-couldnt-raise-venture-capital-so-.html

xli Peter Cohan, "Technion's Brainpower Yields $7.5 Billion in Stock Market Value," *Inc.*, September 8, 2017, https://www.inc.com/peter-cohan/technions-brainpower-yields-75-billion-in-stock-m.html

xlii "Elbit Systems: Quote," Morningstar, accessed September 8, 2017, http://www.morningstar.com/stocks/XNAS/ESLT/quote.html

xliii "Technion's Brainpower Yields $7.5 Billion in Stock Market Value," Ibid.

xliv "Technion's Brainpower Yields $7.5 Billion in Stock Market Value," Ibid.

xlv "ReWalk Robotics Ltd: Quote," *Morningstar*, accessed September 8, 2017, http://www.morningstar.com/stocks/xnas/rwlk/quote.html

xlvi "Breathtec Biomedical: Quote," *Morningstar*, accessed September 8, 2017, http://www.morningstar.com/stocks/pinx/bthcf/quote.html

xlvii "Corindus Vascular Robotics: Quote," *Morningstar*, accessed September 8, 2017, http://www.morningstar.com/stocks/xase/cvrs/quote.html

xlviii "Mazor Robotics: Quote," *Morningstar*, accessed September 8, 2017, http://www.morningstar.com/stocks/xnas/mzor/quote.html

xlix "Microbot Medical: Quote," *Morningstar*, accessed September 8, 2017, http://www.morningstar.com/stocks/xnas/mbot/quote.html

[l] " Novocure: Quote," *Morningstar*, accessed September 8, 2017, http://www.morningstar.com/stocks/xnas/nvcr/quote.html

[li] " Pluristem Therapeutics: Quote," *Morningstar*, accessed September 8, 2017, http://www.morningstar.com/stocks/xnas/psti/quote.html

[lii] "OPKO Health: Quote," *Morningstar*, accessed September 8, 2017, http://www.morningstar.com/stocks/XNAS/OPK/quote.html

[liii] "Technion's Brainpower Yields $7.5 Billion in Stock Market Value," Ibid.

[liv] "Stanford d.school," *Stanford*, accessed September 15, 2017, https://static1.squarespace.com/static/57c6b79629687fde090a0fdd/t/58ab3b659f74561f4dcc75ba/1487616894633/dschool-fact-sheet-2012.pdf

[lv] Peter Cohan, "An Inside Look At Stanford's $2.7 Trillion Turbo-Charged Money Machine," *Inc.*, September 12, 2017, https://www.inc.com/peter-cohan/an-inside-look-at-stanfords-27-trillion-turbo-cha.html

[lvi] "An Inside Look At Stanford's $2.7 Trillion Turbo-Charged Money Machine," Ibid.

[lvii] Peter Cohan, "How Cambridge and Silicon Valley Became Startup Hubs," *Forbes*, July 18, 2017, https://www.forbes.com/sites/petercohan/2017/07/18/how-cambridge-and-silicon-valley-became-startup-hubs/

[lviii] Ken Auletta, "Get Rich U.," *The New Yorker*, April 30, 2012, https://www.newyorker.com/magazine/2012/04/30/get-rich-u

[lix] Peter Cohan, "Theranos Is Made-For-Hollywood Silicon Valley Scandal," *Forbes*, October 16, 2015, https://www.forbes.com/sites/petercohan/2015/10/16/theranos-is-made-for-hollywood-silicon-valley-scandal/

[lx] Peter Cohan, "Why Theranos Could Bleed Out By The End of 2017," *Forbes*, June 30, 2017, https://www.forbes.com/sites/petercohan/2017/06/30/why-theranos-could-bleed-out-by-the-end-of-2017/

[lxi] Tim Walker, "The billionaire factory: Why Stanford University produces so many celebrated web entrepreneurs," *Independent*, July 12, 2013, http://www.independent.co.uk/student/news/the-billionaire-factory-why-stanford-university-produces-so-many-celebrated-web-entrepreneurs-8706573.html

[lxii] Ryan Mac, "Clinkle Up In Smoke As Investors Want Their Money Back," *Forbes*, January 22, 2016, https://www.forbes.com/sites/ryanmac/2016/01/22/clinkle-up-in-smoke-as-investors-want-their-money-back/

[lxiii] Alyson Shontell, "A SILICON VALLEY DISASTER: A 21-Year-Old Stanford Kid Got $30 Million," Then Everything Blew Up," *BusinessInsider*, Apr. 14, 2014, http://www.businessinsider.com/inside-story-of-clinkle-2014-4

[lxiv] "Lucas Duplan," *LinkedIn profile*, accessed September 15, 2017, https://www.linkedin.com/in/lucasduplan/

Chapter 4: Deepening the Human Capital Pool

[i] Peter S. Cohan, "Zephyr Workshop showcases Becker's gaming skills," *Worcester Telegram & Gazette*, http://www.telegram.com/article/20150621/NEWS/150629972

[ii] "Zephyr Workshop showcases Becker's gaming skills," Ibid.

[iii] Peter Cohan, "Grow Produce Anywhere In Freight Farms' $60,000 Shipping Container," *Forbes*, June 27, 2013, https://www.forbes.com/sites/petercohan/2013/06/27/grow-produce-anywhere-in-freight-farms-60000-truck/

[iv] "Grow Produce Anywhere In Freight Farms' $60,000 Shipping Container," Ibid.

[v] "Grow Produce Anywhere In Freight Farms' $60,000 Shipping Container," Ibid.

[vi] Peter Cohan, "Freight Farms' success is Worcester's loss," *Worcester Telegram & Gazette*, September 27, 2015, http://www.telegram.com/article/20150927/NEWS/150929431

[vii] "The Challenges Facing Hong Kong Start-ups: Access to Talent," *The Economist*, August 3, 2017, http://economists-pick-research.hktdc.com/business-news/article/Research-Articles/The-Challenges-Facing-Hong-Kong-Start-ups-Access-to-Talent/rp/en/1/1X000000/1X0AB03X.htm

[viii] Peter Cohan, "Overcoming Startup Obstacles, Hong Kong Style," January 18, 2015, *Entrepreneur*, https://www.entrepreneur.com/article/241618

[ix] "WeLab," *Crunchbase*, accessed September 28, 2017, https://www.crunchbase.com/organization/welab#/entity

[x] "Overcoming Startup Obstacles, Hong Kong Style," Ibid.

[xi] "AfterShip," *Crunchbase*, accessed September 28, 2017, https://www.crunchbase.com/organization/aftership#/entity

[xii] "The Challenges Facing Hong Kong Start-ups: Access to Talent," Ibid.

[xiii] "Peter Cohan, "Hong Kong's Edwin Lee Builds a Mass Incubation Machine," *Forbes*, February 7, 2013, https://www.forbes.com/sites/petercohan/2013/02/07/hong-kongs-edwin-lee-builds-a-mass-incubation-machine/

[xiv] "Hong Kong's Edwin Lee Builds a Mass Incubation Machine," Ibid.

[xv] "Hong Kong's Edwin Lee Builds a Mass Incubation Machine," Ibid.

[xvi] "Hong Kong's Edwin Lee Builds a Mass Incubation Machine," Ibid.

xvii Sandy Li, "Bridgeway founder Edwin Lee carves niche role in Hong Kong street shop property market," *South China Morning Post*, December 13, 2016, http://www.scmp.com/property/hong-kong-china/article/2053942/bridgeway-founder-edwin-lee-carves-niche-role-hong-kong

xviii Peter Cohan, "KTH, The MIT of Stockholm, Produced These Three Mind-Blowing Startups," *Inc.*, September 24, 2017, https://www.inc.com/peter-cohan/kth-mit-of-stockholm-produced-these-three-mind-blowing-startups.html

xix "KTH, The MIT of Stockholm, Produced These Three Mind-Blowing Startups," Ibid.

xx "KTH, The MIT of Stockholm, Produced These Three Mind-Blowing Startups," Ibid.

xxi "KTH, The MIT of Stockholm, Produced These Three Mind-Blowing Startups," Ibid.

xxii Peter Cohan, "Disney And Intel Looking For Growth From This Stockholm Social Robot Maker," *Forbes*, September 21, 2017, https://www.forbes.com/sites/petercohan/2017/09/21/disney-and-intel-looking-for-growth-from-this-stockholm-social-robot-maker/

xxiii "Disney And Intel Looking For Growth From This Stockholm Social Robot Maker," Ibid.

xxiv CupoNation, *Crunchbase*, accessed September 24, 2017, https://www.crunchbase.com/organization/cuponation#/entity

xxv "CUPONATION Group becomes Global Savings Group," *Cuponation*, June 2, 2016, https://www.cuponation.com/cuponation-group-becomes-global-savings-group/

xxvi Stefan Nicola, "Rocket Internet Gets Boost as Its Coupon Startup Has Profit," *Bloomberg*, August 24, 2017, https://www.bloomberg.com/news/articles/2017-08-24/rocket-internet-gets-unit-boost-as-coupon-startup-turns-profit

xxvii Lukas Ohlsson, "We really wanted to move our startup to Stockholm. Here's why we decided not to actually do it," *TechEU*, November 5, 2015, http://tech.eu/features/6467/challenges-moving-startup-stockholm-sweden/

xxviii "Housing for foreign talent: collaborative solutions," *The Local*, November 24, 2015, https://www.thelocal.se/20151124/how-stockholm-solved-a-startups-housing-crisis-stockholmbusinessregion-tlccu

xxix Andy Rosen, "Amazon could find those 50,000 jobs hard to fill in Boston area," *Boston Globe*, September 21, 2017, https://www.bostonglobe.com/business/2017/09/20/would-amazon-suck-all-tech-talent-boston/quW1jXNOePqid5gGjdmwoI/story.html xxx Peter Cohan, "Attention Worcester grads: 4 Boston startups are hiring" *Worcester Telegram & Gazette*, October 2, 2017, http://www.telegram.com/news/20171001/wall-amp-main-attention-worcester-grads-4-boston-startups-are-hiring

xxxi "Attention Worcester grads: 4 Boston startups are hiring," Ibid.

xxxii "Attention Worcester grads: 4 Boston startups are hiring," Ibid.

xxxiii "Attention Worcester grads: 4 Boston startups are hiring," Ibid.

xxxiv "Facebook," *Morningstar*, accessed September 26, 2017, http://www.morningstar.com/stocks/XNAS/FB/quote.html

xxxv Leena Rao, "Facebook's Zuckerberg: If I Were Starting A Company Now, I Would Have Stayed In Boston," *TechCrunch*, October 30, 2011, https://techcrunch.com/2011/10/30/facebooks-zuckerberg-if-i-were-starting-a-company-now-i-would-have-stayed-in-boston/

xxxvi Scott Kirsner, "Why Facebook went west," *Boston Globe*, September 9, 2007, http://archive.boston.com/business/globe/articles/2007/09/09/why_facebook_went_west/

xxxvii Rao, Ibid.

xxxviii Kirsner, Ibid.

xxxix Mike Swift, "Nurturing of Facebook started in Palo Alto house," Mercury News, November 26, 2011, http://www.mercurynews.com/2011/11/26/nurturing-of-facebook-started-in-palo-alto-house/

xl Bloomberg News, "This Startup Is Luring Top Talent With $3 Million Pay Packages," *Bloomberg*, September 24, 2017, https://www.bloomberg.com/news/articles/2017-09-24/in-battle-for-talent-one-startup-founder-tries-unlimited-pay

xli Bloomberg, Ibid.

xlii Peter Cohan, "Theranos Is Made-For-Hollywood Silicon Valley Scandal," *Forbes*, October 16, 2015, https://www.forbes.com/sites/petercohan/2015/10/16/theranos-is-made-for-hollywood-silicon-valley-scandal/

xliii Sarah Buhr, "Theranos slashes another 41 percent of its workforce," *TechCrunch*, January 6, 2017, https://techcrunch.com/2017/01/06/theranos-slashes-another-41-percent-of-its-workforce/

xliv Hugo Daniel and Harriet Alexander, "British head scientist at US maverick's Silicon Valley start-up took own life over 'unworkable' technology," *The Telegraph*, October 22, 2016, http://www.telegraph.co.uk/technology/2016/10/22/british-head-scientist-at-us-mavericks-silicon-valley-start-up-t/

Chapter 5: Sourcing Investment Capital

[i] Peter Cohan, "Disciplined Growth Strategies: Insights from the Growth Trajectories of Successful and Unsuccessful Companies," (New York, NY: Apress, 2017), p. 153.

[ii] Peter Cohan, "Hungry Start-up Strategy: Creating New Ventures With Limited Resources and Unlimited Vision," (Oakland, CA: Berrett-Koehler Publishers, 2012).

[iii] This is a manifestation of confirmation bias. See Peter Cohan, "When the blind lead," *Business Strategy Review,* September 1, 2007, https://www.london.edu/faculty-and-research/lbsr/when-the-blind-lead#.Wh1udXmWy1s

[iv] Peter Cohan, "Wall & Main: StartUp Worcester hosting condom reinvention," *Worcester Telegram & Gazette,* May 14, 2017, http://www.telegram.com/news/20170514/wall-amp-main-startup-worcester-hosting-condom-reinvention

[v] "Wall & Main: StartUp Worcester hosting condom reinvention," Ibid.

[vi] "Wall & Main: StartUp Worcester hosting condom reinvention," Ibid.

[vii] Peter Cohan, "WPI grad learns from startup experience," *Worcester Telegram & Gazette,* November 20, 2011, http://www.telegram.com/article/20111120/COLUMN70/111209978

[viii] "WPI grad learns from startup experience," Ibid.

[ix] Jon Chesto, "Canton-based Network Engines agrees to be sold for $63M," *The Patriot Ledger,* June 20, 2012, http://www.patriotledger.com/x681120923/Canton-based-Network-Engines-agrees-to-be-sold

[x] "Ammasso," *CrunchBase,* accessed October 7, 2017, https://www.crunchbase.com/organization/ammasso

[xi] "WPI grad learns from startup experience," Ibid.

[xii] Don Seiffert, "Terascala expands to Boston, nabs ex-EMC exec," *Boston Business Journal,* October 17, 2012, https://www.bizjournals.com/boston/blog/mass-high-tech/2012/10/terascala-expands-to-boston-nabs-ex-emc-exec.html

[xiii] "Cray Expands Team with Terascala Storage Experts," *Scientific Computing,* July 15, 2015, https://www.scientificcomputing.com/news/2015/07/cray-expands-team-terascala-storage-experts

[xiv] "M&A or more correctly, acqui-hire: Cray bags much of Terascala," *Scalability.org,* July 15, 2015, https://scalability.org/2015/07/ma-or-more-correctly-acqui-hire-cray-bags-much-of-terascala/

[xv] "WPI grad learns from startup experience," Ibid.

xvi "GoGoVan," *CrunchBase*, accessed October 8, 2017, https://www.crunchbase.com/organization/gogovan

xvii Catherine Shu, "GoGoVan Raises $6.5M Series A To Expand In Asia," *CrunchBase*, August 15, 2014, https://techcrunch.com/2014/08/15/gogovan-raises-6-5m-series-a-to-expand-in-asia/

xviii C. Custer, "Hong Kong's Gogovan grabs $10M investment from Renren for China expansion," *TechInAsia*, November 18, 2014, https://www.techinasia.com/hong-kongs-gogovan-grabs-10m-investment-renren-china-expansion

xix Michael Tegos, "Alibaba's Hong Kong fund throws cash at 'Uber for vans' startup Gogovan," *TechInAsia*, May 5, 2016, https://www.techinasia.com/gogovan-series-c-funding

xx Jon Russell, "GoGoVan becomes Hong Kong's first $1 billion startup following merger deal," *TechCrunch*, September 1, 2017, https://techcrunch.com/2017/09/01/gogovan-becomes-hong-kongs-first-1-billion-startup-following-merger-deal/

xxi "WeLab," *CrunchBase*, accessed October 8, 2017, https://www.crunchbase.com/organization/welab

xxii Ron Finberg, "WeLab Grabs $160m Series B Funding as Online Lending Stays Hot in China," *Finance Magnates*, January 20, 2016, https://www.financemagnates.com/fintech/p2p/welab-grabs-160m-series-b-funding-as-online-lending-stays-hot-in-china/

xxiii "Serge Alleyne," *LinkedIn profile*, accessed October 9, 2017, https://www.linkedin.com/in/sergealleyne/?ppe=1

xxiv Steve O'Hear, "Tok Tok Tok, The European Local Delivery Platform Similar To Postmates, Raises $2M To Expand To London," *TechCrunch*, January 22, 2014, https://techcrunch.com/2014/01/22/tok-tok-tok/

xxv Romain Dillet, "Tok Tok Tok Hires Former Carrefour CFO Eric Reiss To Head The European Delivery Startup," *TechCrunch*, July 15, 2014, https://techcrunch.com/2014/07/15/tok-tok-tok-hires-former-carrefour-cfo-eric-reiss-to-head-the-european-delivery-startup/

xxvi Steve O'Hear, "French on-demand delivery startup Tok Tok Tok to close, sells tech assets to Just Eat," September 6, 2016, https://techcrunch.com/2016/09/06/french-on-demand-delivery-startup-tok-tok-tok-to-close-sells-tech-assets-to-just-eat/

xxvii Knowledge@Wharton, "How Stockholm Became A 'Unicorn Factory'," *Forbes*, https://www.forbes.com/sites/knowledgewharton/2015/11/11/how-stockholm-became-a-unicorn-factory/

[xxviii] John Kennedy, "Something is sizzling in the start-up city of Stockholm," *Silicon Republic*, January 20, 2017, https://www.siliconrepublic.com/start-ups/stockholm-startup-city

[xxix] Knowledge@Wharton, Ibid.

[xxx] Knowledge@Wharton, Ibid.

[xxxi] Peter Cohan, "Meet Two Mind-Bending Founders From Stockholm," *Inc.*, October 5, 2017, https://www.inc.com/peter-cohan/meet-two-mind-bending-founders-from-stockholm.html

[xxxii] "Affibody," *Equity.net*, accessed October 6, 2017, https://www.equitynet.com/c/affibody

[xxxiii] "Alligator Bioscience," *CrunchBase*, accessed October 6, 2017, https://www.crunchbase.com/organization/alligator-bioscience#/entity

[xxxiv] "Alligator Bioscience," *Bloomberg Markets*, accessed October 6, 2017, https://www.bloomberg.com/quote/ATORX:SS

[xxxv] "Biotage," *Bloomberg Markets*, accessed October 6, 2017, https://www.bloomberg.com/quote/BIOT:SS

[xxxvi] "Meet Two Mind-Bending Founders From Stockholm," Ibid.

[xxxvii] "Meet Two Mind-Bending Founders From Stockholm," Ibid.

[xxxviii] "Meet Two Mind-Bending Founders From Stockholm," Ibid.

[xxxix] Thomas Ohr, "Stockholm-based Adaptive Simulations secures €1.5 million to democratize the virtual simulations market," *EU Startups*, May 4, 2017, http://www.eu-startups.com/2017/05/stockholm-based-adaptive-simulations-secures-e1-5-million-to-democratize-the-virtual-simulations-market/

[xl] "Moshe Yanai," *CrunchBase*, accessed October 6, 2017, https://www.crunchbase.com/person/moshe-yanai#/entity

[xli] Chris Mellor, "Symmetrix daddy Moshe Yanai on chair-throwing and storage," *The Register*, April, 10 2017, https://www.theregister.co.uk/2017/04/10/moshe_the_storage_mensch/

[xlii] "Infinidat," *CrunchBase*, accessed October 6, 2017, https://www.crunchbase.com/organization/infinidat#/entity

[xliii] Kelly J. O'Brien, "Infinidat worth $1.6B after Goldman investment of $95M," *Boston Business Journal*, https://www.bizjournals.com/boston/blog/startups/2017/10/infinidat-worth-1-6b-after-goldman-investment-of.html

[xliv] "Making moves," *BostInnoBeat*, accessed October 7, 2017, https://www.americaninno.com/boston/restaurant-app-shuts-down-catalant-exec-leaves-for-new-startup/

xlv "Marik Marshak," *LinkedIn* profile, accessed October 7, 2017 https://www.linkedin.com/in/marikmarshak/

xlvi Olivia Vanni, "A Former EMC Director of Engineering Is Starting a 'Hotel Tonight for Restaurants'," *BostonInno*, April 9, 2016, https://www.americaninno.com/boston/2016/04/09/last-minute-restaurant-reservations-and-deals-in-boston/

xlvii Olivia Vanni, "The 'Hotel Tonight for Restaurants' Is Expanding Within Boston's Eatery Scene, *BostonInno*, January 23, 2017, https://www.americaninno.com/boston/gopapaya-restaurant-reservation-discounts-in-boston/

xlviii "Boston-Based Startup GoPapaya Brings Dynamic Pricing to the Takeout Market," *Business Wire*, May 22, 2017, https://finance.yahoo.com/news/boston-based-startup-gopapaya-brings-130500984.html

xlix "Making moves," Ibid.

l Peter Cohan, "Zoom Scoops Customers From Cisco In $16 Billion Video Conferencing Market," *Forbes*, October 3, 2017, https://www.forbes.com/sites/petercohan/2017/10/03/zoom-scoops-customers-from-cisco-in-16-billion-videoconferencing-market/

li "Zoom Scoops Customers From Cisco In $16 Billion Video Conferencing Market," Ibid.

lii "Zoom Scoops Customers From Cisco In $16 Billion Video Conferencing Market," Ibid.

liii "Zoom Video communications," *Pitchbook*, accessed October 11, 2017, https://my.pitchbook.com/profile/56017-63/company/profile#news

liv Cromwell Schubarth, "Zoom Video Communications CEO Eric Yuan raised $100 million more for his downtown San Jose startup," *Silicon Valley Business Journal*, January 17, 2017, https://www.bizjournals.com/sanjose/news/2017/01/17/sequoia-helps-cisco-webex-veteran-raise-100m-for.html

lv "Zoom Scoops Customers From Cisco In $16 Billion Video Conferencing Market," Ibid.

lvi Schubarth, Ibid.

lvii Katherine Rosmannov, "How Organic Avenue Lost All Its Juice," *New York Times*, November 4, 2015, https://www.nytimes.com/2015/11/05/fashion/organic-avenue-close.html

lviii Derek Thompson, "How Juicero's Story Set the Company Up for Humiliation," *The Atlantic*, April 21, 2017, https://www.theatlantic.com/business/archive/2017/04/juicero-lessons/523896/

lix Andrew Meola, "Juicero has set itself apart by creating an IoT integrated 'smart juicer'," *Business Insider*, April 1, 2016, http://www.businessinsider.com/juicero-smart-juicer-brings-fresh-juice-to-the-masses-2016-4

lx Ellen Huet and Olivia Zaleski, "Silicon Valley's $400 Juicer May Be Feeling the Squeeze," *Bloomberg*, https://www.bloomberg.com/news/features/2017-04-19/silicon-valley-s-400-juicer-may-be-feeling-the-squeeze

lxi David Gelles, "Juicero, Start-Up With a $700 Juicer and Top Investors, Shuts Down," *New York Times*, September 1, 2017, https://www.nytimes.com/2017/09/01/technology/juicero-start-up-shuts-down.html

lxii Annie Vainshtein, "Juicero founder reportedly embarking on five-day water fast in Mill Valley," *SFGate*, September 20, 2017, http://www.sfgate.com/news/article/Juicero-founder-reportedly-embarking-on-five-day-12216537.php

Chapter 6: Building Mentor Networks

i Peter Cohan, "What Makes LinkedIn Chairman, Reid Hoffman, a Great Mentor," *Forbes*, December 11, 2012, https://www.forbes.com/sites/petercohan/2012/12/11/what-makes-linkedin-chairman-reid-hoffman-a-great-mentor/

ii Peter Cohan, "Why Elad Gil Gives Back To Silicon Valley," *Forbes*, July 23, 2012, www.forbes.com/sites/petercohan/2012/07/23/why-elad-gil-gives-back-to-silicon-valley/#4b7691ef72db.

iii Peter Cohan, "A Silicon Valley VC Talks Acquisitions," *Forbes*, May 4, 2012, https://www.forbes.com/sites/petercohan/2012/05/04/a-silicon-valley-vc-talks-acquisitions/

iv Peter Cohan, "Silicon Valley's Culture Doctor," *Forbes*, November 4, 2011, https://www.forbes.com/sites/petercohan/2011/11/04/silicon-valleys-culture-doctor/

v Peter Cohan, "Where should you locate your start-up?," *MIT Entrepreneurship Review*, October 7, 2013, http://miter.mit.edu/where-should-you-locate-your-start-up/

vi "Where should you locate your start-up?," Ibid.

vii Edwin Lopez, "Ingram Micro will mentor startups via tech accelerator," August 15, 2016 https://www.supplychaindive.com/news/logistics-tech-accelerator-ingram-startup/424458/

viii Peter Cohan, "12 local startups win space, mentors," *Worcester Telegram & Gazette*, May 31, 2015, http://www.telegram.com/article/20150531/NEWS/150539895

ix "12 local startups win space, mentors," Ibid.

x Michael D. Kane, "Petricore Games wants to help grow a gaming community in Worcester," *Masslive*, May 29, 2015, http://www.masslive.com/news/worcester/index.ssf/2015/05/petricore_games_wants_to_help.html

xi Michael D. Kane, Ibid.

xii Peter Cohan, "Wall & Main: Petricore making it bigger in Worcester," *Worcester Telegram & Gazette*, October 15, 2017, http://www.telegram.com/news/20171015/wall-amp-main-petricore-making-it-bigger-in-worcester

xiii Peter Cohan, "Can WPI's prodigal entrepreneur keep more startups in Worcester?" *Worcester Telegram & Gazette*, April 21, 2014, http://www.telegram.com/article/20140421/column70/304219984

xiv "Can WPI's prodigal entrepreneur keep more startups in Worcester?" Ibid.

xv "Can WPI's prodigal entrepreneur keep more startups in Worcester?" Ibid.

xvi Peter S. Cohan, "Holy Cross start-up leaves town for the hub, raises $700,000," *Worcester Telegram & Gazette*, December 14, 2014, http://www.telegram.com/article/20141214/COLUMN70/312149967

xvii "Holy Cross start-up leaves town for the hub, raises $700,000," Ibid.

xviii Kristin Musulin, "As Wigo app reaches $15M valuation, students leave school to join team," *USA Today*, March 11, 2015, http://college.usatoday.com/2015/03/11/students-leave-school-to-join-wigo-as-app-continues-to-grow/

xix Julie Bort, "After building a $14 million company in 13 months, college party app Wigo is dead," *Business Insider*, September 21, 2015, http://www.businessinsider.com/college-party-app-wigo-is-dead-2015-9

xx Lucas Matney, "Local Discovery App Yeti Acquired By Private Investors, Undergoes Leadership Changes," *TechCrunch*, July 16, 2015, https://techcrunch.com/2015/07/16/local-discovery-app-yeti-acquired-by-private-investors-undergoes-leadership-changes/

xxi Alex Capecelatro, *LinkedIn Profile*, accessed October 21, 2017, https://www.linkedin.com/in/alexcaps/

xxii Peter Cohan, "After Iliad, What's Next For Paris's Startup Scene?," *Forbes*, August 29, 2017, https://www.forbes.com/sites/petercohan/2017/08/29/after-iliad-whats-next-for-pariss-startup-scene/

xxiii Falguni Desai, "Hong Kong's Startup Scene Gains Momentum," *Forbes*, December 17, 2015, https://www.forbes.com/sites/falgunidesai/2015/12/17/hong-kongs-startup-scene-gains-momentum/

xxiv Deng Yanzi and Chai Hua, "HK startups revving up 'significantly'," *China Daily Asia*, January 11, 2017, http://www.chinadailyasia.com/hknews/2017-01/11/content_15555730.html

xxv Jon Russell," Despite challenges, startups see a bright future for tech companies in Hong Kong," *TechCrunch*, June 19, 2017, https://techcrunch.com/2017/06/19/can-hong-kong-become-a-startup-hub/

xxvi Peter Cohan, "KTH, The MIT of Stockholm, Produced These Three Mind-Blowing Startups," *Inc.*, September 24, 2017, https://www.inc.com/peter-cohan/kth-mit-of-stockholm-produced-these-three-mind-blowing-startups.html

xxvii "KTH, The MIT of Stockholm, Produced These Three Mind-Blowing Startups," Ibid.

xxviii "KTH, The MIT of Stockholm, Produced These Three Mind-Blowing Startups," Ibid.

xxix "KTH, The MIT of Stockholm, Produced These Three Mind-Blowing Startups," Ibid.

xxx "KTH, The MIT of Stockholm, Produced These Three Mind-Blowing Startups," Ibid.

xxxi "KTH, The MIT of Stockholm, Produced These Three Mind-Blowing Startups," Ibid.

xxxii Peter Cohan, "Wall & Main: How mentoring can help startups grow," *Worcester Telegram & Gazette*, September 3, 2017, http://www.telegram.com/news/20170903/wall-amp-main-how-mentoring-can-help-startups-grow

xxxiii "Wall & Main: How mentoring can help startups grow," Ibid.

xxxiv "Wall & Main: How mentoring can help startups grow," Ibid.

xxxv "Wall & Main: How mentoring can help startups grow," Ibid.

xxxvi "Wall & Main: How mentoring can help startups grow," Ibid.

xxxvii "Wall & Main: How mentoring can help startups grow," Ibid.

xxxviii Peter Cohan, "3 Ways That Mentoring Helps This Company Grow 100% A Year," *Inc.*, October 24, 2017, https://www.inc.com/peter-cohan/3-ways-that-mentoring-helps-this-company-grow-100-a-year.html

xxxix "3 Ways That Mentoring Helps This Company Grow 100% A Year," Ibid.

xl Peter Cohan, "After Imperva And Mobileye, Here's What's Next For Israeli Startups," *Forbes*, Aug 21, 2017, https://www.forbes.com/sites/petercohan/2017/08/21/after-imperva-and-mobileye-heres-whats-next-for-israeli-startups/

xli Jeffrey Bussgang and Omri Stern, "How Israeli Startups Can Scale," *Harvard Business Review*, September 10, 2015, https://hbr.org/2015/09/how-israeli-startups-can-scale

xlii Peter Cohan, "How Israeli Entrepreneurs Build Mentor Networks," *Inc.*, October 26, 2017, https://www.inc.com/peter-cohan/how-israeli-entrepreneurs-build-mentor-networks.html

xliii Peter Cohan, "How Boston Could Help CyberArk Grow Faster, *Forbes*, August 16, 2017, https://www.forbes.com/sites/petercohan/2017/08/16/how-boston-could-help-cyberark-grow-faster/

xliv "How Boston Could Help CyberArk Grow Faster," Ibid.

xlv Peter Cohan, "4 Reasons to Become a Mentor," *Inc.*, May 14. 2013, https://www.inc.com/peter-cohan/4-reasons-to-become-mentor.html

xlvi "4 Reasons to Become a Mentor," Ibid.

xlvii Peter Cohan, "How Silicon Valley Mentors Turn Engineers Into CEOs," *Inc.*, October 17, 2017, https://www.inc.com/peter-cohan/how-silicon-valley-mentors-turn-engineers-into-ceos.html

xlviii "How Silicon Valley Mentors Turn Engineers Into CEOs," Ibid.

xlix Katie Benner, "SoFi Board Says C.E.O. Is Out Immediately Amid Sexual Harassment Scandal," *New York Times*, September 15, 2017, https://www.nytimes.com/2017/09/15/technology/sofi-cagney-scandal.html

l Peter Cohan, "Silicon Valley's Mentoring Gap," *Forbes*, January 28, 2013, https://www.forbes.com/sites/petercohan/2013/01/28/silicon-valleys-mentoring-gap/

li "Silicon Valley's Mentoring Gap," Ibid.

lii "Silicon Valley's Mentoring Gap," Ibid.

liii David Z. Morris, "SoFi Is Being Sued by an Employee Claiming He Was Fired for Reporting Sexual Harassment," *Fortune*, August 13, 2017, http://fortune.com/2017/08/13/sofi-sexual-harassment-lawsuit/

liv Benner, Ibid.

Chapter 7: Creating Startup-Friendly Shared Values

i Peter Cohan, "How local values shape startup activity," *Worcester Telegram & Gazette*, November 13, 2017, http://www.telegram.com/news/20171113/wall-amp-main-how-local-values-shape-startup-activity

ii "How local values shape startup activity," Ibid.

iii Peter Cohan, "Startups led by Worcester-educated executives," *Worcester Telegram & Gazette*, April 14, 2013, http://www.telegram.com/article/20130414/column70/304149979

iv Peter Cohan, "Where should you locate your start-up?," MIT Entrepreneurship Review, October 7, 2013, http://miter.mit.edu/where-should-you-locate-your-start-up/

v "Where should you locate your start-up?," Ibid.

vi "Where should you locate your start-up?," Ibid. Salesforce.com acquired Clipboard in May 2013 for $12 million.

vii "Where should you locate your start-up?," Ibid.

viii Peter Cohan, "Blue Skies Ahead for Worcester Contract Researcher," *Worcester Telegram & Gazette*, June 16, 2013, http://www.telegram.com/article/20130616/column70/306169984

ix "Blue Skies Ahead for Worcester Contract Researcher," Ibid.

x Peter Cohan, "Blue Sky investor brings in outside CEO," *Worcester Telegram & Gazette*, July 14, 2013, http://www.telegram.com/article/20130714/column70/307149980

xi Peter Cohan, "Blue Sky executives' abilities helped make LakePharma deal," *Worcester Telegram & Gazette*, March 28, 2016, http://www.telegram.com/article/20160328/NEWS/160329373

xii Peter S. Cohan, "LakePharma offers hope for Worcester's growth," *Worcester Telegram & Gazette*, February 13, 2017, http://www.telegram.com/news/20170213/wall-and-main-lakepharma-offers-hope-for-worcesters-growth

xiii Peter Cohan, "Lack of lab space constrains LakePharma's Worcester growth," July 17, 2017, *Worcester Telegram & Gazette*, July 17, 2017, http://www.telegram.com/news/20170717/wall-amp-main-lack-of-lab-space-constrains-lakepharmas-worcester-growth

xiv Peter Cohan, "WPI professor developing health care apps," *Worcester Telegram & Gazette*, June 9, 2013, http://www.telegram.com/article/20130609/COLUMN70/306099990

xv "WPI professor developing health care apps," Ibid.

xvi Bonnie Russell, "College Town: WPI-developed app aids diabetics," *Worcester Telegram & Gazette*, April 18, 2015, http://www.telegram.com/article/20150418/news/304189721

xvii Hiawatha Bray, "WPI develops an app to make drunk drivers toe the line," *Boston Globe*, December 20, 2016, https://www.bostonglobe.com/business/2016/12/19/app-make-drunk-drivers-toe-line/jTpGccVnyn7upXgKpSJD5N/story.html [xviii] Jordan Kimmel, "BU professor receives $320,000 grant to test app that detects alcohol intoxication," *Daily Free Press*, September 27, 2017, http://dailyfreepress.com/2017/09/27/bu-professor-receives-320000-grant-to-test-app-that-detects-alcohol-intoxication/

[xix] "The world's best start-up hubs: Paris, France," Virgin.com, accessed November 14, 2017, https://www.virgin.com/entrepreneur/worlds-best-start-hubs-paris-france

[xx] Christopher F. Schuetze, "In Paris, Wine, Brie and … Silicon?," *US News & World Report*, April 24, 2017, https://www.usnews.com/news/best-countries/articles/2017-04-24/paris-sets-its-sights-on-being-a-start-up-hub

[xxi] Thomas Husson, "After Brexit, Will Paris Become The New Startup Hub In Europe?," *Forrester Research*, June 30, 2016, https://go.forrester.com/blogs/16-06-30-after_brexit_will_paris_become_the_new_startup_hub_in_europe/

[xxii] Laura Feinstein, "French Girls Are Reinventing the Tech Scene in Paris," *Harper's Bazaar*, July 14, 2017, http://www.harpersbazaar.com/culture/a10302219/french-girls-rising-in-tech/

[xxiii] Jon Russell, "Despite challenges, startups see a bright future for tech companies in Hong Kong," *TechCrunch*, June 19, 2017, https://techcrunch.com/2017/06/19/can-hong-kong-become-a-startup-hub/

[xxiv] Jon Russell, Ibid.

[xxv] Zolzaya Erdenebileg, "Hong Kong's Startup Scene: the Future of Mainland–Hong Kong Economic Cooperation," *China Briefing*, August 8, 2017, http://www.china-briefing.com/news/2017/08/08/hong-kongs-startup-scene-future-mainland-hong-kong-economic-cooperation.html

[xxvi] Peter Cohan, "Stockholm's startups may interest locals whose ancestors hail from Sweden," *Worcester Telegram & Gazette*, August 27, 2017, http://www.telegram.com/news/20170827/wall-amp-main-stockholms-startups-may-interest-locals-whose-ancestors-hail-from-sweden

[xxvii] "Stockholm's startups may interest locals whose ancestors hail from Sweden," Ibid.

[xxviii] "Stockholm's startups may interest locals whose ancestors hail from Sweden," Ibid.

[xxix] "Stockholm's startups may interest locals whose ancestors hail from Sweden," Ibid.

[xxx] Ryan Mac, David M. Ewalt and Max Jedeur-Palmgren, "Inside The Post-Minecraft Life Of Billionaire Gamer God Markus Persson." *Forbes*, March 3, 2015, https://www.forbes.com/sites/ryanmac/2015/03/03/minecraft-markus-persson-life-after-microsoft-sale/

xxxi Simon Parkin. "The Creator." *The New Yorker,* April 5, 2013, https://www.newyorker.com/tech/elements/the-creator

xxxii Ryan Mac, David M. Ewalt and Max Jedeur-Palmgren, Ibid.

xxxiii The Blast staff, "Creator Markus 'Notch' Persson Threw The Spookiest, Most Insane Party," *The Blast,* October 29, 2017, https://theblast.com/minecraft-notch-halloween-party-beverly-hills/Minecraft

xxxiv Peter Cohan, "Is Startup Nation Catching Up With Silicon Valley?," *Inc.,* November 9, 2017, https://www.inc.com/peter-cohan/is-startup-nation-gaining-ground-on-silicon-valley.html

xxxv "Is Startup Nation Catching Up With Silicon Valley?," Ibid.

xxxvi "Is Startup Nation Catching Up With Silicon Valley?," Ibid.

xxxvii "Is Startup Nation Catching Up With Silicon Valley?," Ibid.

xxxviii "Is Startup Nation Catching Up With Silicon Valley?," Ibid.

xxxix Peter Cohan, "Can Boston Catch Up With Silicon Valley?," *Forbes,* August 14, 2017, https://www.forbes.com/sites/petercohan/2017/08/14/can-boston-catch-up-with-silicon-valley/

xl "Can Boston Catch Up With Silicon Valley?," Ibid.

xli "Can Boston Catch Up With Silicon Valley?," Ibid.

xlii Peter Cohan, "Clark grad makes big bank in Boston tech," *Worcester Telegram & Gazette,* November 12, 2017, http://www.telegram.com/news/20171112/wall-amp-main-clark-grad-makes-big-bank-in-boston-tech

xliii "Clark grad makes big bank in Boston tech," Ibid.

xliv "Clark grad makes big bank in Boston tech," Ibid.

xlv "Clark grad makes big bank in Boston tech," Ibid.

xlvi "How local values shape startup activity," Ibid.

xlvii "How local values shape startup activity," Ibid.

xlviii "How local values shape startup activity," Ibid.

xlix Peter Cohan, "How This Salesforce Investor Created $100B In Value," *Forbes,* November 10, 2017, https://www.forbes.com/sites/petercohan/2017/11/10/how-this-salesforce-investor-created-100b-in-value/

l "How This Salesforce Investor Created $100B In Value," *Forbes,* November 10, 2017, Ibid.

li "How This Salesforce Investor Created $100B In Value," *Forbes,* November 10, 2017, Ibid.

[lii] "How This Salesforce Investor Created $100B In Value," *Forbes*, November 10, 2017, Ibid.

[liii] "How This Salesforce Investor Created $100B In Value," *Forbes*, November 10, 2017, Ibid.

[liv] "How This Salesforce Investor Created $100B In Value," *Forbes*, November 10, 2017, Ibid.

[lv] Wolf Richter, "Silicon Valley's 'death by overfunding' spreads as another unicorn collapses," *Business Insider*, July 11, 2017, http://www.businessinsider.com/silicon-valley-jawbone-liquidation-overfunding-2017-Wolf Street

[lvi] Peter Cohan, "7 Unraveling Rings To Flush $60 Billion In Venture Investment," *Forbes*, March 6, 2016, https://www.forbes.com/sites/petercohan/2016/03/06/7-unraveling-rings-to-flush-60-billion-in-venture-investment/

[lvii] Erin Griffith, "Jawbone Failed, But Its Founder Remains Determined," *Fortune*, July 7, 2017, http://fortune.com/2017/07/07/jawbone-failed-but-its-founder-remains-determined/

[lviii] Tim Bradshaw, Jawbone reaches end of the road as it goes into liquidation," *Financial Times*, July 6, 2017, https://www.ft.com/content/c146f144-62ad-11e7-8814-0ac7eb84e5f1

[lix] Heather Somerville, "Jawbone's demise a case of 'death by overfunding' in Silicon Valley," *Reuters*. July 10, 2017, https://www.reuters.com/article/us-jawbone-failure/jawbones-demise-a-case-of-death-by-overfunding-in-silicon-valley-idUSKBN19V0BS

Chapter 8: Boosting Your Startup Common

[i] Peter Cohan, "5 Steps That Made Israel a Start-up Haven," *Inc.*, March 26, 2013, https://www.inc.com/peter-cohan/israel-from-socialism-to-start-up-haven.html

[ii] AJ Agrawal, "Countries That Pay You to Move Your Startup to Their Country," *Huffington Post*, May 24, 2017, https://www.huffingtonpost.com/aj-agrawal/countries-that-pay-you-to_b_10105502.html

[iii] Peter Cohan, "Stockholm's startups may interest locals whose ancestors hail from Sweden," *Worcester Telegram & Gazette*, August 27, 2017, http://www.telegram.com/news/20170827/wall-amp-main-stockholms-startups-may-interest-locals-whose-ancestors-hail-from-sweden

[iv] Peter Cohan, "Don't Try To Make Your City The Next Silicon Valley," *Forbes*, July 21, 2017, https://www.forbes.com/sites/petercohan/2017/07/21/dont-try-to-make-your-city-the-next-silicon-valley/

[v] "Don't Try To Make Your City The Next Silicon Valley," Ibid.

[vi] "Don't Try To Make Your City The Next Silicon Valley," Ibid.

[vii] "Don't Try To Make Your City The Next Silicon Valley," Ibid.

[viii] Edward Wyatt, "Fast Internet Is Chattanooga's New Locomotive," *New York Times*, February 3, 2014, https://www.nytimes.com/2014/02/04/technology/fast-internet-service-speeds-business-development-in-chattanooga.html

[ix] Edward Wyatt, Ibid.

[x] "Don't Try To Make Your City The Next Silicon Valley," Ibid.

[xi] Cadie Thompson, "Three growing start-up cities in South America," *CNBC*, May 7, 2015, https://www.cnbc.com/2015/05/07/three-growing-start-up-cities-in-south-america.html

[xii] Conrad Egusa and Victoria O'Shee, "A Look into Chile's innovative startup government," *TechCrunch*, October 16, 2016, https://techcrunch.com/2016/10/16/a-look-into-chiles-innovative-startup-government/

[xiii] Egusa and O'Shee, Ibid.

[xiv] Tia Burton, "11 Chilean Startups You Need to Know," *Launchway Media*, May 25, 2017, https://www.launchwaymedia.com/blog/2017/5/24/10-chilean-startups-you-need-to-know

Index

© Peter S. Cohan 2018
P. S. Cohan, *Startup Cities*, https://doi.org/10.1007/978-1-4842-3393-1

Get the eBook for only $5!

Why limit yourself?

With most of our titles available in both PDF and ePUB format, you can access your content wherever and however you wish—on your PC, phone, tablet, or reader.

Since you've purchased this print book, we are happy to offer you the eBook for just $5.

To learn more, go to http://www.apress.com/companion or contact support@apress.com.

Apress®

Printed by Printforce, the Netherlands